CHRISTIAN LIGHT EDUCATION
Reading Series

Calls to Courage

Sixth Grade Reader

Compiled by Tim Kennedy

CHRISTIAN LIGHT

EDUCATION

Harrisonburg, Virginia
(540) 434-0750   www.christianlight.org

CHRISTIAN LIGHT
Reading Series

Grade 1
I Wonder

Grade 2, book 1
Helping Hands

Grade 2, book 2
Happy Hearts

Grade 3
Doors to Discovery

Grade 4
Bridges Beyond

Grade 5
Open Windows

Grade 6
Calls to Courage

Grade 7
The Road Less Traveled

Grade 8
Where Roads Diverge

CALLS TO COURAGE

Christian Light Education, a division of
Christian Light Publications, Harrisonburg, VA 22802
©2003 Christian Light Publications, Inc.
All Rights Reserved.
Printed in China

ISBN: 978-0-87813-851-7

Seventh Printing, 2020

Table *of* Contents

601 **So Many Things to Learn**

Happy Is the Man	*Proverbs 3:13-15*	1
The Honor Box	*Betty Steele Everett*	2
A Harvest of Gold	*Bonnie Abbs*	7
September	*Helen Hunt Jackson*	12
Making Joe's Lunch	*Author Unknown*	13
Rebellion in September	*Rachel Field*	17
So Many Things to Learn	*James B. Garfield*	18
Call of the Wild Geese	*Todd Lee*	27
Something Told the Wild Geese	*Rachel Field*	32
Created to Fly	*Robert Doolan*	33
Beavers!	*Tim Kennedy*	37
Pilgrims of the Wild	*Grey Owl*	44
Starfish	*Winifred Welles*	51
Looking Mature	*Author Unknown*	52
Check	*James Stephens*	59

602 **Contentment**

Beautiful	*Author Unknown*	61
The Prodigal Son	*Luke 15:11-32*	62
A Prodigal Son	*Christina Rossetti*	64
The King and the Shirt	*Leo Tolstoy*	65
The Tale of Bramble the King	*Judges 9:7-15*	66
Crossing the Ice	*Thomas H. Raddall*	68
Jack's Foolishness	*E. Hammond*	76

Slaves . . . . *James Russell Lowell*   84

Be Like the Bird . . . . *Victor Hugo*   85

The Road to Canada . . . . *Anna L. Curtis*   86

Elias . . . . *Leo Tolstoy*   90

Always 'Ungry . . . . *Frances Hodgson Burnett*   96

603   Courage

What Have We Done Today? . . . . *Nixon Waterman*   103

The Carolers of Bethlehem Center . . . . *Frederick Hall*   104

Ola and the Wooden Tub . . . . *Ragnhild Chevelier*   114

The Wolf . . . . *Georgia R. Durston*   120

Escape at Bedtime . . . . *Robert Louis Stevenson*   121

A Dangerous Errand . . . . *Elmo Stoll*   122

I-ho Ch'üan . . . . *Author Unknown*   130

R Is for *Remarkable* . . . . *Walter E. Andrews*   136

It Couldn't Be Done . . . . *Edgar A. Guest*   146

Putting Fear to Flight . . . . *Joseph B. Ames*   147

The Baker's Neighbor . . . . *retold by Jennifer Crider*   156

Advertising for a Thief . . . . *Author Unknown*   161

The Sari With the Silver Border . . . . *Dorothy C. Haskin*   166

The Flies and the Honey Pot . . . . *Aesop*   172

604   In All Thy Ways

I Know Christ . . . . *E. Margaret Clarkson*   173

The Ichthyosaur . . . . *Helen Bush*   174

The Earth Abideth . . . . *Ecclesiastes 1:4-7*   182

God Provides Water . . . . *Psalm 104*   183

Could It Be Done? Part 1: Secrets of the Soil . . . . *David Collins*   185

Could It Be Done? Part 2: The School in a Wagon . . . . . *David Collins*   191

A Chance to Escape . . . . *David Luthy* 199

Dirk Mieuwess, A.D. 1571 . . . . *Thieleman J. van Braght* 207

An Ill Wind. . . . . *Author Unknown* 209

Thar She Blo-o-ows!. . . . . *Edith Dorian and W. N. Wilson* 215

The Quakers of Nantucket . . . . *J. Hector St. John* 222

I Treated Him; God Healed Him . . . . *John Hudson Tiner* 224

Going to Market . . . . *Sydney Taylor* 230

Varifrån Kommer Språken?. . . . . *Genesis 11:1-9* 239

   A Jingle of Words . . . . *Betty Scott Stam* 241

   Words . . . . *George Gordon, Lord Byron* 243

   A Word . . . . *Emily Dickinson* 244

Responsibility

   Myself. . . . . *Edgar A. Guest* 245

In the Sugar Bush, Part 1. . . . . *Elizabeth Yates* 246

In the Sugar Bush, Part 2. . . . . *Elizabeth Yates* 254

   The Pasture . . . . *Robert Frost* 259

The Meaning of the Word . . . . *Mildred Geiger Gilbertson* 260

   The Runaway . . . . *Robert Frost* 271

Hunting Graybeard . . . . *Robin Collins* 272

Henry's Own Story . . . . *Tim Kennedy* 277

   The Easy Road Crowded . . . . *Messick* 285

   A Smile as Small as Mine. . . . . *Emily Dickinson* 286

Not Meant for Bullets, Part 1 . . . . *Elmo Stoll* 287

Not Meant for Bullets, Part 2 . . . . *Elmo Stoll* 296

Race Against Death . . . . *Irma H. Taylor* 305

Glossary 315

605

So Many Things to Learn

Happy Is the Man

Happy is the man that findeth wisdom,
And the man that getteth understanding.
   For the merchandise of it is better
   Than the merchandise of silver,
   And the gain thereof than fine gold.
     She is more precious than rubies:
     And all the things thou canst desire
     Are not to be compared unto her.

– Proverbs 3:13-15

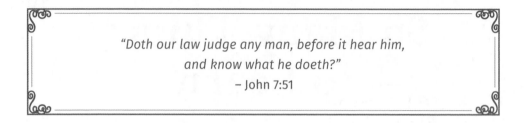

*"Doth our law judge any man, before it hear him,
and know what he doeth?"*
– John 7:51

The Honor Box

Wayne Fisher was whistling as he and Jack Gorman turned onto Lake Street, their sneakers crunching the black **cinders** now that there was no more sidewalk. To their left the rays of the late afternoon sun bounced off the water, sending out sparks of light in all directions.

"Guess you have a right to be happy." Jack grinned at him. "Having this stand to sell bait to the fishermen and using an honor box to pay was your idea. And it sure has worked! We'll be able to make our **pledge** to the Sunday school class in no time and have money coming in for ourselves for the rest of the summer."

Wayne smiled back. Jack was almost as tall as he was, but Jack's dark hair and eyes contrasted precisely with Wayne's sun-bleached towhead and blue eyes. Both boys were tanned from the weeks in the summer sun.

"Don't forget about Curly Lewis," Wayne reminded his friend. "He has just about promised to come to Sunday school and church with me this week. That's something to be glad about too."

Jack nodded, but he was frowning. "I guess so. But I'm surprised you ever got any Lewis that close. You can't trust any of them! Curly's big brother's still in prison. People will really be surprised to see one of them in church!"

"But maybe Curly's different," Wayne insisted.

They stopped in front of the stand they had constructed the week before. They had salvaged some old crates from a peach orchard and placed a wide plank across them. An old blue sheet draped over the plank shielded the bait from the midday sun. Wayne had painted the BAIT FOR SALE sign and nailed it to a post in front of the stand. A green metal box sat on the stand, a sign taped to it: "This is the honor box. Please put the money for the bait here; then take your bait from under the stand." On the sign Jack had written the price of each type of bait.

"A real good idea," Jack said again. "The fishermen can get their bait practically on the lake, the prices are cheap enough, and all we have to do is come with more bait and pick up the cash twice a day. This way we can still work at other things too."

Wayne picked up the honor box. "Hey," he said as he opened it, "there's hardly any money here at all!"

Jack squinted against the sun and looked out over the lake. "That's funny; there are as many boats as ever. Think we're losing customers?"

Wayne checked the worms, crickets, and other bait that were in the jars and dirt-filled boxes beneath the stand.

"They're about gone." He stood up.

"But if no one bought them, they should still be there!"

"Maybe someone stole them!" Wayne finished. "Either stole the bait or took the money from the box! Smart though—whoever it was didn't take *all* the money."

"Let's call the police!" Jack's eyes were wide with excitement.

Wayne shook his head slowly. "The police need clues before they can do much. And this is just little stuff to them." They stared over the lake for a long hot minute, then Wayne exclaimed, "I know! Let's catch the thief ourselves!"

"How?"

Wayne hesitated, a plan forming in his mind. "We'll hide where we can watch the stand. When the thief comes back, we'll catch him! Or at least be able to tell the police what he looks like."

"What if he doesn't come back?"

"We'll watch all day, every day, if we have to. He'll come back sometime and try again."

Finding a place was easy. Between the road and the lakeside were two maple trees, thickly covered with leaves. Wayne climbed into one of them, Jack into the other. They waited, watching the stand across the road.

After a long while two fishermen came. One took some worms, but the other put money into the honor box. Wayne saw the coins flash in the sun.

When the two men had gone, Wayne eased himself into another position, rubbing his cramped legs. *I wonder how long this'll take,* he thought.

A woman and a little boy came to the stand. The little boy looked all over the bait, but they didn't take any.

Next, someone came toward the stand from the little store that sold ice, pop, and snacks to fishermen. Wayne gasped; it was Curly Lewis!

Wayne saw Curly glance around quickly, then go up to the stand. Without looking at the bait, Curly opened the honor box. He swiftly thrust his hand in, pulled it out, and started jogging down the street.

Wayne sat in the tree, stunned. He had thought Curly was almost ready to come to Sunday school and church with him, but here was Curly, stealing from the honor box!

Anger flashed through Wayne. He dropped from the tree, sprinting after Curly as fast as he could.

"Wait, Curly!" Wayne yelled.

Jack was at his side, puffing. "Curly stole the money! Then he came back for more. I told you not to trust a Lewis. Curly!" he yelled.

The other boy stopped and turned around.

Wayne was running at full speed. He was the fastest runner in the school, so he was not surprised that Curly stopped. He knew he couldn't outrun Wayne.

Curly waited, a smile on his face. "Hi, Wayne, I didn't see you. Hi, Jack."

"You sure didn't see me!" Wayne snapped. "I want my money back! Don't look so surprised. You know—the money from the honor box. You stole it—some before and just now some more. Come on, Jack and I both saw you take it."

"Saw me take money? But I—"

"Don't try to lie out of it," Wayne warned. "I sure was **gullible**, wasn't I? You acted interested in church just to throw me off, didn't you? Thought I'd never think it was you who took money from our box. But I saw you with my own eyes. From the tree. So did Jack."

Curly seemed to pale, then a rush of angry red spread over his face. "Wait a minute. You mean you saw me at the box just now, and—"

"We both did," Jack put in. "You stole the money from the honor box."

"You're a thief. Give us back our money," Wayne demanded.

"I didn't take your money!" Curly said.

"If you won't give it, we'll have to take it from you," Wayne said threateningly.

Angrily Curly responded, "You're just like my brother said—"

"Hey, what's going on here?"

Wayne looked up to see a tall man in fishing gear approaching them.

"You tell 'em, Mister," Curly said fiercely.

The fisherman frowned. "I was coming to see if this young man put the money I gave him in that box. Did he?"

Wayne and Jack watched in surprise as Curly nodded. "Just a few minutes ago."

"Thanks." The stranger turned to Wayne. "No one in our group had the right change to pay for the bait we took, so we went into the store to get some. But we got to talking, and when we finally remembered your money, we were busy. I asked this boy to bring it over for us. Just wanted to be sure he did, so I came over to check."

They all walked back to the stand, and Wayne lifted the lid of the honor box. There were plenty of coins there now. Each one accused him!

"Well, thanks, fellow." The stranger nodded at Curly and left.

Wayne looked down at his feet. "Curly—" he started.

"Forget it!" Curly snapped. "Forget the church stuff too. My brother always said church people were just a bunch of big talkers. Underneath they aren't any different from anyone else. Maybe worse. I was almost fooled for a while, but no more. You didn't even check the box or give a *Lewis* a chance to explain. Thanks for *nothing*."

Curly turned and ran away from them down the street.

Wayne and Jack looked at each other, then started running after Curly.

"Curly!" Wayne shouted. "Curly, wait! Please wait!"

But even as he called, Wayne knew it was too late. Curly was beyond his reach.

– Betty Steele Everett

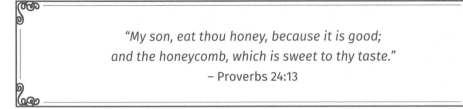

A Harvest of Gold

There's something I've always wondered: how does the beekeeper get the honey out of the hives? Every day when I look out my bedroom window, I see my neighbor's hives, like three stacks of wooden boxes. With my binoculars, I can see bees flying in and out. I know there's honey in there, but how . . . Oh, my name's Joshua. I'm twelve years old, and I wonder about a lot of things. So last weekend when I was wondering about the honey, I happened to see my neighbor, Mr. Carter, out picking tomatoes. I thought I'd just wander over and ask him. Whew! Did I ever learn a lot!

"Oh, *that*," said Mr. Carter. "It's really quite simple. About one week before you want to **extract** the honey, you put in the escape. Then on extracting day, you smoke the hives, remove the frames from the supers, uncap the foundations, extract, fill your jars, and you're done for another year!"

He smiled. "Do you understand?"

Understand? *Escape? Uncap? Extract?* I didn't understand a word of it. *This must be what they mean by a specialized vocabulary,* I thought. *Strictly beekeeper language.*

I must have looked puzzled, because Mr. Carter wrinkled his brow and gave a long "Hmmm . . ."

"I can see that you don't understand," he continued. "I'll tell you what. I've just put in the escape. That's a bee-sized, one-way swinging door. It lets the bees out of the honey-storage area but not back in. So in a few days, with most of the bees gone, it will be safe to harvest the honey. How would you like to help?"

"Like to help? *Me?* Well sure." It sounded like a real hands-on experience, like my teachers always say. But what about the bees? I don't know a whole lot about how insects are designed, but I do know that bees have stingers. So I asked.

Mr. Carter laughed. "Don't you worry," he said. "I'll get you outfitted so the bees can't sting you. Just be here about nine o'clock the next sunny morning this week."

On Friday the sun woke me up early. I remembered the bees and was knocking on Mr. Carter's door before nine o'clock. He still had a cup of tea in his hand when he greeted me.

"Come in, come in," he said, sounding excited. "I'm glad you remembered. Extracting honey is hard work. I can really use your help."

Work? Well, maybe if you'd done it a lot of times. To me it sounded like fun.

Mr. Carter handed me a one-piece suit that zipped up the front, heavy gloves that went past my elbows, and a hat that looked like a hard hat with a wide brim. It was covered by a veil that hung around my shoulders and zipped onto the suit. I suppose I looked like an astronaut. Mr. Carter sure did as he motioned for me to follow him.

"There are a few bees left in the hive," he said. "First we must calm them."

In the garage he stuffed small rags into what looked like an oil can with part of an accordion attached. "This is the smoker," he explained. "You light these rags, then pump the bellows to blow smoke into the hives. First the bees panic and fill themselves with honey. God gave them the instinct to save their honey if their tree catches on fire. Later, the smoke makes the bees lazy. Docile, they call it—the way we feel after eating a big meal. Then they're not as likely to sting."

That sounded good to me. As long as they wouldn't sting, I was ready to take on the bees. I guess Mr. Carter could tell that I was getting keyed-up, because he said in a very serious voice, "Joshua, there's one thing that I want you to remember. When we work around the hives, we have to move *slowly and gently.* The bees sense our movements and react to them."

I took a deep breath and tried to calm down by picturing the gentle, floating motion of astronauts walking in space. I think it worked. Mr. Carter looked at me.

"Think you're ready?" he asked.

I nodded.

"Good. Grab that wheelbarrow and let's harvest some honey."

The wheelbarrow held a brush, a towel, and part of a hive that looked like a box without a top or bottom. Mr. Carter told me it was called a super.

He took the top off the hive and blew the smoke into it. He lifted out a frame filled with honeycomb. With the soft brush, he brushed a few bees off of it. Like an orchestra conductor directing a lullaby, he moved so slowly and **rhythmically** that I felt calm just watching him.

But this feeling didn't last long. Suddenly I knew I wasn't alone. I was an **invader** in the queendom of the bees. Bees were buzzing all around me, crawling on my suit, marching across my veil. Their loud sound, like the *zzzzzz!* of my alarm clock, filled my ears, and I became a statue, frozen in time next to the beehives. I knew I would never move again! Then the sharp command of Mr. Carter's voice snapped me out of it.

"Joshua! Take this. Put this frame in the empty super and cover it with the towel. Quickly! Before the bees find it again."

I did as I was told. Gently I dropped the frame into the super. And I did it again . . . and again . . . for ten supers that each held nine frames. That's ninety frames and five trips to the garage. Because each time we had two full supers in the wheelbarrow, we'd take them to the garage, slide them under the door, and close it quickly—bees are smart about finding their honey. By this time I was starting to see what Mr. Carter meant about work. And we still hadn't touched a drop of that tasty golden honey.

We unsuited, ate lunch, then headed back to the garage and its waiting supers. I heard the buzzing of bees and suspiciously looked around for a swarm.

"Don't worry," said Mr. Carter. "They're just a few stragglers. They shouldn't bother us."

He set up a table and placed a large pan on it. Then he plugged in a long narrow tool that looked like a trowel for spreading concrete.

"This is the uncapping knife," he explained. "It's hot and it's sharp. After the bees fill their six-sided wax cells with honey, they seal, or *cap,* the top. This knife makes it easy to slice off the cappings."

Mr. Carter showed me how to use it. It looked easy, and it was. Slice, scrape the cappings into the pan, then the honey at last! It smelled sweet, like brown sugar frosting, as it sizzled on the knife.

While I was uncapping, Mr. Carter was dusting off the extractor. That's a fancy name for a garbage-can-sized pail with a wire basket in it. The basket holds the frames. You crank a handle that spins the basket, and the honey flies out. The honey runs down the inside walls of the extractor barrel and collects in the bottom of the pail where there's a spigot. You drain the honey out through the spigot into jars.

When Mr. Carter had the extractor ready, I handed him my first uncapped frame. He looked at it, then handed it back.

"This isn't done," he said with a smile.

I could see that it wasn't. It was still waxed-over. But I was *sure* that I had uncapped it. Then I turned it over. There was the side that I had done.

"See, I *did* uncap it," I said.

"But you did only half," Mr. Carter said, laughing. "The bees fill in both sides of the frame."

With twice as much to do, I got back to work. I worked and I worked. I felt my arm and shoulder getting sore from all of that back and forth motion. I got up to stretch.

"Would you like to crank the extractor for a while?"

Mr. Carter knew just what I needed. Some circular movements would help loosen up my arm. I grabbed the handle and cranked as hard as I could.

"Whoa," called Mr. Carter. "Slow it down! Going too fast will ruin the frames. It'll pull out the wax foundations." He took the handle and demonstrated. "First, crank slowly to start the honey flowing, then a little faster to empty the frames, then slow it down again and stop."

When we took the empty frame from the extractor, I could see what he meant by a foundation. Lining each frame was a sheet of hundreds of now empty wax cells. "We want only the honey, not the wax," Mr. Carter pointed out. "When we put these frames back in the hives, the bees will fill the foundations with honey and recap them."

We worked all afternoon, uncapping, extracting, and putting honey in jars. When we were finished, Mr. Carter thanked me and said, "Now I'll pay you with gold. The golden treasure of the bees."

As I walked home carrying my jars of honey, I thought about my adventure. I'd learned the language of the beekeeper and how to get the honey from the hives. But I still wondered about some things. Like, what would those bees think when they flew home and found their honey missing? And what do bees do in the hive all winter?

Oh, well, I knew Mr. Carter would take good care of all his bee colonies. And I'd find all that out later—after I'd eaten my fill of peanut butter and honey sandwiches.

– *Bonnie Abbs*

September

The goldenrod is yellow;
    The corn is turning brown;
The trees in apple orchards
    With fruit are bending down.

The gentian's bluest fringes
    Are curling in the sun;
In dusty pods the milkweed
    Its hidden silk has spun.

    The sedges flaunt their harvest
        In every meadow nook;
    And asters by the brook side
        Make asters in the brook.

From dewy lanes at morning
    The grapes' sweet odors rise;
At noon the roads all flutter
    With yellow butterflies.

    By all these lovely tokens
        September days are here,
    With summer's best of weather,
        And autumn's best of cheer.

– Helen Hunt Jackson

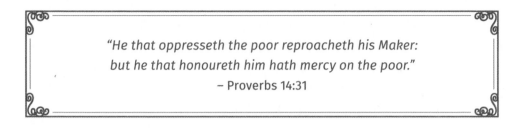

Making Joe's Lunch

The boys lounged comfortably on the grass under the sycamore trees. Soon they would be playing very hard at a game of softball, but first they had to take care of their well-filled lunch pails and brown bags.

"Why—" wondered Howard, "why doesn't Joseph Hadley come out and eat his dinner with us? Seems like he always sneaks off somewhere until we're through."

"Probably afraid we'll ask him for some of his goodies," answered Chris.

"Nah!" said Will, laying back on the grass, a little too full of his oversized lunch, "more likely he doesn't have anything at all. Probably too proud to let anyone know! Dad says their family doesn't have much since Mr. Hadley died. And Mom says they're too proud—probably always will be poor."

"Mary Hadley asked my mother if she had sewing she could do," put in Samuel. "But sometimes people do that who aren't poor."

"Joseph's wearing patched pants," Howard added.

"Hey," Will said, "let's spy on old Joe tomorrow and see what he brings. He's always in his seat before the first bell. We can get a peek into his bag before the final bell."

The boys nodded their agreement, all except Alan Collins. Alan hadn't taken part in the conversation. Now he said simply, as he brushed the crumbs off his lap, "I can't see what fun there will be in that. It seems mean and sneaky to me. It's none of our business what Joe brings for dinner or where he goes to eat it."

"You're always the *nice guy,* Alan Collins," Will **scoffed**. A couple of the younger boys giggled.

Alan didn't like to be laughed at. His eyes flashed for a minute. Then he sprang up and shouted, "We bat first!" In five minutes everyone was absorbed in a game of softball.

The next morning just before the first bell, a half dozen mischievous faces peered into the classroom. Sure enough, there was Joseph Hadley, working on his math lesson. It took only a minute to hurry into the coat closet, and soon the whole group was pressing around Will as he held the mysterious brown bag in his hand. Among them, in spite of his protest the day before, was Alan Collins.

"That thing's big enough to hold a day's **ration** for an army!" Chris said as Will opened the big grocery bag and pulled out a clean white napkin. After that, he drew out a large wad of folded paper. In the bottom of the bag, at last, Will found one cold potato. That was all. He held it up between two fingers, grimacing. The others laughed.

"Hey," said Will, "let's toss out the potato and stick some coal in. It'll be a laugh to see him open it!"

The boys agreed. Will set the potato on a shelf while Howard brought some coal from the coal bucket. Will dropped a few lumps of hard coal into the sack. He stuffed the paper back in and carefully laid the white napkin on top. Before the bell rang, they were all in their seats. Alan Collins was the last to leave the coat closet, slipping into his seat just as the bell rang.

Noon came around and the children rushed to the closet for their dinner pails. Instead of going out to the playground, the boys lingered at the door. Alan Collins, however, marched straight past them and down the hall, his pail under his arm.

"Psst! Alan," Samuel whispered loudly. "Where you going now?"

"Home!" Alan said, laughing. "I saw Mom making cookies when I left this morning. I'm not going to miss out on those!"

"Ask me to go too," Howard shouted after Alan, who was already through the double doors and headed across the lawn toward home. Just then the boys saw Joe carrying his bag up to his desk.

"Think he suspects something, with that heavy coal in there?" Chris chuckled.

The boys leaned in at the back of the room to watch Joe open his lunch bag.

"Hope his dinner doesn't lie too hard on his stomach," Will whispered. First Joe pulled at the paper, which seemed stuck beneath something. He looked in the bag with surprise and then with a bewildered look on his face, he took out one of Mrs. Collins' delicious ham sandwiches, and then a little home-baked apple pie, a thermos of milk, and a bag full of almonds and raisins. It was a dinner fit for a king, the watching boys thought.

But Joe made no move to taste his lunch; he only sat there and looked at it. At last, he laid his head on his desk. One of the smaller boys whispered, "Look, he's praying."

The boys sneaked away toward the playground without a word.

"Hum," said Will when they reached the bright sunshine. "Wonder what happened?"

"I'm glad, whatever it was," Howard remarked. "I've felt mean all morning. The Hadleys aren't to blame for having only cold potatoes to eat, and I don't blame Joe for being embarrassed."

"Dad says Mr. Hadley was a fine man, and it was one of the worst things for the community when he got killed," Samuel said.

Will suddenly noticed that it began to feel unusually warm as the boys sat on the lawn and guessed at what had happened.

As soon as he finished eating, Will jumped up. "Let's play. Same teams as yesterday—they were fair." Without waiting for Alan, the boys rushed to the diamond. Pitches flew and bats swung as usual, but comments about Alan, and about Joe's lunch, passed back and forth from catcher to batter and first baseman to runner.

After the first half inning, Howard shouted from shortstop, "Hey, Alan. Come on!"

The others turned to look at Alan coming toward the field, and they were surprised to see Joseph Hadley walking timidly at his side.

"Hey, Joe," Howard called, "you play second for us. We're shy on infielders."

The game resumed, Alan on one team, Joe on the other. Alan and Will were standing behind the backstop, watching their team hit, when one of their players smacked a line drive straight at Joe Hadley. Joe snagged it out of the air and fired it to first, catching the player who had already run halfway to second base.

"Double play!" Alan admired. "Joe must have played a little baseball before, eh?"

Will poked Alan in the ribs and said, half in teasing and half in spite, "You're always the *nice guy,* Alan Collins."

"Nah, Will, I just remembered the proverb that says, 'He that oppresseth the poor reproacheth his Maker; but he that honoureth him hath mercy on the poor.' "

– Author Unknown

The poem "September" on page 12 spoke of the beauty of autumn.
This poem does too—but something is different!

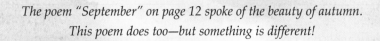

Rebellion in September

Five and twelve make? Oh, dear me,
How the red leaves shine on the maple tree.

Wild geese fly in a long dark line!
Seven times seven are forty-nine.

Crickets chirp where the grass grows brown—
Which is the verb and which the noun?

Asters grow white and gentians blue—
What are the boundaries of Peru?

How can I name the Presidents,
When cornstalks rise like golden tents?

Eleven times three are thirty-three—
Why wasn't I born a bird or a tree?

– Rachel Field

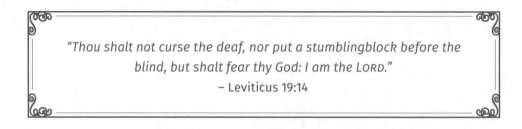

So Many Things to Learn

This story is one chapter taken from a longer book. Can you guess what happened in the earlier part of the book, before this chapter?

Mother and Aunt Martha took Jimmy to the bus station. Jimmy tried not to show how worried he was, and the excitement around him helped to keep his mind away from the trip ahead of him.

He heard the announcer call the different buses over the loud-speaker while his mother and Aunt Martha calmly talked together, their voices blending with the hum of confusion in the waiting room.

"Mom, why don't they call my bus?" Jimmy asked.

"It isn't time yet, Jimmy."

"But you're not listening; you're talking to Aunt Martha."

"Don't worry, Jimmy. We'll see that you don't get left behind," Aunt Martha assured him.

Just then a porter came up to Mrs. Carter. "Your bus is ready now, ma'am," he said. "Just follow me."

"But they haven't called it yet," Jimmy protested. "I was listening."

"We take you out before it's called," the porter explained, "to get ahead of the crowd."

"Come along, Jimmy," his mother said. "I'm putting your baggage check in the envelope with your ticket." She handed him the envelope. "Take good care of it."

"Mom, how will I know when to get off?"

"Don't worry about that." The porter laughed. "They won't let you ride any farther than you paid for."

Jimmy clung to his mother as they went through the gate and out onto the platform, his white cane dangling useless at his side.

"Here's your passenger," the porter called.

Jimmy felt a strong hand grasp his arm. "All right, young man," the driver said. "Let me get you seated before the rush."

A quick hug and kiss from his mother and Aunt Martha, a breathless walk across the platform; then, half carried, half led, he stumbled up a couple of steps into the bus and felt himself being eased onto a soft cushion.

"You're sitting right behind me, fellow, where I can keep an eye on you. Now I've got to go out and collect my tickets," the driver told him, and Jimmy was alone in the large empty bus.

He sat by a window, and as the passengers came into the bus, Jimmy felt a man sit down beside him. "I guess that's your mother outside waving to you," he told Jimmy.

"Where?" Jimmy asked.

"Right over there," the man said. Jimmy guessed he was pointing. Jimmy waved as the bus started, but he didn't know in which direction to wave. He sat very tense, very straight in his seat, gripping his white cane as tightly as he had the first time he crossed the street.

The bus had gone just a short distance when the man beside Jimmy asked, "Do you make this trip often?"

"No, sir. I've never traveled alone before, but the school says I have to."

A lady in the seat behind them had overheard. "But isn't that dangerous, young man? Why must you do that?"

"It's one of the rules of the school," Jimmy explained. "The bus driver promised to take care of me."

"Where are you going?" she asked.

"I'm going to the guide dog school. I'm going to get a dog," Jimmy said proudly.

The lady turned to a passenger across the aisle. "This young man is going to a guide dog school, traveling all by himself. Isn't that wonderful?"

"How far are you going?" someone asked.

"About four hundred miles," Jimmy answered. "I won't get there until night."

"What's your name?" another passenger asked.

"I'm Jimmy Carter," he said. And from then on the bus adopted him.

The conversation was interrupted when they stopped for lunch and the driver turned to him. "If you'll come with me, we'll go to the lunchroom."

"We'll take him with us," several passengers said, and Jimmy found himself the center of a friendly group of people who had not known each other before. They all wanted to order for him.

"I think I'd like a hamburger," Jimmy said, "and a glass of milk."

"Bring him two hamburgers," the voice next to him ordered.

"Wait a minute!" Jimmy was confused. "How much will all this cost?"

"You're my guest," several said at once and then argued with one another about it.

"Thank you," said Jimmy, "but Mother gave me expense money."

"How do you handle money?" someone asked. "How can you tell a one-dollar bill from a ten?"

"I can't," Jimmy said, "but I'm not supposed to carry anything larger than a five so the change will be in ones, and I fold them different."

"That's clever. But how do you recognize change?"

"Oh, that's easy," said Jimmy. "Half-dollars, quarters, and dimes are rough around the edge. A nickel is kind of like a quarter, but smooth around the edge. And you won't mix pennies and dimes because the edge of the penny is smooth."

"I never noticed that," one of the men said, and they all dug into their pockets to discover if they could tell what coins they had by the feel of them.

"You keep your money in your pocket," someone told Jimmy. "I've got your check."

"Thank you ever so much, sir."

"All aboard," the driver shouted, and Jimmy was led back to the bus and showered with more candy bars than were good for him.

The trainer was at the station to meet Jimmy. "I'm Mr. Weeks from the school," he said. "I suppose you are Mr. James Carter."

"Did you bring my dog?" was Jimmy's first question.

Mr. Weeks laughed. "Not yet. There's a lot to do before you get the dog."

"Oh!" Jimmy was disappointed but had no time to show it.

"Take my arm and we'll go to the station wagon," Mr. Weeks said. "We'll drive out to the school."

They got into the station wagon. "Did you have any trouble on the trip, Mr. Carter?" Mr. Weeks asked.

Jimmy listened for someone to answer. Then, after a pause, "Oh, you mean me? I'm Jimmy."

"No. You are Mr. Carter while at the school," Mr. Weeks explained. "You see, most of our students feel helpless because they are newly blind. By treating them with respect, we make them feel like grown men and women again."

"And everybody calls me Mister?" Jimmy asked.

"Just the members of the school staff. The students may call each other by their first names."

Jimmy settled back in his seat. His lips moved. "Mister Carter," he almost whispered. It sounded good. He felt very grown-up.

When they arrived at the school, Mr. Weeks took Jimmy's suitcase and led him up a short flight of stairs into a wide hall.

"Oh, Mr. McDonald," he called to someone standing there. "This is Mr. James Carter. He's your roommate. Will you take his suitcase and show him around? I have some other things I must do."

Jimmy felt a strong handclasp as a deep voice said, "Hello Jim, glad to know you. Call me Mack. Come along and I'll take you to our room."

Mack led Jimmy down the hall and into their bedroom.

"This is my bed," Mack explained. "Yours is by the window. Give me your hand. This is your chest of drawers."

Jimmy felt his hand laid gently on a piece of furniture. Before he had time to inspect it, Mack tucked Jimmy's arm under his own and started across the room.

"I'll Braille the room for you. Your closet is next to mine, and there are coat hangers in it. Here it is. You can look at it later. This next door leads to our bathroom, and this door over here leads outside to a fenced-in runway for our dogs. Here's a window. Now you're back to your chest of drawers again. Your chair is between it and your bed. I put your suitcase on your bed. You had better unpack and put your things away. I'll come for you when the dinner gong rings. You've got about an hour."

"Well, w-e-l-l." Jimmy's mind was spinning. "Who's going to help me unpack?"

"You'd better do that for yourself," Mack advised. "How can you find your clothes if someone else puts them away?"

Jimmy felt very lost, very much alone, and for the first time since he had started to work with Miss Thompson, he felt very, very blind. "Can't you at least show me what to do?" he asked.

"What do you want to know?" Mack inquired. "Put your shirts in the second drawer, underwear in the third drawer; hang your clothes in the closet and use the top drawer for your handkerchiefs, socks, and small items. And, oh yes, put your toothpaste on the third shelf in the medicine cabinet. I'm using the second shelf from the bottom for mine. Put your shaving cream and razor to the left on the bottom shelf."

"Razor?"

"Sure," Mack said. "What do you use, electric or safety?"

"Not—not either one. You're kidding me," Jimmy said. "I—I don't shave yet."

"Well, enjoy not having to, while it lasts. How old are you?" Mack asked.

"I'm 11, going on 12," Jimmy said. "How old are you?"

"I'm 28," Mack replied. "Now you better get busy and put your things away. You can do that, can't you?"

"Not without help," Jimmy stammered. "You seem to forget I'm blind."

"Well," Mack said quietly, "what do you think I am?"

Then Jimmy realized that this confident, steady chap was also blind.

When the gong rang for dinner, Mack rescued Jimmy, who was still struggling with his unpacking. Jimmy dumped the things into the chest of drawers and put the empty suitcase on the floor of his closet.

Mack led him into the dining room, and Jimmy remembered some of the things Miss Thompson had taught him about feeling the size of a room. He heard footsteps coming from quite a distance on the linoleum-covered floor, and the sound of those footsteps bounced back from walls that seemed far apart.

"This is a large room," Jimmy said to himself.

His thoughts were interrupted as Mack put Jimmy's hand on the back of a chair. "This is your place," Mack told him. "I'm across the table from you."

The footsteps Jimmy had heard approaching now reached the end of the table, and a chair scraped on the floor as someone sat down. "I'm Mr. Weeks, your trainer," the voice said from that end of the table. He introduced the students and Jimmy learned that there were seven other men and two girls in the class.

By this time a plate had been quietly laid on the table in front of Jimmy, and he waited for someone to cut up his food as his mother had done. He heard the rest of the blind students eating, laughing, and talking.

Miss Young, the social secretary, came over to Jimmy's side. "What's the matter, Mr. Carter? You aren't eating."

"Mother always cut up my food," he answered.

"You will learn to do that for yourself," she told him. "Let me show you. We use the face of a clock for directions."

"Oh, I know about that," Jimmy said.

"Good. Now take your fork, and I will hold your hand. Your slice of meat is down here at six o'clock." Guiding his hand, she touched the meat with the tip of his fork. "Your mashed potatoes are at nine o'clock, here. The carrots are from two to four o'clock over here, and string beans are up at twelve o'clock." She touched each vegetable with his fork as she spoke. "Your salad is in a small dish at nine o'clock, your bread and butter is at eleven, and your glass of water at twelve o'clock."

Nora, the cook, came in to inquire who wanted coffee, tea, or milk. Jimmy was tempted to take coffee. He wanted to be grown-up but realized his mother would not approve, so he chose the milk and Miss Young explained, "Nora will put the milk at one o'clock next to your plate."

Miss Young showed him how to cut the meat for himself and then went back to her own place at the table. Jimmy's knife felt awkward in his hand; he wasn't sure whether he was cutting with the sharp or the dull edge. He turned it over and then turned it back again. Both edges seemed dull—or else the meat was tough.

Finally he got a bite cut off and started to lift it up, only to find that he had put an empty fork into his mouth. Jimmy hoped nobody was looking and then remembered that the rest of the students were blind also. He fished around gently in his plate until his fork came in contact with a piece of meat; he started to lift it, and this time the whole slice came up. Little beads of **perspiration** formed at the back of his neck and began to run like a miniature Niagara Falls down his spine. He felt nervous and **flustered**. Holding the meat firmly with his fork, he stabbed at it, making a powerful thrust with his knife. His plate tilted forward, and the slice of meat slid into his lap.

Jimmy was horrified. "What will I do now?" he asked himself. "Shall I sneak it back to my plate or wrap it up in my napkin and pretend I have eaten it?" He wished he were back at home where his mother could fuss over him. Then he heard Miss Young at his side.

"Don't let that bother you, Mr. Carter," she said so quietly that no one else could hear. "That can happen just as easily to people who can see. Many a person carving a Thanksgiving turkey has had the turkey fly across the table."

She gathered up Jimmy's napkin with the slice of meat in it and said quietly, "Eat your vegetables until I get back." He heard her footsteps fade down the length of the room toward the kitchen door.

Jimmy ate his vegetables. The mashed potatoes were easy, but the string beans tried to play a game with him. If he tried to scoop them up on his fork they slid off, and time after time he brought an empty fork to his mouth. He decided to spear them, and they stuck to his fork like jackstraws sticking out at various angles. As he brought the fork to his mouth, one of the beans struck his upper lip, one **dribbled** against his chin, and a couple stuck out like fingers at either side of his mouth. Jimmy wished he had a funnel. He wondered how the other students were able to eat and laugh and talk at the same time without washing their faces in vegetable juice.

He thought of Mack and how **capable** he was, then said to himself, "They've all been blind longer and had more training than I have."

Miss Young returned with a fresh slice of meat and again showed Jimmy how to measure off a bite size, cut it, and bring it up to his mouth. He didn't know how much of his food slid off his plate onto the table while he was eating. Miss Young didn't tell him, and the blind students never knew. He made up his mind that he, too, would learn to eat nicely. But there were so many things to learn!

Jimmy did learn to eat nicely and to do more things for himself. And he got his guide dog, a German shepherd named Leader.

– James B. Garfield

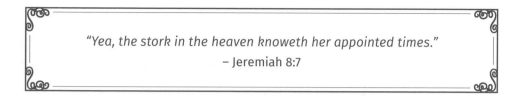

> *"Yea, the stork in the heaven knoweth her appointed times."*
> – Jeremiah 8:7

Call of the Wild Geese

"Say, Bob, do you know where you're going?" For some time we had walked along single file without seeing a familiar landmark.

"Now that you mention it, I'm not sure that I do," Bob replied sheepishly. "I thought we were headed south, but it seems to me we should have come out onto the road by now if we were going in the right direction."

"I think home is *that* way," I suggested, pointing.

"But that's only a guess," Bob replied. "From the slope of the land, I'd say you're turned around at least a quarter of a circle!"

It was dark and getting darker with the shortness of a late October day. To make matters worse, a thick overcast shut out the stars, and an unseasonable flurry of snow added to our difficulties.

We could not have been more than three miles from home, but because our ranch was very remote, we could wander for miles if we headed in the wrong direction.

Suddenly, above the moaning of the wind in the treetops, I heard a familiar sound. I gripped Bob's arm and drew him to a stop.

"Listen!"

The snow flurries had turned into a great swirling sea of snow and darkness. We stood close together and strained to identify the new sound. Then it came again:

"Alonk! Honk! Alaw-onk!"

"Canada geese!" said Bob excitedly. "Hundreds of them! Say, do you know what?"

"Sure," I replied. "They're **migrating**, and a good thing too—the lakes will be freezing over pretty soon."

"You're right. They're pulling out of the country. But it's *where* they're heading, not *why,* that interests me. Geese go *south* in the winter, remember?"

Now I understood what Bob was talking about. Of course! The geese moved across the sky above us for nearly an hour, perhaps thousands of them flocking together for their great trip. And following this feathered compass, we made our way south through the stormy night until finally we saw the lights of home.

A mighty wanderer is the Canada goose. His familiar "honk-alonk" can be heard all the way from the Gulf of Mexico to the Arctic Circle. In early spring the chief gander leads his flock in their annual trek across the continent. In late autumn when the young have become strong enough flyers, he leads them south again to leave the **frigid** winter behind.

One summer day Bob and I were exploring the edge of a marshy lake. Duke, our collie, ranged ahead of us, letting his curious nose lead him here and there on the track of some wild inhabitant of the marsh. While we stopped to pluck cattail canes, Duke disappeared from sight in a clump of lush swamp grass.

Suddenly there was a tremendous commotion, a great squawking and hissing, then Duke shot out of the grass with a pair of angry geese in close pursuit. They stopped a few yards short of us while Duke crouched behind our legs. Then, uttering threatening honks, they took to the air and circled over our heads.

"Say, I wonder if they are nesting!" Bob said. "Must be something like that to make them so angry."

Keeping a watchful eye on the circling geese, we moved forward until we could see beyond the clump of grass. Sure enough, there was a nest in a mound of moss and feathers. We could make out the outline of four large eggs buried in down. It was exciting to know that a family of geese would be raised in our area.

One of the geese had an unusual pattern of white markings on its head and throat. Because of this, we were able to discover that the same pair came back to nest year after year.

The young geese were dependent on the safety of the lake and the fierceness of their protective parents until they were almost grown. Only then would the feathers of their wings be developed sufficiently to carry their large bodies into the air.

One summer day a tragedy befell our goose family. We never did find out what happened, but the parent birds disappeared, and there were only two of the young left on the lake. They seemed terrified, for when we approached they swam rapidly to the far shore and ran into the woods, using their spread wings to speed them along. Bob and I held a hurried discussion. How would these two young geese survive without their parents? It seemed likely that they would soon fall victim to a fox or dog since they were not yet able to fly. We decided at last that we would try to fill the role of parents.

Quickly we circled the lake until we reached the point where the geese had entered the woods. They had not gone far, and when we came upon them, we discovered how easily some coyote or fox could have captured them. Bob went after one while I closed in on the other.

Once caught, the goslings proved to be surprisingly tame. We must have presented an amusing sight when we later walked into the house, each with a long goose neck craning up out of our arms.

"Mother, just look what we've got! May we keep them?" we shouted in unison.

"Wherever did you get those birds?" Mother asked. "Have you been bothering that goose family?"

"Oh, no, we didn't take them away from their parents," we protested. When we had told the story of the tragedy, Mother said that we could try to look after the husky youngsters.

Our task was not too difficult. We found that the goslings would eat almost anything we gave them. Named Willy and Nilly, they took up residence with our flock of chickens and soon had the chicken yard completely in their control. Eventually they became so fierce with the hens that it was necessary to **banish** them from the chicken yard. They then roamed at will about the ranch.

When Bob and I left the house, the two mischievous geese would come flapping and squawking to meet us, knowing that we usually carried a crust of bread or a handful of grain to reward them. Often they would follow us about, craning their necks around our ankles or gaggling together behind us.

September came with crisp, frosty nights. Willy and Nilly learned to fly. At first they went only short distances, often flying across the yard to meet us, instead of running. As their wings grew stronger, they grew more daring, rising to soar around the barnyard, to the dismay of the chickens, who mistook them for hunting hawks.

September gave way to October. Flocks of crows and blackbirds gathered in the stubble and discussed travel plans in noisy committees. Then the first flocks of wild geese flew over in great wedges against the blue autumn sky.

Willy and Nilly were excited. They craned their long necks skyward and honked anxiously whenever a new flock went by. Sometimes they would rise to the air and fly aimlessly around the barnyard.

One night a flock of Canada geese spent the night in the stubble of our grain field. We could hear them talking among themselves through the evening hours. In the morning they rose in a body, but instead of leaving directly, they circled over our barnyard. Willy and Nilly took to the air, honking frantically. The leader of the wild birds brought his flock around for one more circuit. There was an unmistakable invitation to his honking. Our two pets circled back over us, craning their heads down, honking—almost sadly, we thought. Then they rose higher, climbing swiftly after their wild cousins.

The call of the wild was strong enough to overcome the bond formed between us and our unusual feathered pets. Although we were sad to see Willy and Nilly go, we would not have wanted it otherwise. We were thankful that we had become better acquainted with these noble birds who, with the wisdom granted by the wise Creator, follow their paths of migration across our land.

– Todd Lee

What is the something in the poem?

Something Told the Wild Geese

Something told the wild geese
    It was time to go.
Though the fields lay golden,
    Something whispered, "Snow."
Leaves were green and stirring,
    Berries, luster-glossed,
But beneath warm feathers
    Something cautioned, "Frost."
All the sagging orchards
    Steamed with amber spice,
But each wild breast stiffened
    At remembered ice.
Something told the wild geese
    It was time to fly—
Summer sun was on their wings,
    Winter in their cry.

– Rachel Field

> *"And God said, Let the waters bring forth abundantly the moving creature that hath life, and fowl that may fly above the earth in the open firmament of heaven."* – Genesis 1:20

Created to Fly

Made for Flight

If an award were given to the bird with the clumsiest landing, there is little doubt which bird would win—the gooney bird. In the sky the gooney bird is powerful and beautifully graceful. By skillful use of wind currents, it can glide over the ocean for hours without even a flap of its wings. But it often makes a three-point landing—two legs down and flat on its face! It has earned the nickname *gooney bird* partly because of its clumsy landings.

If landing is not the strong point of this bird—properly known as the *albatross*—flying certainly is. With a wingspan that may reach 11 feet (3.35 m), the albatross can spend months flying enormous distances over the seas. It sometimes may not touch land more than a few times in four or five years. It sleeps on the surface of the ocean, drinks seawater, and feeds on small marine creatures and garbage thrown from ships.

Sailors have long been fascinated by the ability of some species of albatross to fly zigzag right into a strong wind. These graceful birds will soar and glide above a ship for days, diving steeply into the water to claim garbage from its wake.[1] The albatross is perfectly designed for flight.

---

1 wake: the track left by a moving ship in water

The evolution theory teaches that flying birds evolved from a nonflying reptile. For this to happen, almost every structure in the nonflying animal would have to change. There is no living or fossil evidence for this. And there is much evidence against it.

Consider yourself. It is claimed that you have evolved from the same ancestor as birds did long ago, but clearly, you can't fly.

Down through the centuries people have sought ways to fly. Many imaginative flapping devices, such as light, feathered boards tied to someone's arms, have quickly brought their inventors back to earth. "Why?" the disappointed flappers ask. "Why can't humans fly?"

Bones for Flight

Seeking an answer, some people have compared the bones in a bird's wing with those in their own arm. They are obviously similar. Yet there is also an important difference: the wing was designed to fly, the human arm was not.

Even if you could cover your arms with feathers, you still couldn't fly. Your arm bones may *look* like those in a bird's wing, but they can never serve the same flight function.

To be aerodynamically successful, your skeleton would need to be strong, but light. A bird's bones are hollow, like strands of macaroni or straw. They are supported by struts and honeycombed with air sacs. These lightweight bones of a bird are designed so well for flight that the bird's feathers usually weigh more than its whole skeleton! Our human bones are not like this. Why? Because they are designed to support the weight of our bodies when standing, walking, running, and so on.

Even a bird's beak is designed to save weight and make flying easier. Unlike the human jaw, which is made of heavy bone, a bird's beak is made of lightweight horn. This is another feature that shows perfect planning in the creation of birds.

Muscles and Air Sacs for Flight

To be able to fly, you would need enormous wings. But how could you flap them? Your muscles would tire too easily. Birds have two strong sets of breast muscles—a large set to control the wings' down-strokes, and a smaller set to control the upstrokes.

But let's suppose you somehow had wings of the required length. Let's say you even had those amazing muscles to flap them. You still couldn't fly like a bird! You don't have air-filled sacs in your body like those that lie between the bird's heart, lungs, stomach, and other organs. These air sacs are connected to the bird's lungs, and during flight air flows through them. This arrangement rapidly feeds the bird's body tissues with life-supporting oxygen while keeping it light in the air.

Just as the albatross might win the title for the most beautiful soaring skills, there is another bird that would probably win the title of master of maneuvering. The tiny hummingbird can hover in the air, staying in one place in mid-flight. It makes sharp turns, and even flies backwards! How does it do this? A circular action of the hummingbird's wings makes such astonishing skills possible.

All hummingbirds are small, with long slender bills. The smallest is the bee hummingbird, which is not much bigger than a bumblebee. Twelve of these hummingbirds could sit together comfortably on the page you are reading.

This tiny bird's strong wing muscles make up about 30 percent of its weight. A hummingbird may visit up to 2,000 flowers a day to briefly sip the high-energy sugars it needs to fuel its spectacular flying abilities. It will hover in front of a flower, beating its wings an incredible 60 to 90 times a second. Such rapid wingbeats create a humming sound, which is how the hummingbird got its name. A hummingbird cannot walk on the ground. Its legs are small and weak. But the hummingbird has little need to walk—it is designed for skillful maneuvering in the air.

Feathers for Flight

All birds have been created with one thing that no other creature has: feathers. Feathers protect birds from the sun's heat. They also warm birds against the cold. They prevent them from getting too wet and form an important part of the wings so necessary for flying. Tail feathers help birds balance in the air. Feathers steer flight and act as a brake when a bird slows down to land.

A bird must keep its feathers in good working order. It does this by preening—running its beak over its feathers—which cleans and straightens out the feathers. In this process the bird oils its feathers by pressing its beak on an oil gland near the base of its tail.

Another cleaning process used by some birds, such as jays, is called *anting.* Jays sit on the ground with wings outstretched and encourage ants to crawl all over them. The jays twitch in apparent delight as the ants crawl through their feathers. Scientists think the powerful formic acid in the ants' saliva helps remove tiny creatures that cling to the birds' feathers and skin in large numbers.

So there are many obvious reasons why birds can fly and you cannot. Birds have a lightweight skeleton; your body is too heavy. Flying birds have strong sets of muscles to carefully control their flight; your muscles tire too easily. Birds have air sacs, light beaks, small lungs, feathers, and wings designed for flying; your body is simply not designed for flight.

It is clear that there is one overall reason why birds have always been able to fly, and why man's attempts have taken off only with the invention of flying planes. What is it? The birds got off to a flying start at the time of their creation. Flight, like birds, could not and did not evolve. It was created complete in the beginning.

– Robert Doolan

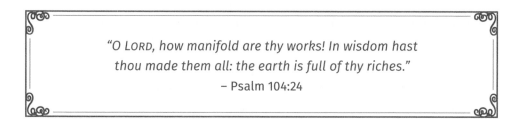

"O LORD, how manifold are thy works! In wisdom hast thou made them all: the earth is full of thy riches."
– Psalm 104:24

Beavers!

As I came up the hillside to the pond, a sharp *smack!* resounded through the woods. I jumped and my heart thumped out of rhythm as I scanned the surface of the pond.

I had come to the woods to soak up the quiet and beauty. The maple trees' fiery reds and the lustrous yellow of the autumn ash trees were bursting over the forest before winter's gray descended on the world.

Autumn is a good time to catch beavers at work as they make last-minute repairs to their dams and lodges and store up food for the coming winter. Today I had startled a beaver, and he had smacked a warning to his fellows before he dived into the pond.

"He's as busy as a beaver!" "What an eager beaver!" folks say. What makes people think beavers are *busy* and *eager?* Maybe it is the way beavers change their surroundings—more than any other animal does. When a beaver is active in an area, we see the results of his work. Beavers cut down trees. They gnaw them into logs. Then they haul their logs downhill or float them in their own canals. They construct log dams to form large ponds. Then, in the center of their ponds, they build timber houses. They are busy, eager beavers!

I like to walk in the state game lands and the Erie National Wildlife

Refuge near our home in Guys Mills, Pennsylvania. It is perfect beaver **habitat**. Near the center of the game lands, a grove of young alder trees is growing on a hillside above a beaver pond. A muddy trail connects this alder grove to the bank of the pond: evidence that beavers have been logging the trees. White pointed stumps, like freshly sharpened pencils, are surrounded by thick curlicues of wood. The felled trees and the branches cut from them are nowhere to be seen. The beavers have dragged everything, even the smallest twigs, down their logging trail to the pond. They have strengthened their house with new logs and safely stored the branches and twigs underwater—food for the winter ahead.

Seeing those sharpened tree stumps reminds me of the mountain man's nickname for the beaver: chiseltooth. It is a fitting name. Chiseltooth's large front teeth never stop growing! If they did, he would soon wear them out. He would not be able to build or eat. A beaver's teeth are also self-sharpening. As he gnaws, his lower teeth automatically grind a sharp edge on his long upper teeth. God has perfectly **equipped** the beaver for his role as the forest's logger.

After he chops down a tree, the beaver cuts the trunk and the large limbs into logs. With these logs he will build a dam across a stream. First, however, he must drag his timber to the water. On my walk I spot what appears to be an abandoned logging canal. Beavers are very clever, you see. If they cannot find suitable trees nearby, these hard workers dig a canal and float their logs to their building site. Sometimes beaver canals are very long—up to 700 feet (213 m) long.

The stout beavers—one may weigh as much as a large dog—pile timber in the stream or lake where they plan to build. To create a dam, they add branches, leaves, and grass. Workers scoop up mud from the bottom of the pond and carry it to the dam with their front feet. The building team finishes the engineering feat[1] by coating the

1 feat: accomplishment

dam with the mud and some stones. The water backs up behind the dam, forming a pond.

The largest dam near our home in Guys Mills stretches over 100 feet. But that's not huge by beaver standards. Across the Jefferson River in Montana, beavers once built a dam 2,140 feet (652 m) long.

In the newly formed pond, the beavers build their lodge. They pile logs in the pond and add smaller branches to make a strong house. When the top of the pile is a few feet above the pond surface, they dive underwater and dig passages into their new home. They make from two to five entrances, all hidden under the water to keep wolves, bears, lynx, and wolverines out. Finally, they chew out a den in the middle, above the water line, and coat the whole lodge with mud and stones.

Beavers build larger houses than do other rodents.[2] The biggest lodge near our home is about 15 feet (4.5 m) across. When the house is ready to live in, the beavers gather branches and twigs for food. The family drags them into the pond to store. Beaver lodges must be built in water deep enough not to freeze solid in the winter because beavers store their food supply in the water next to their lodge.

If you could explore a beaver lodge during the winter, you would find the father and mother beaver there with two to six *kits*—the name for beaver young. In the lodge they doze away the coldest months, swimming out once in a while to take a meal from their hidden food supply.

A new pair of kits will be born in the spring. They will live in their parents' lodge for two years. So, beaver families are made up of the father and mother and two sets of young. When the kits are two years old, the parents chase them away. Off they waddle to build their own lodges and begin a new beaver clan.

---

2 rodent: animal with sharp front teeth used for gnawing. Common rodents are mice, squirrels, and porcupines.

How does the beaver accomplish his astonishing engineering feats? How does a mammal like the beaver eat and work underwater? The answers to these questions are found in God's wonderful design of the beaver.

Let's start with the beaver's big flat tail, which is as famous as his chompers are. His unique tail serves several purposes. For one thing, it serves as a powerful paddle that helps him swim well. It also helps the beaver to build. With his tail, the beaver packs the mud walls of his dam and lodge. In the wintertime, the tightly packed lodge walls freeze as hard as concrete to protect the beaver family from hungry foes. And don't forget, the beaver's tail provides him with a superior alarm. Chiseltooth *smacks!* his flat, heavy tail on the water to warn that intruders are approaching.

Folks know about the beaver's handy tail, but often they are unaware of the beauty of his feet. His hind paws are fully webbed, like ducks' feet—precisely what a strong swimmer needs. His front paws are not. God has designed them like little hands, useful in dam and lodge construction. The beaver uses his hands to roll logs, to hold small twigs while he nibbles off the tender bark, and to clutch mud and sticks against his chest so that he can move them around his building site.

The beaver's wonderful design does not end with his hands. Consider those big teeth. Have you ever seen a picture of a beaver's front teeth? If so, you may have thought that he needs a new toothbrush! A special, very hard orange coating covers the beaver's front chisel-like chompers. The backs of his big cutting teeth are much softer. When the beaver chomps, the soft backside of his top teeth is worn away by the hard front surface of his lower teeth. This means that his top teeth always remain sharp, ready to whittle away at his favorite trees: alder, willow, and cottonwood.

Have you ever tried to swim underwater while holding something between your teeth? How would you like to eat your lunch at the bottom of a pond? The beaver can do both. He holds branches in his mouth while he swims and even gnaws twigs and cuts branches underwater. How does he do it? He's designed that way. God has given the beaver special flaps of skin behind his teeth. With these flaps he can seal the water out of his mouth while he chews.

How long can you hold your breath? A minute? The beaver can swim or work underwater for up to fifteen minutes at a time without taking a breath. He has unusual muscles in his ears and nose. When he dives beneath the water, these muscles close and seal the water out. God also equipped the beaver with a transparent inner eyelid, which permits him to see underwater. The beaver's lungs and liver are extra large for his size too. They provide him with plenty of oxygen while he works beneath the pond. Repairing dams underwater and storing food on the bottom of a pond are easy work for the brilliantly designed beaver.

Part of his design almost led to the end of the beaver forever. His fur is dense and soft, both waterproof and warm. People prize beaver furs for making coats and other articles of clothing. Can you believe that wars have been fought over the beaver's fur? First Dutch and then English settlers fought wars with the French over the right to trap beavers in Canadian streams.

Someone once said that "the map of the West was drawn on a beaver skin." Americans' desire for beaver pelts sped up settlement of the United States. A pioneer could trade one beaver skin for an iron kettle or four pounds of bullets. For twelve skins he could get a rifle. By the time Lewis and Clark made their 1803 expedition through the Louisiana Territory, beavers had become scarce in the eastern United States. But Lewis and Clark found plenty of beavers west of the Mississippi River. When news of their discovery spread, trappers rushed "out West" to find beaver pelts. After only forty years of trapping, however, the report from the West came back: "Beaver gone!" The beaver's warm, waterproof coat had almost led to his extinction.

It's a good thing the trappers didn't kill them all. While beaver damming may occasionally flood farm fields, the beaver's work is mostly helpful. Beaver ponds slow down runoff from rain, which keeps soil from being carried away into streams and rivers. Ponds sometimes collect soil carried away by heavy rains. Leaves and other material also collect on the bottom and rot. After many years, abandoned ponds become rich meadowland.

Ponds also attract wildlife, especially birds, which nest in trees killed by the flooding behind beaver dams. Ponds support frogs, fish, and turtles. These animals attract larger birds, such as hawks and great blue herons. Many larger animals **benefit** from beaver ponds too. Bears hunt for fish at beaver dams, and wildcats prey on mink or raccoons that drink or feed around ponds. Deer sometimes depend on beaver ponds for water.

Last winter we had a big snowfall. Heavy spring rains followed and brought on a swift melt. The little creek that runs through Guys Mills swelled with rushing water and then overflowed its banks. One morning we looked out to see that the creek had turned our neighbor's backyard into a small lake. I knew that the big beaver dam must have broken.

Later in the week, I went upstream to survey the damages. I found the beaver pond nearly empty. Drained, it was only a giant mud hole—a thin rivulet snaked through its wide flat bottom. The lodge was fully exposed, the secret entrances open to view. Another dam, downstream from the big one, had given way too. It could not hold up when the big dam let loose the torrent of water.

I was sad to see the big dam go. But I have found an encouraging sign upstream. Someone, or something, has been cutting—I should say *chewing*—low branches from the willows along the streambed. The beavers are not gone. Perhaps they will choose to build again along our creek. That would be good news, because they are good neighbors. The changes they make in the woods benefit both men and animals, and their eager busyness teaches us the importance of hard work. The beaver's design helps us to admire God's creative wisdom and power. It's not hard to understand why folks like old Chiseltooth so well.

– *Tim Kennedy*

Pilgrims of the Wild

In 1928 the editor of the British magazine Country Life *received a story from Canada. The author said he was a half-breed Scots-Indian and wondered if the editor would be interested in publishing the story.*

The editor was. He sent the author, Wa-sha-quon-asin, a check for the story. The check arrived just in time to save Wa-sha-quon-asin and his wife Anahareo from starvation.

Wa-sha-quon-asin, or Grey Owl, as the English-speaking backwoods folk called him, had been a noted guide and trapper. But that winter, he had suddenly given up trapping. His old friends thought him foolish—a trapper who refused to trap would soon starve. But the check and the letter from the magazine editor gave Grey Owl encouragement. He bought some supplies and spent the winter writing his book—a book that told what had happened to make him give up trapping.

Grey Owl was not all that he said he was. His name was Archibald Belaney, and he was actually an Englishman. But he did live and work in the Canadian wilderness, and the Ojibway tribe that adopted him called him Grey Owl. The rest of his story is true.

This story is from his book.

My wife Anahareo and I were hunting in an area that had been "trapped over" by a noted hunter the winter before. He had already trapped most of the grown fur-bearing animals. Between that and the low prices, we took only about six hundred dollars worth of furs.

We would have little money left after we had paid our debts and purchased our summer's provisions. So I decided on a spring hunt to make some money, something that went against my principles, because a hunt at that time of year was both destructive and cruel. But I knew of a beaver family remaining from the year's hunt, and I **salved** my conscience by saying that I might as well clean them out before someone else stepped in and took them.

We were delayed over a week at the trading post by the late arrival of a fur buyer, so we did not arrive back at our trapping ground until the last of May. The hunt should have been over by then, and I was a little disturbed over the hardship I knew I would now **inflict** on the young beavers. The young beavers had surely been born by this time, and they would die after the parents were trapped.

I was setting a trap at an old beaver lodge where I knew a big female to be when I heard the thin musical voices of beaver kits. Anahareo heard them too, and she begged me to lift the trap and let the babies have their mother and live. I had never killed a beaver at this time of year, so I felt a pang of conscience myself. In spite of my conscience though, I continued with my work. We needed the money.

The next morning I hauled up the bodies of three drowned beavers. The mother was missing, however, and one trap was unaccounted for. I found where she had broken the chain on the trap. I broke down the dam and partly drained the pond to look for her. I dragged for the body, but I was unsuccessful. The mother would have been the largest and most valuable, so I regretted my loss and tried to forget the animals that I had destroyed for nothing and the helpless kittens that would be left to starve.

After a day of searching, we collected our traps and equipment and were about to leave for camp, when I heard a splash behind me. I looked back and saw what I thought was a muskrat, lying on top of the water beside the beaver lodge. Determined to make this wasted day pay, I threw up my gun and stood up in the canoe to get better aim. I was just about to press the trigger when the creature gave a low cry. At the same moment I saw, right in my line of fire, another creature that gave out the same peculiar call. They could both be hit with the one charge of shot. They cried again, and this time the sound was unmistakable. They were young beavers.

I lowered my gun. "There are your kittens," I said.

"Let us save them," cried Anahareo excitedly. Then, in a lower voice, "It is up to us after what we've done."

And truly what I had done there now looked like an act of brutal cruelty. With some confused thought of giving back what I had taken, some dim idea of making up for what I had done, I answered, "Yes. We must. Let's take them home." It seemed the only fitting thing to do.

It wasn't an easy matter to catch the young beavers; they were well able to take care of themselves in the water. However, we finally caught them and dropped them into the canoe. What a spectacle they were! Two funny-looking furry creatures with little scaly tails and large hind feet. They weighed less than half a pound apiece, and they tramped soberly up and down the bottom of the canoe with their steady, purposeful beaver walk. We looked at them in bewilderment, feeling like we had caught a pair of white elephants.[1] We certainly had no idea of the far-reaching effects they would have on our life.

From the very first it was plain that this experiment would be no picnic. We quickly changed our ideas about raising and handling pets. Our beavers were no wild things **cowering** fearfully in dark corners. They were a pair of very wide-awake personalities! They fastened themselves onto us as their protectors and began to make constant demands on us. Not letting us forget the responsibilities we had

---

1 white elephant: something very rare or valuable that is troublesome and expensive to take care of. It refers to a rare type of elephant that in some parts of Asia was held sacred.

taken on, they had us trained before long to sleep with one eye open and one hand on the milk can.

Feeding them was a problem. Beaver kits will not drink milk out of a dish, and we had no feeding bottle. We got the idea of loading a slim twig with the sweet milk out of a can, closing the beaver's mouth over it with our fingers, and pulling out the stick. Chewing this sticky mass kept them entertained for long periods at a time, so this scheme simplified matters.

After feeding, they wanted to be picked up and petted. This became a regular habit. After being petted, our little friends would fall asleep in odd places like the inside of my shirt, halfway up a sleeve, or draped around my neck. If I removed them, they would immediately awaken and scramble back. When we laid them in their box, they awoke at once, and with piercing outcries demanded to be picked up again.

Their voices were really the most remarkable thing about them. They resembled the cries of a human infant, without the volume but with greater expression. At all hours of the day and night, we heard some new sound issuing from their box. The easiest to recognize was the loud, long call for lunch. This chorus broke out about every two hours.

It was not long before our little beavers became attached to us—and we to them. One always preferred Anahareo, and the other liked me best. They showed affection for us in a number of curious ways. They crept into our blankets at night and cuddled up to us. They would lie, one on each of us; their favorite position being an inconvenient one across the throat! Often they were ready to rise before we were. We would lie perfectly still, faking sleep and hoping they would keep still. But they liked to see everybody getting up early and would pick at our eyebrows and lips and otherwise bother us until, in self-defense, we had to get up.

They were keenly aware of our moods too. When Anahareo and I were in a bustle, they also became very active. When we were making our bed, they would run around us pulling at the blankets, and sometimes make off with the pillows. If we laughed a great deal, or held a more lively conversation than usual, they got excited. I felt a little self-reproach and learned to guard my tongue and temper better when I found that they kept out of sight when I complained loudly about something that bothered me.

Our beaver pets continually wandered away. The first few times this happened, we hunted for them high and low. But our anxiety was quite unnecessary because we discovered that when they heard us coming through the brush they would run toward us of their own choice.

We became a little too overconfident of this, and one morning we awoke to find their box empty. There was no sign of a beaver anywhere. We hunted all that day both by canoe and on land, but we couldn't find our little beavers. We remained out all night, checking back at the tent often, in the hope that they might have returned while we were gone. It seemed hard to believe that they would desert us like that, but after all they were wild animals. They were well able to travel and feed themselves and could now probably get along without us. We felt a little hurt about it. But then, I thought, maybe they could not return. There were plenty of hawks and owls about, and an otter would make short work of them.

When they had been gone over thirty hours, we gave up the search and went home sadly to get some sleep. There in the tent, all unconscious of the anxiety they had caused, sat the two runaways on the bed, soaking wet, and squeezing the water out of their coats onto the blankets.

After this experience we simply pitched our camp near a lake and let the young beavers come and go as they pleased. They would walk down to the lake, bathe, swim, play in the reeds awhile, and return, plodding solemnly up and down the water trail together, like two little old men out for a walk.

If we went away up the lake for a while, we would call them on our return, while yet some distance away. They would come to meet the canoe with outstretched hands, grasping our fingers and making the most uncommon sounds. We would bring them little bits of sweets, and they would lie in the water eating these with loud enjoyment and a very **audible** smacking of lips. Then they would try to get aboard the canoe, and after I lifted them in, they would climb all over us with pleasure. Maybe the treats improved our welcome, but show me the good friend whose heart isn't warmer toward you when you sit him at your table!

By three months of age we had only to feed them porridge once a day. They were clean, gentle, and good-natured. They were good housekeepers too. Each had his own dish, which when empty, he pushed over to the side of the tent. The instinct for stacking used material as far out of the way as possible caused them to try to stand plates on edge against the wall. This wasn't easy to do, but they persevered and very often succeeded.

Their hands—I don't know what else to call them—were almost as effective as ours. They could pick up very small objects with them and handle sticks and stones or strike, push, and heave with them. They had a firm grasp that was difficult to loosen. When peeling a stick, they used both hands to twist the stem, flexing their wrists while their teeth rapidly whittled off the juicy bark as it went by.

Our beavers were very quiet and most of the time were neither to be seen nor heard. But in the evenings they needed attention, and we made a point of giving it to them. They would utter little bleats and play with our hands, nibble our fingertips, and climb on us with many silly but very real signs of affection. When satisfied, they would go about their business and perhaps not show up again till daylight—weary, wet, and very sleepy.

In a few months they had grown rapidly, weighing in the neighborhood of fifteen pounds apiece. Their fur had come in full, rich, and shiny. Although they were growing up, they were as much attached to us as ever.

And we were attached to them: to their little sneezes, their childish whimpers and coughs, and their eager responses to every kindness. We marveled at their tiny, clinging, hand-like forepaws and impatiently stamping feet. All of these things made them seem childlike. That Anahareo should become devoted to them is not all that remarkable, but my own feeling toward them was likely to have a serious effect on our chief means of livelihood—the beaver hunt. I wondered at times how manly it was to feel as I did toward these small beasts. But their utter dependence on us had touched in us the chord of tenderness that lies in every human heart for the small and helpless.

– Grey Owl

As you read this poem, try to decide if the speaker is young or old.

Starfish

Last night I saw you in the sky.
I watched you jumping from so high,
Falling so far it made me cry.
I said that star will be so hurt,
Cut on stones and buried in the dirt,
He'll wish he had not been so pert,
So proud, so sure. I said no star
Should take such chances, it's too far,
Even for stars. Yet there you are,
Quietly curling. You are found
Upon this soft and sandy mound,
Cooled by the spray, all safe and sound.
And not one point in all your five
Is even nicked; you sprawl alive,
Not even dented by your dive.
Brave star, I hope that you will lie
Lazily here and never try
To jump back up into the sky.

– Winifred Welles

51

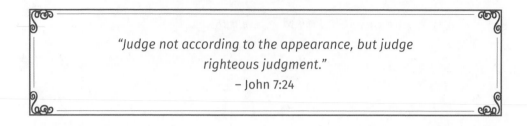

Looking Mature

Sarah and I both gulped when we met Elaine outside the school gate one morning. "Whatever happened to you?" I asked.

"Whose spectacles are you wearing?" Sarah gasped between giggles.

"Mine." Elaine laughed back.

"Why didn't you tell us you were getting glasses?"

"Well—" Elaine folded her arms. "Because I wanted to surprise you."

"You certainly did," I said. "But what happened? Why'd you need glasses?"

"I've been having headaches. So my parents took me to the optometrist, and he said I needed glasses."

Sarah leaned against the gatepost and surveyed Elaine critically. Finally she pronounced, "I like you in glasses. You look so mature."

"I think so too," I echoed, though I hadn't really thought about it at all. Though now that Sarah mentioned it, it was true—the dark plastic frames nicely complemented Elaine's smooth olive complexion and dark hair.

Elaine grimaced. "Don't call me names," she teased and led the way up the sidewalk.

It didn't seem to make Elaine proud that Sarah had told her she looked nice in glasses. But I knew a compliment like that would have puffed me up. In fact, I felt a twinge of jealousy—Sarah had never complimented *me* like that.

Stowing my lunch bucket on the shelf in the coat closet, I thought how sweet it would be to hear Sarah say I looked mature. *Mature.* The word lodged in my mind, and somehow the word *eyeglasses* was stuck right up beside *mature.* By the end of the day, as I walked down our lane, a plan had taken shape in my mind.

I decided to wait a week. It would be too obvious to carry out my plan the same day Elaine first appeared with her glasses. I didn't want Mom to think my plan had sprung from jealousy or anything like that. So, a week later, when I got home from school and found Mom in the kitchen, I reported my news to her.

"I can't see the blackboard at school very well, Mom."

Her eyebrows lifted slightly. "Aren't you sitting in the front row anymore?"

I nodded deliberately. It had been hard for me to see the board for a couple of years now. That's why I had been given a seat in the front. And even from the front row, I sometimes had to strain to read what the teacher wrote on the board.

"Sometimes my eyes just ache from trying so hard."

Mom responded just as I had hoped she would—

"Maybe you need glasses," she said, looking at my eyes.

"I think so," I said, nodding even more vigorously. "When can we make an appointment with the optometrist?"

"Not so fast! I have to talk with Dad and with your teacher. If she agrees that you're having trouble with the board, we'll have to look into glasses."

I tried not to show my elation, for fear Mother would guess that I had other motives for wanting glasses.

"Mind you, Judith," she said, "glasses aren't fun. I remember them being a real nuisance."

"*You* do?" I tried to imagine my mom wearing glasses. Would they make *her* look mature? But of course, she was mature, even without glasses.

"It gets to be bothersome, having something always sitting on the bridge of your nose."

"Uh-huh," I said absently. Bothersome? Hardly.

Well, my plan worked. Dad made an appointment with Doctor Borling, the optometrist, and Dad and I rode the bus into town.

The optometrist's chair looked like a dentist's chair: long and covered with brown slippery leather. I had to assure myself as I sat back into the big chair that Doctor Borling would not do to my eyes the kinds of things that Doctor Wentworth had done to my teeth.

Dr. Borling asked me questions in his **jovial** voice and swung the big eyepiece in front of my eyes. Rapid-fire he threw out his questions and almost as quickly switched lenses—asking me to read first these letters, then those words on the far wall. I perspired, trying to keep it all straight.

"Well," the optometrist finally said, "this young lady's eyes need some help. I'm surprised she has been able to get along without glasses."

My heart pounded. What would Dad say? There was the money to think about . . .

"I guess we'll choose a frame then, and you'll order the lenses?"

I nearly slipped right off the chair.

What a mind-boggling **array** of frames to choose from! The glasses gleamed invitingly on their racks, glossy or glinting beneath the florescent lights.

"These, Dad! How about these?" I said, lifting a pair like Elaine's from their place.

Dad frowned. "I was looking at these," he said, touching a plain pair of frames with thin metal rims.

"Ooooh, not *those*," I groaned. Suddenly I caught myself. I had contradicted Dad.

He only shook his head slowly. "Judith, you know we can't buy glasses for decoration. These metal rims are less likely to get broken than those plastic ones."

"Have you these frames in her size?" he asked the doctor.

We went out into the brilliant February sun. We tramped through the dirty city snow toward the bus terminal. Though I felt like pouting, I asked Dad meekly, "How long will it take until my glasses are ready?"

"Three or four weeks, I guess. He'll send them by mail."

Like Elaine, I decided I would keep my glasses a secret until I had them. At first I was disappointed about the frames, but as the weeks passed, I consoled myself with the thought that metal rims would probably make me look mature too. Maybe even more than plastic ones, I thought, since a lot of grown-ups wear metal-rimmed glasses.

One evening when I came home from school, there they were. I lifted them carefully out of the box and tried them on. They felt funny! I looked in the mirror over the sink at the stranger in the glasses. Who was she? She looked funny!

I forced myself to keep on looking at the image in the glass, because I had to know something. Did the glasses make me look more mature? I stared—my nose, my eyes, my mouth—the glasses. Was I more grown-up?

"I hope those new glasses aren't making you vain!" My sister Mary laughed behind me.

"I'm not vain!" *Where did she come from?* I wondered, as I went upstairs to the mirror in my bedroom.

It took about ten minutes of studying myself in the mirror before I knew it. My new glasses did make me look more mature! But at supper time I approached the table hesitantly, because my brothers quite often did not see things the way I did. And they could be quite frank!

I will not allow their remarks to bother me, I told myself as I descended the stairs. *I must concentrate on how bright and clear and sharp-edged everything looks through my new glasses. Why, I can even see the dust particles on the ledges of the door panels. And that cobweb in the corner of the stairwell—did I see that this morning?*

Noah and Oscar were seated at the table when I came into the dining room. Noah wrinkled his nose. "You look funny."

I pretended not to hear him. Turning the other way, my eyes met Oscar's, opened **grotesquely** wide, under arched eyebrows. "Who is this young lady taking Judith's place at the supper table?" he intoned.

Everyone laughed. At first, I held back, but then I couldn't help it, and I laughed too. Dad and Mom just smiled, and Dad asked us to quiet down so that we might say grace.

That night, lying in bed, I mulled over Oscar's words. He'd called me a *young lady.* A compliment, really. A *young lady* is more mature than just a girl. But in the morning I lingered before setting out for school. I wasn't sure why I was hesitant, because I could hardly wait for the girls to compliment me on my glasses. At last I pushed the fear aside and walked to school.

I met the first boys on the stairs as I went down into the basement to hang up my things. "Oho! Look at Judith!" They laughed. I didn't care. What else could you expect from boys?

I slipped into the cloakroom, and like a switch being turned off, all the girls' voices dropped, silent. They stared at me. **Nonchalantly**, I slipped off my coat and wraps and began hanging them up.

The girls burst into giggles—that was all right, we had giggled at

Elaine too. I giggled with them, and a warm feeling rose inside—a feeling of belonging. I waited for the comment . . .

"Why, Judith!" Sarah gasped between giggles, "do you know who you look exactly like?"

I tried to keep on giggling, tension rising in my throat.

"Exactly like your grandmother!"

My throat closed. The girls laughed harder. Tears swelled in my eyes, and I spun around for the stairs. I could hear Sarah behind me, coming after me with apologies.

"Judith, I didn't mean to hurt your—I shouldn't have said—Judith?"

I shook my head. "It's nothing," I said thickly through the lump in my throat. Then the bell rang, rescuing me.

I couldn't imagine the hurt ever going away. Somehow I struggled through the day, managing to act normal, pretending that I had forgotten Sarah's remark.

That evening Noah caught up to me after Sarah had turned off into her lane.

"What did the girls say about your glasses?" he asked.

I don't know why I confided in Noah, but I did. He and I had always been good friends, and I sobbed the whole story out to him. "They said I looked like Grandmother!"

He couldn't understand what that meant to me. He laughed and said that was a nice compliment. I tried to explain that it wasn't that I didn't love Grandmother, but . . . Finally, I gave up trying to explain.

In the morning I left the glasses on my dresser top.

"Where are your glasses, Judith?" Mom asked as I was leaving for school.

"They make my eyes kind of tired," I said. "I want to get used to them gradually."

Day after day passed, and the glasses gathered dust on the dresser. At first, the girls asked why I wasn't wearing them, but then they forgot about it.

But Mom didn't forget.

"Here are your glasses!" She said one morning, cornering me in my room. "They're dusty, aren't they!" Mom looked straight into my eyes.

I stammered, but could make no excuse.

"We got them so that you could see better at school," Mother said quietly. "A few thoughtless remarks shouldn't keep you from seeing better, Judith."

I blinked. Noah! Then the feelings that had been simmering so long inside bubbled over. "They all liked Elaine's glasses, Mom. They told her she looked so mature. Why didn't they think I looked mature?"

Mom pulled me down to sit beside her on the bed. "Wanting to be mature isn't a bad idea, Judith. Maturity is a virtue. But," she went on after a pause, "do you think you can be mature just by looking mature?"

It was all rather ridiculous, I suddenly realized. "No, I guess not."

"Experience—like the one you've recently had—brings maturity. Mature people learn not to be overly concerned about their appearance or to be easily put out by thoughtless remarks."

After a while she added, "True maturity comes through acknowledging our weaknesses and turning to Christ for help in overcoming them."

I nodded, beginning to get a glimpse of *being* mature and understanding that it has very little to do with wearing glasses.

– Author Unknown

Why do you think the author used "Check" as the title for this poem?

Check

The Night was creeping on the ground!
She crept and did not make a sound,

Until she reached the tree: And then
She covered it, and stole again

Along the grass beside the wall!
—I heard the rustling of her shawl

As she threw blackness everywhere
Along the sky, the ground, the air,

And in the room where I was hid!
But no matter what she did

To everything that was *without*
She could not put my candle out!

So I stared at the Night! And she
Stared back solemnly at me!

– *James Stephens*

Contentment

Beautiful

Beautiful faces are they that wear
The light of a pleasant spirit there;
Beautiful hands are they that do
Deeds that are noble, good, and true;
Beautiful feet are they that go
Swiftly to lighten another's woe.

– Author Unknown

The Prodigal Son

[11] And he said, A certain man had two sons: [12] And the younger of them said to his father, Father, give me the portion of goods that falleth to me. And he divided unto them his living.

[13] And not many days after the younger son gathered all together, and took his journey into a far country, and there wasted his substance[1] with riotous living. [14] And when he had spent all, there arose a mighty **famine** in that land; and he began to be in want.

[15] And he went and joined himself to a citizen of that country; and he sent him into his fields to feed swine. [16] And he would fain have filled his belly with the husks that the swine did eat: and no man gave unto him.

[17] And when he came to himself, he said, How many hired servants of my father's have bread enough and to spare, and I perish with hunger! [18] I will arise and go to my father, and will say unto him, Father, I have sinned against heaven, and before thee, [19] And am no more worthy to be called thy son: make me as one of thy hired servants.

[20] And he arose, and came to his father. But when he was yet a great way off, his father saw him, and had **compassion**, and ran, and fell on his neck, and kissed him.

---

1 substance: wealth

²¹ And the son said unto him, Father, I have sinned against heaven, and in thy sight, and am no more worthy to be called thy son.

²² But the father said to his servants, Bring forth the best robe, and put it on him; and put a ring on his hand, and shoes on his feet: ²³ And bring hither the fatted calf, and kill it; and let us eat, and be merry: ²⁴ For this my son was dead, and is alive again; he was lost, and is found. And they began to be merry.

²⁵ Now his elder son was in the field: and as he came and drew nigh to the house, he heard music and dancing. ²⁶ And he called one of the servants, and asked what these things meant.

²⁷ And he said unto him, Thy brother is come; and thy father hath killed the fatted calf, because he hath received him safe and sound.

²⁸ And he was angry, and would not go in: therefore came his father out, and entreated² him. ²⁹ And he answering said to his father, Lo, these many years do I serve thee, neither transgressed³ I at any time thy commandment: and yet thou never gavest me a kid⁴, that I might make merry with my friends: ³⁰ But as soon as this thy son was come, which hath devoured thy living with harlots, thou hast killed for him the fatted calf.

³¹ And he said unto him, Son, thou art ever with me, and all that I have is thine. ³² It was meet that we should make merry, and be glad: for this thy brother was dead, and is alive again; and was lost, and is found.

– Luke 15:11-32

---

2 entreated: begged
3 transgressed: deliberately disobeyed
4 kid: a young goat; not as nice a gift as the calf that the father gave the younger son

A Prodigal Son

Does that lamp still burn in my Father's house,
    Which he kindled the night I went away?
I turned once beneath the cedar boughs,
    And marked it gleam with a golden ray;
    Did he think to light me home some day?

Hungry here with the crunching swine,
    Hungry harvest have I to reap;
In a dream I count my Father's kine,[1]
    I hear the tinkling bells of his sheep,
    I watch his lambs that **browse** and leap.

There is plenty of bread at home,
    His servants have bread enough and to spare;
The purple wine vat froths with foam,
    Oil and spices make sweet the air,
    While I perish hungry and bare.

Rich and blessed those servants, rather
    Than I who see not my Father's face!
I will arise and go to my Father:
    "Fallen from sonship, beggared of grace,
    Grant me, Father, a servant's place."

– *Christina Rossetti*

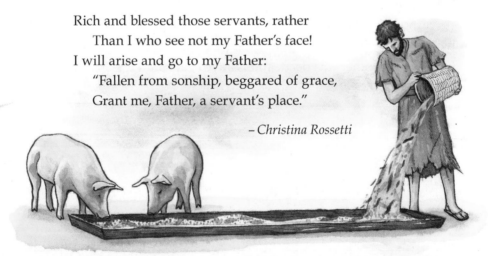

1 kine: cattle

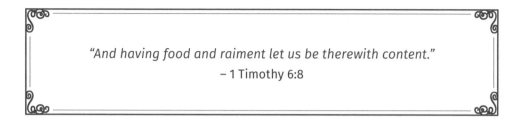

The King and the Shirt

A king once fell ill.

"I will give half my kingdom to the man who can cure me," he said.

All his wise men gathered to decide how the king could be cured. But no one knew. Only one of the wise men said what he thought would cure the king:

"If you can find a happy man, take his shirt, put it on the king— and the king will be cured."

The king sent his emissaries to search for a happy man. They traveled far and wide throughout his kingdom, but they could not find a happy man. There was no one who was completely satisfied: if a man was rich, he was ailing; if he was healthy, he was poor; if he was rich and healthy, he said he had a bad wife; or if he had children, they were bad—everyone had something to complain about.

Finally, late one night, the king's son was passing by a poor little hut and he heard someone say,

"Now, God be praised, I have finished my work, I have eaten my fill, and I can lie down and sleep! What more could I want?"

The king's son rejoiced and gave orders that the man's shirt be taken and carried to the king and that the man be given as much money as he wanted.

The emissaries went in to take off the man's shirt, but the happy man was so poor that he had no shirt.

– Leo Tolstoy

65

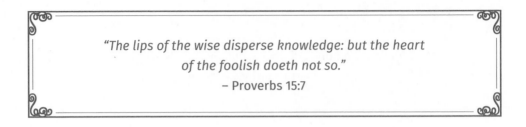

The Tale of Bramble the King

Jotham, the man who told this story, lived in Israel during the time of the judges. This was a sad time, because the people of Israel sinned greatly against God.

Why did Jotham tell the fable about the bramble who wanted to be king?

Do you remember Gideon, who defeated a huge army with his little band of 300 men? Gideon had 71 sons. When Gideon died, one of them, Abimelech, wanted to be king of Israel. He wanted to reign over the people.

To make sure he would be king, Abimelech did a terrible thing—he murdered his brothers. Only one escaped—Jotham. The people of the city made Abimelech their king. When Jotham heard that Abimelech had been anointed king, he went to the top of the hill beside the city. He called to the people of Shechem and told them the story of the bramble bush who wanted to be king of the trees.

What kind of king was Jotham saying Abimelech would be?

⁷ And when they told it to Jotham, he went and stood in the top of mount Gerizim, and lifted up his voice, and cried, and said unto them, Hearken unto me, ye men of Shechem, that God may hearken unto you.

⁸ The trees went forth on a time to anoint a king over them; and they said unto the olive tree, **Reign** thou over us.

⁹ But the olive tree said unto them, Should I leave my fatness,

66

wherewith by me they honour God and man, and go to be **promoted** over the trees?

¹⁰ And the trees said to the fig tree, Come thou, and reign over us.

¹¹ But the fig tree said unto them, Should I **forsake** my sweetness, and my good fruit, and go to be promoted over the trees?

¹² Then said the trees unto the vine, Come thou, and reign over us.

¹³ And the vine said unto them, Should I leave my wine, which cheereth God and man, and go to be promoted over the trees?

¹⁴ Then said all the trees unto the bramble,[1] Come thou, and reign over us.

¹⁵ And the bramble said unto the trees, If in truth ye anoint me king over you, then come and put your trust in my shadow: and if not, let fire come out of the bramble, and devour the cedars of Lebanon.

– Judges 9:7-15

---

1 bramble: a shrub that is covered with sharp, pricking thorns, like the blackberry

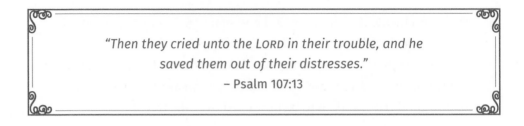

Crossing the Ice

This is a true story that happened many years ago. Greta, a widow, and her young son lived on a small farm in the woods west of the La Have River, near the coast of Nova Scotia. They were very poor, but Greta was rich in faith.

Greta was a tall Nova Scotia girl with the heart of a man. She had not the strength of a man though, and no men lived near enough to help her. That was why, though she worked hard, the house and barn needed repair and the fences were falling down. That was why each year the crops were smaller. But Greta would not give up.

One winter she thought of a way to earn some money. A fishing village toward the mouth of the La Have was not many miles away. When the fishermen fitted out their vessels each spring, they needed a supply of good brooms. She would make some brooms.

Greta had grown up in a shore village and had seen the stiff, strong fishermen's brooms made. You take a stick of birch about four feet long and three or four inches thick. Then you take a good sharp jackknife. First you remove the bark. Then you start at one end of the stick, cutting a **splint** or shaving about half an inch wide and as thick as the knife blade. You keep pushing the knife blade to within eight inches of the other end. There you stop. Go back and start another splint. Keep doing that round and round the stick until it is no more than an inch and a half thick. And there is your broom handle.

68

Now you take the bush of splints hanging near the other end and bend them back over the eight inches of solid wood remaining there. Bind them together tightly in that position with strong fishing line. With an axe, cut them off about twelve inches below the cord. There is your broom, all in one piece.

The Bank Fleet[1] was very large in those days, and in the course of a season each vessel used a number of brooms. So each winter the outfitters bought a good supply.

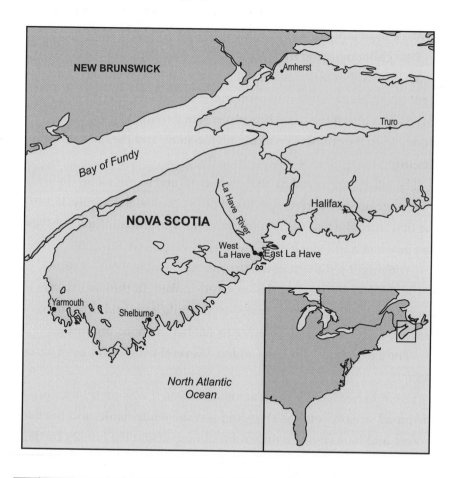

1 Bank Fleet: the fleet of fishing boats that catch fish in the Grand Banks, an area in the Atlantic Ocean between Nova Scotia and Newfoundland where there are many fish

But Greta's days were short and busy. She would have to do this extra chore after dark.

So every evening after her son fell asleep, Greta went to the barn, lit a fire in a rusty tin stove, and cut splints by the light of a lantern. Her hands were used to hard work, but after a time the grip on the knife made them sore. She tried wearing gloves, but that was awkward. So she tied a strip of linen over the blisters and went on. But at last her palms were rough and hard, and she could work without a bandage. Sometimes she made four or five brooms before midnight. By the end of January she had two hundred and forty brooms.

One chilly morning in February, she hitched the mare Judy to the sleigh, loaded her brooms, helped her boy into the seat, and started for West La Have. She left her son in the care of her nearest neighbors, three miles down the road. It was pleasant driving through the woods with the runners creaking on the snow and the harness bells ringing.

The village appeared, with its wharves[2] and stores along the wide frozen surface of the river. Greta got out of the sleigh happily. But in the first store she had disappointing news. The ship outfitters at West La Have had a full stock of brooms. They could buy no more.

"You might sell them down the river at East La Have," a storekeeper said, pointing over the ice. Greta looked. In the clear winter air the river did not seem very wide—half a mile, say. And three miles down the east shore was a chance to sell her precious brooms.

"The ice is good," the man added. "Several teams have been across today."

So Greta headed the mare across the river. It was pretty—ice on the broad stream as far as she could see, the white banks and the dark woods, and blue smoke rising in small wisps from the houses by the shore.

---

2 wharves: structures built along the shore where ships unload cargo

When she reached East La Have, she was stiff from her long drive in the cold, but she entered the store with a quick step and an eager face. The storekeeper listened to her request and shook his head.

"Sorry, lady, but it seems everybody's been making brooms this winter. We've got too many now."

Half a dozen fishing captains sat by the stove, talking over the coming season on the Banks. They looked at the woman from up the river. Her coat was cheap and old, too thin for this sort of weather. They saw the worn overshoes, the home-knit woolen cap, the hands twisting anxiously inside the gray mittens. They looked at her tight mouth and her eyes holding back the tears.

One of them said quietly, "Buy her brooms. If you don't, we will." The storekeeper called one of his clerks to carry the brooms inside. They made a great heap on the floor.

"Let's see now. Two hundred and forty brooms at twenty-five cents . . ."

"Forty cents," the fishing captain said. "Those are good brooms. I'd say you made them yourself, didn't you, ma'am?"

"Yes," said Greta.

The storekeeper counted out ninety-six dollars—nine tens, a five, and a one. Greta thanked him and the captains in a small choked voice. As she went out the door, one of them said, "You'd better drive home smart, ma'am. Looks like snow." She noticed then that the sunshine was dimming. The sky was filling with a gray **scud** of heavy clouds. An uneasy wind blew.

Greta had no purse. She stooped and fastened the money to the inside hem of her skirt, using a big safety pin. She drove off, humming and thinking of the things she could buy now. Before she had gone far, snow began to fly in small hard specks. When she reached the crossing place, a blizzard was blowing. She could not see across the river.

She turned off the road onto the ice, following the faint tracks of other teams. After ten minutes the old tracks disappeared, buried in the new soft snow sweeping along the ice. She had to trust the horse to find the way. But Greta was not afraid. After all, it was only half a mile or so.

The snow was now so thick that she could not see past Judy's ears. She let the reins go slack and crouched down in the seat, trying to find a little comfort in the storm. There was none. The snow whirled and stung; it seemed to come from every side. Sometimes it stopped her breath, like a cold white cloth laid over her mouth and nose. The little mare kept plunging her head and snorting in the blasts.

The way seemed strangely long. Greta noticed that the light was growing dim. The afternoon had gone. Soon now, surely, she must see the west shore looming through the storm. The horse went on and on, slipping here and there on patches of bare ice. Greta began to pray in earnest.

At last Judy stopped. Greta peered into the whirling snow and saw a dim, pale shape ahead. She shielded her eyes with her mittened hand for a better look. Through the snow gusts she could see that the thing was large, with three slim objects standing upon it and reaching up into the murk. Trees, of course! She cried thankfully, "Good girl, Judy! There's the shore. I knew you'd find it! Thank You, Lord!"

She urged the horse on with a jerk at the reins. Judy took three steps and stopped again. The object stretched right across her path. It was close and clear now, and Greta gasped. Her heart seemed to stop beating. For there, like a ghost risen out of the ice, lay a ship. A ship, of all things! A big schooner with three tall masts, all crusted with snow. What was it doing there? Slowly her mind filled with an awful suspicion. She tried to put it aside, but it came back. At last she faced the truth.

The little mare had been lost all this time. Instead of crossing the ice, they had been wandering down the river, toward the open sea. They were now somewhere near the mouth, where the ice was never safe. To prove it, here was the big three-master, frozen where the crew had left it moored for the winter.

Greta's heart began beating again in slow, hard thumps. She did not know which way to turn. Were vessels anchored with their bows upstream or down or any way at all? She could not remember. All she could do was press on and continue to pray.

It was quite dark now. Greta's arms and legs felt numb. One thing was certain, she was freezing there in the bitter wind and snow. So was the little horse. They must move or perish. Greta made up her mind. She got down and took hold of Judy's bridle, turned the sleigh carefully, and began to walk, leading the horse straight away from the long pointing bowsprit of the schooner.

The strongest blasts of the storm seemed to come from the right, so Greta kept the wind on her right cheek. In that way at least she might avoid moving in a circle.

"Suppose the wind changes?" asked a small cold voice inside her. But that was the voice of fear, and she refused to listen.

The effort of walking took some of the cold ache out of her legs, but there was no feeling in her hands and feet. Her cheeks felt like wood. She kept changing her hold on Judy's bridle and rubbing her face with the other hand. The storm tore at her long full skirts and darted icy fingers through her thin coat. The world seemed full of snow, driving in a sharp slant on the wind and sweeping along the ice with a hiss like escaping steam.

The mare was not shod for this sort of footing. She slipped and stumbled and seemed very tired. And Greta herself felt weary and empty. She had eaten nothing since the hasty breakfast at the farm. Sometimes the wind lulled, and the cloud of snow drifted heavily about them. Its touch then was soft upon her cheek, and Greta was tempted to let Judy go, to lie down on the ice and let that cold white powder go on brushing her face. Somehow the snow made her think of clean, cool bed sheets. How nice it would be to lie down and sleep away the night!

But whenever Greta's eyes closed, she saw a picture of her son, waiting, staring anxiously from the neighbor's window. She would open her eyes and cry to God for a little more strength, and step forward strongly in the darkness.

As the night wore on, this happened many times. Greta became more and more drowsy with the cold, and more weary, and the little horse lagged and stumbled. Finally, after one of those dreamy pauses, as Greta began to lead the horse again, she came upon a black patch in the ice ahead. It extended to the right and left as far as she could see. She moved closer—then stepped back in alarm. It was water— open water. She could hear it lapping against the edge of the ice.

She thought, *This is the end. We have come to the sea.*

She closed her eyes, praying slowly and silently. She stood there a long time. At last she put her chin up. She looked toward the sky in silent appeal to the Father. Aloud she said, "Judy, it's all or nothing now. Suppose this isn't the sea—suppose it's just the flooded ice along the shore! You know, where the ice sinks and buckles when the tide falls down the river. There's only one way to prove it, Judy. I must go to the edge and let my feet down into the water. Come, girl! Steady now! Come!"

Greta led the mare to the edge of the ice. The water looked very black. The snow was blowing harder than ever.

If only I could see, she thought, *just for a minute. Just for a second. If only I could be sure.* But there was only one way to be sure in this stormy darkness. She took a turn of the reins about her wrist, stooped, and lowered her left foot into the water. It came to her ankle, to her knee. The cold grip of the water sent a pain to her very bones.

She gasped and lost her balance.

For one wild moment Greta thought she was gone. The sea! She was plunging into the sea. But her feet came upon something solid now, something slippery but solid—the sunken ice. She paused to gather her courage and her breath. She waded out to the length of the reins. The flooded ice held firm. It tilted against hidden rocks, and now the water barely reached her trembling knees.

"Come, Judy!" she cried and pulled on the reins. The mare snorted and would not move. Greta threw her whole weight on the reins. Judy tried to draw back, but her worn iron shoes had no grip on the ice. Snorting with fear, she came over the edge into the water. The horse floundered past Greta, and she caught hold of the lurching sleigh. Dimly she saw a solid whiteness looming out of the windy dark. It was the shore—a pasture deep in snow.

Greta took the mare's head and led her up the bank. The fence was low and the poles rotten. She broke them down. She led Judy along inside the fence, wading through the drifts until she came to a gate and saw a light. Then she was standing at Judy's head outside a house and crying for help.

A man and a woman came to the door. She cried again, and they ran out to her. The man unhitched Judy quickly and took her off to his barn. The woman half-led, half-carried Greta into her kitchen. Greta's clothes were crusted with snow, her wet skirts frozen stiff. But before she would let the woman do anything for her, she stooped and turned up the icy hem of her skirt.

She laughed shakily. It was all there—the money that would buy new shoes for her boy and help repair the house. She gave thanks to God while the woman stood beside her, listening. God had heard her prayers on the frozen river. He had brought her safely back, and He had protected her earnings.

– *Thomas H. Raddall*

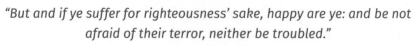

"But and if ye suffer for righteousness' sake, happy are ye: and be not afraid of their terror, neither be troubled."
– 1 Peter 3:14

Jack's Foolishness

Is it possible that what one man calls foolish, another might call wise? Is it possible that what God says is wisdom might be called foolishness by men?

The master was gone and the house servants working in the summer kitchen, so Jack stole up quietly to the porch. The master's son sat on the porch rail with his back against a massive pillar, a book propped against his knees.

"Whatcha got there?" Jack asked loudly, standing just below the other boy's perch.

Willie nearly fell off the porch rail. "Hey! Ya scared me, Jack!"

"Sorry," Jack said, grinning. Then he asked again, "Whatcha got there?"

"This is my spelling book. I'm learning my school words." Willie held up the speller for the slave's son to see. A puzzled look passed over Jack's face.

"What's a spelling book for?"

"Helps you learn how to read," the master's son said, jumping down from the porch rail. "See here, that's the word *Sam*."

"Sam . . . " Jack repeated. "How do you do it? How do you learn to read?" He craned his neck to get a look at the pages. They were filled with strange figures.

Willie opened the book wider, and the boys peered into it together.

76

"First we learn the ABCs," Willie explained. He pointed to the letters on the first page. "See. Each word is made with letters from the ABCs, so we have to learn those first. Then we learn to read."

"Could I learn the ABCs too?" Jack asked hopefully.

"Yep. Sure. I don't see why not."

Neither boy knew anything about slave laws. Neither knew that the law forbade slaves to learn how to read and write. In innocence the little plantation school began under a weeping willow on the front lawn: one teacher and one pupil. Soon Jack knew the alphabet as well as his teacher did. Willie gladly shared his readers with Jack, and the boys laughed over the poems and stories they read together.

The school had been going for a long time when one day Willie brought a little black book to the willow.

"What's that, Will?"

"It's a New Testament, Jack! It tells about Jesus."

Before long Jack had learned to read the New Testament. Sitting under the willow one muggy[1] summer afternoon, he read, "For God so loved the world, that He gave His only begotten Son, that whoso-ever believeth in Him should not perish, but have everlasting life."

Just think, Jack pondered. *God loves the whole world that much. Even the slaves, even me, a little slave boy.*

Jack grew older and his love for God's Word grew till at last he surrendered his heart to Jesus. He became a contented, growing Christian, in spite of the dirty cabin where his family crowded together to eat and sleep, in spite of the harsh work, bending over the cotton in the sweltering southern sun.

Though he was just a young man, Jack began to tell other slaves on the plantation about Jesus. Many of them learned to love the Lord too. As Jack grew, his zeal[2] grew. On Sundays, the only day when the

---

1 muggy: hot and very humid, sticky

2 zeal: enthusiasm

slaves' backs and fingers had rest, Jack began traveling to neighboring plantations. Down dusty red roads, into **bleak**, crowded hovels,[3] he carried the good news: Jesus loves even the slave!

One Monday morning as Jack walked with the crowd of slaves into a green field spotted with ripe white fluffs of cotton, the master, Mr. Hawkins, rode up on his favorite white horse.

"Jack!" he called.

"Yes, sir." Jack looked up at the man sitting on horseback.

"Jack, I hear you've been traveling on Sundays."

Jack studied the hard face. *Don't say too much,* he told himself. *Just tell the truth.*

"Yes, sir."

"Preaching?"

"Well, sir . . ." The young man hesitated. "I just been telling people Jesus died on the cross for them."

"Jack." Mr. Hawkins looked away over the fields for what seemed a long time. "Jack, if you go off preaching on Sunday again, I tell you what I'm going to do on Monday."

"What's that, sir?"

"I'm going to tie you to that tree over there," he pointed with his black whip out across the field to the great oak, "and I'm going to take this here whip and beat that religion right out of you."

Mr. Hawkins rode away, and Jack found a place among the pickers where he could think and pray. He knew that Mr. Hawkins was a determined man. He would do just what he'd said.

Jack listened to the other workers around him, singing—"Were you there when they crucified my Lord?" One side of the field sang the question and then paused while the answer came from the workers on the other side, singing the question over again. Then the field rang

3 hovel: a small poor shack

as they all sang the chorus—"Sometimes, it causes me to tremble, tremble, tremble."

They sing because they know about Jesus, Jack thought. *I have to tell the slaves on other plantations so they can sing too. Jesus suffered so much for us. If He wants me to tell others the Good News, I got to do it.* He resolved to go again next Sunday.

And the next Sunday Jack went. He carried his little New Testament and went down to a nearby plantation. People had gathered together in a split-log **shanty**, waiting for him. He gave them the words of life, and they listened like hungry folks sitting down to a feast.

"My master might beat me tomorrow for coming down here to you," he told them, "but if he do, it won't be nothing compared to what Christ suffered for us all."

The next morning Mr. Hawkins called Jack before he went into the fields.

"Jack, I hear you preached over at Wynette's place yesterday."

"Yes, sir. I have to go and tell sinners how Jesus was whipped for us so that we could go free."

"I told you, boy, how if you didn't stop preaching, I'd whip you. Now I will."

Jack closed his eyes and clung to the tree while the leather slashed across his back. While Mr. Hawkins cursed, Jack cried out to Jesus, and it seemed that Jesus was holding him up in His arms.

Mr. Hawkins finally dropped the whip. "Now, Jack, I don't believe you'll be preaching next Sunday. Get on down to the cotton field. You got work to do."

Next Sunday came. Jack's back had not healed from Monday's whipping. Still, that morning he stood before another audience, opened the little black Testament, and explained the words of life.

Negro Spirituals—Slave Songs

Swing Low, Sweet Chariot

I looked over Jordan, and what did I see—
    Comin' for to carry me home?
A band of angels comin' after me—
    Comin' for to carry me home!
Swing low, sweet chariot, Comin' for to carry me home!
Swing low, sweet chariot, Comin' for to carry me home!

If you get there before I do,
    Comin' for to carry me home.
Please tell my friends I'm comin' too—
    Comin' for to carry me home!
Swing low, sweet chariot, Comin' for to carry me home!
Swing low, sweet chariot, Comin' for to carry me home!

Deep River

Deep river,
My home is over Jordan—
Deep river, Lord,
I want to cross over into campground.

Oh, don't you want to go
To that Gospel feast—
That Promised Land
Where all is peace?

Deep river, Lord,
I want to cross over into campground.

Word had reached these folks about Jack's whipping. They listened, full of wonder—what message did he have, so important he would suffer whipping for it?

When he had finished, he told them, "Master whipped me sore last Monday. I don't know but that he'll kill me tomorrow. But if he do, I won't suffer as much as Jesus did when He died for you and me on the cross."

Jack expected Mr. Hawkins the next morning; and, sure enough, he was waiting when the long line of bent black people trudged down the path toward the far fields, where the dark green cotton leaves already shimmered in the hot morning sun. Jack went directly to the man on the white horse.

"I hear you been preaching again, Jack."

"Yes, sir. I told them how Christ was wounded for our transgressions. I told how He sweat drops of blood, praying in the garden. I told how He wore a crown of thorns, so we could wear a crown of joy when—"

"Don't preach to me, boy!" interrupted Mr. Hawkins angrily. "Just come here."

Mr. Hawkins' whip flew, lashing harder and longer, until Jack nearly collapsed from the pain.

"Go down to that field—you got work to do. And don't you *ever* preach again, do you hear? Or it'll be worse for you!"

Jack worked as well as he could. The field boss, knowing the condition of Jack's back, did not make him work hard. Still, when Sunday came, Jack could hardly walk the distance to the next plantation where he would share God's Good News. The people who had crowded into the slave's quarters wept, knowing what Jack was suffering so that they could hear what Jesus had done for them.

"Master whipped me sore last Monday," he told them. "But if I can

get you to come to Jesus and love Him, I'll gladly die tomorrow."
Some of those people did come to Jesus when they saw how Jack was
willing to suffer for Him.

When Jack stooped to walk out of the low cabin door Monday
morning on his way to the fields, he saw Mr. Hawkins waiting.
Without a word, the master turned and rode toward the oak. Jack
followed.

"Bare your back," was all Mr. Hawkins said. But when he raised
the whip, he could find no place to strike that was not full of wounds.

"What's wrong with you, Jack? You know I'm going to whip you
next day—why do you insist on this foolishness?"

"Why?" Jack smiled at Mr. Hawkins. "You ask me—I'll tell you, sir.
I'm going to take these stripes up to Jesus, and I'm going show Him
how I been faithful to Him—'cause He loved me, and you, sir; and He
bled and died on the cross for me, and you, sir. That's why."

The whip dropped. "Go down to the cotton field, Jack," Mr.
Hawkins said weakly.

Jack went to his work, his heart bounding with joy and full of
a prayer for Mr. Hawkins: "Lord, forgive Mr. Hawkins, for Jesus
Christ's sake."

That Monday passed quickly for Jack. Though his back still
throbbed, his heart sang. Then at three o'clock, a messenger came flying down the road, shouting, "Jack! Jack! Come fast! Master's calling
you! Come on, now!"

Dread gripped the pit of his stomach, but Jack dropped his cotton
bag. He knew he mustn't make the master wait. He hurried with all
that was in him. But no angry master greeted him. Instead the messenger led him into Mr. Hawkins' room, where he found the master
writhing on the floor.

"Oh," he cried out, "Oh, Jack. Pray for me. I'm dying. I'm dying."

"I been praying for you all the time, sir," Jack told him, kneeling beside Mr. Hawkins on the floor. "Now you got to pray for yourself."

"I don't know how to pray. I don't know how . . . help me, Jack!"

Jack began to pray aloud for Mr. Hawkins. He prayed and again he urged Mr. Hawkins to pray. The master called out to the Saviour, begging for Him to save him.

Mr. Hawkins did not die that afternoon. But he became a new man. He **yielded** to the Master of all men—both slave and free—and his life was changed.

One of the first things Mr. Hawkins did was call Jack into his office a few days later. He asked Jack to forgive him; then he said, "Jack, here are your freedom papers. You are a free man. I want you to go and preach the Good News wherever you like. Tell people what the Saviour has done for us, Jack. And may His blessing go with you."

– E. Hammond

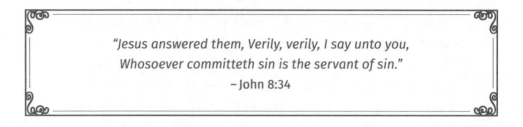

Slaves

They are slaves who fear to speak
    For the fallen and the weak;
They are slaves who will not choose
    Hatred, scoffing, and abuse
Rather than in silence shrink
    From the truth they needs must think;
They are slaves who dare not be
    In the right with two or three.

– James Russell Lowell

Be Like the Bird

Be like the bird, who
Halting in his flight
On limb too slight
Feels it give way beneath him,
Yet sings,
Knowing he has wings.

– Victor Hugo

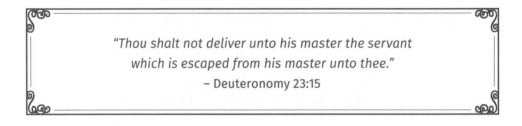

The Road to Canada

Allen looked down the road toward the south.

That morning his father had said, "Allen, I am going to the far field to work. If any Negro should come along, thee can take him down to the cornfield, if thee like, and hide him under the big walnut tree. But do not tell me about it or Mother or anybody else."

So Allen had played by the roadside all morning, watching for the runaway slave who might come along.

And now, sure enough, here came a poor fellow. His clothes were ragged and his feet bleeding from the rough roads he had traveled and the underbrush he had broken through. The man hurried along, turning every now and then to listen, then hurrying on again.

Allen ran out into the road to meet him. The man froze in terror and looked around for a hiding place. Allen spoke quickly: "Is someone after thee? I'll hide thee so that they cannot find thee."

"You will? Can you, for sure? Is you Mister Jay's boy?"

Allen nodded and the man grinned. "They told me I'd get help here. I'll go just where you say."

Allen quickly led the way through the pear trees. When they were out of sight of the road, the Negro looked back and sighed with relief. They left the orchard and entered the big cornfield. The rows of corn stood higher than a man's head.

"Nobody can find thee here," said Allen.

" 'Deed, they can't. I feel perfectly safe now."

Farther and deeper in among the rows of corn they shoved their way, until at last they came out under the great walnut tree. Its branches spread wide in every direction.

"Now, will thee stay right here and wait for me?" Allen asked. "I will come for thee at the right time."

"I won't stir from here," the man answered. "I been walking all day yesterday and all night. I'm tired enough to sleep till tomorrow comes. If only I wasn't so hungry."

"I will get thee something to eat." Allen started off for the house, intending to go into the pantry and find some food. But when he reached the kitchen, he found his mother spreading butter on slices of bread and laying cold meat between them. She smiled at Allen but said nothing. He sat down and watched. Mother packed a basket with the sandwiches and added some cake and pieces of fruit. She filled a jug with rich, creamy milk.

"Allen, if thee knows of anybody who is hungry, thee might take this basket to him."

Allen could hardly **restrain** his eagerness. He slipped off his chair and seized the basket and the jug. Trying not to smile, he answered, "I'll try to find someone; but if I don't, I'll eat the lunch myself!"

"Very well," answered Mother, and Allen hurried out across the backyard and through the corn to the walnut tree where the man lay resting and watching for Allen's return.

The man ate as though starved. Little remained in the basket when he at last paused and poured out his thanks to Allen.

For a time the boy and the man spoke about the "railroad." Allen's people, the Quakers, thought it a wicked thing to buy and sell men and women as though they were cows and horses. Many Quakers were willing to run great risks to help slaves to their freedom. Many slaves escaped from their owners in the South, crossed the Ohio River, and sought a hiding place in the home of Quakers, who called themselves Friends. The Friends would transport them from one place to another across the state and then into Canada where they would be free. Even when the slave's "master" was close behind him and knew exactly where he had gone, the slave would seem to disappear. People came to say that the Friends sent slaves by the "Underground Railroad."

"I can sleep now," the man finally said. "I haven't had my stomach full since I left Virginia." He stretched himself out on the ground as Allen pushed back into the cornfield.

Allen returned to the house and his own dinner. Father and Mother chatted as usual, but Allen was thinking about the man lying under the walnut tree. He wondered what to do next. How could he help the man arrive safely in Canada? He didn't know the next station. And there were people who would do anything to stop a runaway slave from finding freedom.

He was still thinking hard when three rough-looking men rode up to the gate and called gruffly for Mr. Jay. Father went out to talk to them, saying as he left the room, "They look like slave-catchers. I suppose they are searching for some escaped Negro. But even if I had one sitting here, I would never give him up."

Allen slipped into the front room and stood out of sight by the open window. There he could hear all that was said.

"Have you seen an escaped slave going by here today?" one man asked.

"No, I have not," Father replied.

"Don't let him fool you, Jim," interrupted another rider. "Of course he didn't see that runaway go past, because he came in! Look here, Quaker, that slave's in your house, and we're going in to look for him."

"There is no Negro in my house," Father said, "but if you wish to look for him, you may—if you have the proper authority."

But this they did not have. They could only **bluster** and threaten and finally ride away in disgust.

The afternoon and evening passed as usual. Allen wondered again what to do with the man. He couldn't leave him under the tree all night!

Then Father spoke. "Allen, I have a basket of apples to send to Grandfather. It is getting a little dark, but I think thee can drive over with old Ned, can thee not?"

"Oh, yes," exclaimed Allen, smiling all over his face. Here was his answer!

"I will harness the horse for thee," Father went on, "and put the apples in the wagon. It is only five miles, of course, but if thee would like to take anybody along, thee may."

"Thank thee, Father," said Allen. Then catching up his cap, he ran out the door, across the yard, and through the corn to the walnut tree. The Negro was asleep, but Allen shook him awake.

"Come," he said. "We're going on."

The man sprang to his feet, caught up the basket with its remains of lunch, and followed Allen to the barnyard. There stood old Ned, harnessed and tied.

Night had fallen, but Ned knew the road even better than Allen did. He trotted along at his own **moderate** pace. Soon they reached the home of Allen's grandfather.

And half an hour later, the escaped slave was astride a good horse trotting northward with another Quaker to the next station on the Underground Railroad.

– Anna L. Curtis

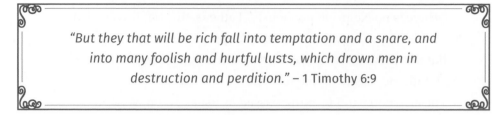

"But they that will be rich fall into temptation and a snare, and into many foolish and hurtful lusts, which drown men in destruction and perdition." – 1 Timothy 6:9

Elias

There once lived, in the city of Ufa,[1] a Bashkir[2] named Elias. His father, who died a year after he had found his son a wife, did not leave him much property. Elias then had only seven mares, two cows, and about a score of sheep. He was a good manager, however, and soon began to **acquire** more. He and his wife worked from morn till night, rising earlier than others and going later to bed. His possessions increased year by year.

Living in this way, Elias little by little acquired great wealth. At the end of thirty-five years, he had 200 horses, 150 head of cattle, and 1,000 sheep. Hired laborers tended his flocks and herds, and hired women milked his mares and cows, and made kumiss,[3] butter, and cheese. Elias had much of everything, and everyone in the district envied him.

They said of him: "Elias is a fortunate man: he has plenty of everything. This world must be a pleasant place for him."

People of position heard of Elias and sought his acquaintance. Visitors came to him from afar, and he welcomed every one and

---

1 Ufa (ü fä'): a city in central Russia, in the western foothills of the Ural Mountains
2 The Bashkirs (bash kirz') live in eastern Russia, especially in the Ural Mountains. They were once a nomadic people who tended livestock throughout eastern Russia.
3 kumiss (kü' mis): a traditional beverage of central Asia made from mare's (horse's) milk

gave them food and drink. Whoever might come, there was always kumiss, tea, sherbet, and mutton to set before them. Whenever visitors arrived, a sheep would be killed or sometimes two; and if many guests came, he would even slaughter a mare for them.

Elias had three children: two sons and a daughter; and he married them all off. While he was poor, his sons worked with him and looked after the flocks and herds themselves; but when he grew rich, they got spoiled, and one of them took to drink. The elder was killed in a brawl; and the younger, who had married a self-willed woman, ceased to obey his father, and they could not live together anymore.

So they parted, and Elias gave his son a house and some of the cattle, and this reduced his wealth. Soon after that, a disease broke out among Elias's sheep, and many died. Then followed a bad harvest, and the hay crop failed. Many cattle died that winter. Then the Kyrgyz[4] captured his best herd of horses.

Elias's property dwindled away, becoming smaller and smaller, while at the same time his strength grew less. By the time he was seventy years old, he had begun to sell his furs, carpets, saddles, and tents. At last he had to part with his remaining cattle, and he found himself face to face with poverty. Before he knew how it had happened, Elias had lost everything, and in their old age he and his wife had to become servants. Elias had nothing left, except the clothes on his back, a fur cloak, a cup, his indoor shoes and overshoes, and his wife Sham-Shemagi, who by this time was old. The son who had parted from him had gone into a far country, and his daughter was dead, so that there was no one to help the old couple.

Their neighbor, Hamid-Shah, took pity on them. Hamid-Shah was neither rich nor poor, but lived comfortably and was a good man. He

---

4 The Kyrgyz (kir gēz') were a nomadic people of Central Asia. They now live in Kyrgyzstan, which is named after their tribe.

remembered Elias's **hospitality**, and pitying him, said: "Come and live with me, Elias, you and Sham-Shemagi. In summer you can work in my melon garden as much as your strength allows, and in winter feed my cattle. Sham-Shemagi can milk my mares and make kumiss. I will feed and clothe you both. When you need anything, tell me and you shall have it."

Elias thanked his neighbor, and he and his wife became servants of Hamid-Shah. At first the position seemed hard to them, but they got used to it and lived on, working as much as their strength allowed.

Hamid-Shah found it was to his advantage to keep such people because, having been masters themselves, they knew how to manage. They were not lazy but did all the work they could. Yet it grieved Hamid-Shah to see people brought so low who had been of such high standing.

It happened once that some of Hamid-Shah's relatives came from a great distance to visit him, and a teacher came too. Hamid-Shah told Elias to catch a sheep and kill it. Elias skinned the sheep and boiled it and sent it in to the guests. The guests ate the mutton, had some tea, and then began drinking kumiss. As they were sitting with their host on down cushions on a carpet, talking together and sipping kumiss from their cups, Elias, having finished his work, passed by the open door. Hamid-Shah, seeing him pass, said to one of the guests: "Did you notice that old man who passed just now?"

"Yes," said the visitor, "what is there remarkable about him?"

"Only this—that he was once the richest man among us," replied the host. "His name is Elias. You may have heard of him."

"Of course I have heard of him," the guest answered. "I never saw him before, but his fame has spread far and wide."

"Yes, and now he has nothing left," said Hamid-Shah, "and he lives with me as my laborer, and his wife is here too—she milks the mares."

The guest was astonished: he clicked his tongue, shook his head, and said: "Life turns like a wheel. One man it lifts, another it sets down! Does not the old man grieve over all he has lost?"

"Who can tell? He lives quietly and peacefully and works well."

"May I speak to him?" asked the guest. "I should like to ask him about his life."

"Why not?" replied the master, and he called from the tent in which they were sitting: "Babay" (which in the Bashkir tongue means *Grandfather*), "come in here and have a cup of kumiss with us and call your wife here also."

Elias entered with his wife; and after exchanging greetings with his master and the guests, he repeated a prayer and seated himself near the door. His wife passed in behind a curtain and sat down with her mistress.

They handed Elias a cup of kumiss. He bowed, drank a little, and put down the cup.

"Well, Daddy," said the guest who had wished to speak to him, "I suppose you feel rather sad at the sight of us. It must remind you of your former success and of your present sorrows."

Elias smiled and said: "If I were to tell you what is happiness and what is misery, you would not believe me. You had better ask my wife. She is a woman, and what is in her heart is on her tongue. She will tell you the whole truth."

The guest turned toward the curtain. "Well, Granny," he cried, "tell me how your former happiness compares with your present misery."

And Sham-Shemagi answered from behind the curtain: "This is what I think about it: My husband and I lived for fifty years seeking happiness and not finding it; and it is only now, these last two years, since we had nothing left and have lived as laborers, that we have found real happiness. We wish for nothing better than our present lot."

The guests were astonished, and so was the master. He even rose and drew back the curtain so he could see the old woman's face.

There she stood with her arms folded, looking at her old husband and smiling. He smiled back at her.

The old woman went on: "I speak the truth and do not **jest**. For half a century we sought for happiness, and as long as we were rich, we never found it. Now that we have nothing left and we have taken service as laborers, we have found such happiness that we want nothing better."

"But what makes up your happiness?" asked the guest.

"Why, this," she replied, "when we were rich, my husband and I had so many cares that we had no time to talk to one another or to think of our souls or to pray to God. Now we had visitors and had to consider what food to set before them and what presents to give them, lest they should speak ill of us.

"When they left, we had to look after our workers, who were always trying to neglect their work but eat the best food, while we wanted to get all we could out of them. So we sinned.

"Then we were in fear lest a wolf should kill a foal or a calf, or thieves steal our horses. We lay awake at night worrying lest the ewes should lie on their lambs, and we got up again and again to see that all was well. As soon as we attended to one thing, another care would spring up: how, for instance, to get enough feed for the winter. And besides that, my husband and I used to disagree. He would say we must do so and so, and I would differ with him; and then we disputed—sinning again. So we passed from one trouble to another, from one sin to another, and found no happiness."

"Well, and now?"

"Now, when my husband and I wake in the morning, we always have a loving word for one another, and we live peacefully, having nothing to quarrel about. We have no care but how best to serve our master. We work as much as our strength allows, and do it with a will, that our master may not lose but profit by us. When we come in, dinner or supper is ready and there is kumiss to drink. We have fuel to burn when it is cold, and we have our fur cloak. And we have time to talk, time to think of our souls, and time to pray. For fifty years we sought happiness, but only now at last we have found it."

The guests laughed.

But Elias said: "Do not laugh, friends. It is not a matter for jesting—it is the truth of life. We also were foolish at first and wept at the loss of our wealth; but now God has shown us the truth, and we tell it, not for our own comfort, but for your good."

And the teacher said: "That is a wise speech. Elias has spoken the exact truth. The same is said in Holy Writ."

And the guests ceased laughing and became thoughtful.

– Leo Tolstoy

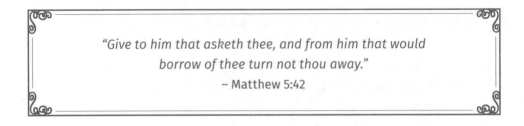
Always 'Ungry

Sara's father raised her in India, where he worked for the British government. Her mother had died when she was born. When Sara was eight years old, her father took her to London and enrolled her in Miss Minchin's school. Then he returned to his work, planning to return and take her back to India when she finished her education.

But then he died in India, leaving her alone in London. She had no other family and no money: her father had lost all his money before he died. Sara could no longer study at Miss Minchin's expensive school, but Miss Minchin agreed to keep her as a servant. She treated Sara cruelly. Sara slept in a bare, unheated attic. She was overworked and underfed. But Sara insisted on being a "giver," helping others and showing kindness to the weak. Because Sara was a giver, she always lived like the princess her father had told her she was. This story comes from the book about Sara, A Little Princess.

For several days it had rained continuously. The streets were chilly and sloppy; there was mud everywhere—sticky London mud, and over everything a **pall** of fog and drizzle. Of course there were several long and tiresome errands to be done—there always were on days like this—and Sara was sent out again and again, until her shabby clothes were damp through. Her worn shoes were so wet they could not hold any more water. Added to this, she had been denied her dinner because Miss Minchin wished to punish her. She was very hungry—so hungry and cold and tired that her joyous little face had a pinched look, and now and then some kind-hearted person passing her in the crowded street glanced at her with compassion.

But she did not know that. She hurried on, trying to comfort herself in that strange way of hers by pretending and supposing. But really this time it was harder than she had ever found it, and once or twice she thought it almost made her more cold and hungry instead of less so. But she persevered.

"Suppose I had dry clothes on," she imagined. "Suppose I had good shoes and a long thick coat and merino[1] stockings and a whole umbrella. And suppose . . . suppose, just when I was near a baker's where they sold hot buns, I should find sixpence[2] —which belonged to nobody. Suppose, if I did, I should go into the shop and buy six of the hottest buns and should eat them all without stopping."

Some very splendid things happen in this world sometimes. It certainly was a wonderful thing that happened to Sara. She had to cross the street just then as she was saying this to herself—the mud was dreadful—she almost had to wade. She picked her way as carefully as she could. In picking her way, she had to look down at her feet and the mud, and in looking down—just as she reached the sidewalk—she saw something shining in the gutter. A piece of silver—a tiny piece trodden upon by many feet, but still with spirit enough to shine a little. Not quite a sixpence, but the next thing to it—a four-penny piece! In one second she had it in her cold hand.

"Oh!" she gasped. "It is true!"

And then she looked straight before her at the shop directly facing her. It was a baker's shop, and a cheerful, motherly woman with rosy cheeks was just putting into the window a tray of delicious hot buns—large, plump, shiny buns with currants in them.

---

1 merino: a fine wool and cotton material used for socks and stockings

2 sixpence: a six-penny piece. *Pence*, a word used in England, is plural for *penny*. In the past the English used two-penny, four-penny, and six-penny coins.

It almost made Sara feel faint for a few seconds—the shock and the sight of the buns and the delightful odors of warm bread floating up through the baker's cellar windows.

She knew that she need not hesitate to use the little piece of money. It had evidently been lying in the mud for some time, and its owner would be completely lost in the streams of passing people who crowded and jostled each other all through the day.

"But I'll go and ask the baker's woman if she has lost a piece of money," she said to herself rather faintly.

So she crossed the pavement and put her wet foot on the step of the shop; and as she did so, she saw something which made her stop.

It was a little figure more miserable than her own—a little figure which was not much more than a bundle of rags, from which small, bare, red, and muddy feet peeped out—only because the rags with which the wearer was trying to cover them were not long enough. Above the rags appeared a shock of tangled hair and a dirty face with big, hollow, hungry eyes.

Sara knew they were hungry eyes the moment she saw them, and she felt a sudden sympathy. "This," she said to herself with a sigh, "is one of the Poor—and she is hungrier than I am."

The child—this "one of the Poor"—stared up at Sara Crewe and shuffled herself aside a little, so as to give her more room. She was used to being made to give room to everybody. She knew that if a policeman chanced to meet her, he would tell her to move on.

Sara clutched her four-penny piece and hesitated a few seconds. Then she spoke to her. "Are you hungry?" she asked.

"Ain't I jist!" she said in a hoarse voice. "Jist ain't I!"

"Haven't you any dinner?" said Sara.

"No dinner," more hoarsely still and with more shuffling, "nor yet no bre'fast—nor yet no supper—nor nothin'!"

"Since when?" asked Sara.

"I dun'no. Never got nothin' today—nowhere. I've axed and axed."

Just to look at her made Sara more hungry and faint. But those strange little thoughts were at work in her brain, and she was talking to herself, though she was sick at heart.

"If I'm a princess," she was saying to herself, "if I'm a princess . . . When they were poor and driven from their thrones, they always shared with the poor—if they met one poorer and hungrier. They always shared. Buns are a penny each. If it had been sixpence, I could have eaten six! It won't be enough for either of us—but it will be better than nothing."

"Wait a minute," she said to the beggar child. She went into the shop. It was warm and smelled delightful. The woman was just going to put more hot buns in the window. "If you please," said Sara, "have you lost fourpence—a silver fourpence?" She held out the **forlorn** little piece of money.

The woman looked at it and at her—at her intense, winsome face and draggled, once-fine clothes.

"Well, no," she answered. "Did you find it?"

"In the gutter," said Sara.

"Keep it then," said the woman. "It may have been there a week. Who knows who lost it? You could never find out!"

"I know that," said Sara, "but I thought I'd ask you."

"Not many would," said the woman, looking puzzled and interested and good-natured all at once. "Do you want to buy something?" she added as she saw Sara glance toward the buns.

"Four buns, if you please," said Sara, "those at a penny each."

The woman went to the window and put some in a paper bag. Sara noticed that she put in six.

"I said four, if you please," she explained. "I have only fourpence."

"I'll throw in two for good measure," said the woman with her good-natured look. "I dare say you can eat them some time. Aren't you hungry?"

A mist rose before Sara's eyes.

"Yes," she answered. "I am very hungry, and I am much obliged to you for your kindness." She was going to add: "And there's a child outside who is hungrier than I am." But just at that moment two or three customers came in at once and each one seemed in a hurry, so she could only thank the woman again and go out.

The child was still huddled up on one corner of the steps. She looked frightful in her wet and dirty rags. She was staring with a dull look of suffering straight ahead, and Sara saw her suddenly draw the back of her chapped hand across her eyes to rub away the tears which seemed to have surprised her by forcing their way from under her lids. She was muttering to herself.

Sara opened the paper bag and took out one of the hot buns, which had already warmed her cold hands a little.

"See," she said, putting the bun on the ragged lap, "that is nice and hot. Eat it, and you will not be so hungry."

The child started and stared up at her; then she snatched up the bun and began to cram it into her mouth with great wolfish bites.

"Oh!" Sara heard her say hoarsely, in wild delight.

Sara took out two more buns and put them down.

"She is hungrier than I am," she said to herself. "She's starving." But her hand trembled when she put down the fourth bun.

"I'm not starving," she said. She put down the fifth.

The starving girl was still snatching and devouring when Sara turned away. She was too **ravenous** to give any thanks, even if she had been taught politeness, which she had not. She was only a poor little wild girl.

"Good-bye," said Sara.

When she reached the other side of the street, she looked back.

The child had a bun in each hand and had stopped in the middle of a bite to watch her. Sara gave her a little nod, and the child, after another stare—a curious, longing stare—jerked her shaggy head in response. Until Sara was out of sight, she did not take another bite or even finish the one she had begun.

At that moment the baker woman glanced out of her shop window. "Well!" she exclaimed. "If that young-un hasn't given her buns to a beggar child! It wasn't because she didn't want them, either. She looked hungry enough! I'd give something to know what she did that for." She stood behind her window for a few moments and pondered. Then her curiosity got the better of her. She went to the door and spoke to the beggar child.

"Who gave you those buns?"

The child nodded her head toward Sara's vanishing figure.

"What did she say?" inquired the woman.

"Axed me if I was 'ungry," replied the hoarse voice.

"What did you say?"

"Said I was jist!"

"And then she came in and got buns and came out and gave them to you, did she?"

The child nodded.

"How many?"

"Five."

The woman thought it over. "Left just one for herself," she said in a low voice. "And she could have eaten all six—I saw it in her eyes."

She looked awhile after the little, draggled, faraway figure and felt more disturbed in her usually comfortable mind than she had for many days.

"I wish she hadn't gone so quickly," she said. "I'm sure she should have had a dozen."

Then she turned to the child.

"Are you hungry, yet?"

"I'm always 'ungry. But 'tain't so bad now as it was."

"Come in here," said the woman, and she held open the shop door.

The child got up and shuffled in. To be invited into a warm place full of bread seemed an incredible thing. She did not know what was going to happen. She did not care even.

"Get yourself warm," said the woman, pointing to a fire in a tiny back room. "And look here, when you're needing a bite of bread, you can come here and ask for it. I'll give it to you for that girl's sake."

– Frances Hodgson Burnett

Courage

What Have We Done Today?

We shall do much in the years to come,
    But what have we done today?
We shall give our gold in a princely sum,
    But what did we give today?
We shall lift the heart and dry the tear,
We shall plant a hope in the place of fear,
We shall speak the words of love and cheer,
    But what did we speak today?

– Nixon Waterman

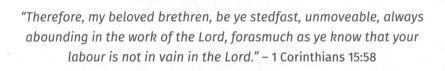

> *"Therefore, my beloved brethren, be ye stedfast, unmoveable, always abounding in the work of the Lord, forasmuch as ye know that your labour is not in vain in the Lord."* – 1 Corinthians 15:58

The Carolers of Bethlehem Center

There might have been no church had not the minister, James McKenzie, come just when the few regulars seemed ready to give up in despair. There might have been no Sunday school had not Harold Thornton tended it as carefully as he tended his own orchard. There might have been no class for the sixth grade boys, had it not been for Gertrude Windsor. But there would have been no glad tidings in one wintry heart if not for the voices that sang the carols that morning in the snow. The voices belonged to Eddie, the two Willies, Charlie, Harry, and little Phil, and they came straight from Him who gave the angels their song: "On earth peace, good will toward men."

Gertrude was ill. At the end of the winter term in Gertrude's junior year,[1] the doctor had **prescribed** a year of rest for her. So she came to find it with her aunt Melinda in the quiet village of Bethlehem Center.

On her first Sunday she attended the little church and Sunday school. At the close of the service the pastor and superintendent held a conference.

"She would be just the one, if she *would*," said Pastor McKenzie.

---

1 junior year: the third year in college

"It can't go on as it is," answered Harold Thornton. "The teacher means well—but he just doesn't know boys. Not one of the boys came this morning. Only Eddie came last week. We may lose them all—"

"I was told her health nearly broke down in college. She's here to rest."

"Yes, so Mr. Thompson told me. But we do need her help."

"Well," the pastor said thoughtfully at last. "I will call on Gertrude. I'll let you know what I find out."

When the pastor called to ask Gertrude about helping out in the sixth grade Sunday school class, she hesitated. Hadn't the doctor said—"Perhaps it's not so much your schoolwork that's gotten you down, but all of your other activities: your Sunday school class and your student volunteer work, on top of your classes"?

But the wistful face of Harry, who brought Aunt Melinda's milk, convinced her. So on her second Sunday in Bethlehem Center, Gertrude taught the class, **consisting** of Eddie and little Phil.

The lesson was on drunkenness and sobriety. Eddie joined right in, but Gertrude didn't know what to make of little Phil's silence. She kept wondering through the afternoon—*did I say something to offend little Phil?* Then on Monday she met Phil and his father on the street. She tried to atone for her mistake, whatever it might have been.

"Are you Phil's father?" she asked, smiling.

Some folks in Bethlehem Center said of Tim Shartow that he regarded neither God nor man. But Phil's father grew strangely embarrassed as he shook Gertrude's hand.

"Yes'm," he answered.

"I am to be his Sunday school teacher," she went on. "And of course I want to know the fathers and mothers of my boys. I hope Phil can come regularly. We are going to have some very interesting lessons."

"I guess he can come," answered his father. "It's a better place for him than on the street anyway."

This was faint praise, but well meant. Gertrude smiled her appreciation and in that brief meeting won not only Phil's lifelong regard, but that of his father as well. From that time on, Tim Shartow felt that he had two friends in Bethlehem Center of whom he need not be ashamed.

Tim's other friend was Pastor James McKenzie. These two very different men had a **mutual** but qualified respect for each other that dated from their first meeting. Pastor McKenzie had walked into Shartow's saloon and asked permission to tack up an announcement of revival services to be held at the chapel.

"I guess you can," the proprietor[2] had grumbled, standing on his guard.

The poster was displayed, and the unusual visitor turned to Tim Shartow, staring from behind the bar. They were alone, since it was still early in the day.

"We'd be very glad, Mr. Shartow, if you would attend some of the meetings."

"Wouldn't go if you paid me," answered the saloon keeper.

Mr. McKenzie did not reply.

"The worst enemies I have are in that church," added Tim, by way of explanation.

A smile lighted up the pastor's earnest face. "No, Mr. Shartow," he said, "you're wrong. They don't like your business—*I* don't like your business—but you haven't an enemy in our church. And I want to tell you now"—his foot was on the bar rail and he was looking straight into the eyes of the man to whom he spoke— "that every night, as I pray that God will remove this saloon, I pray that He will bring you to

2 proprietor: owner of a store or business

know my Saviour. And if ever you need any help that I can give, I want you to feel free to come to me. We are traveling different roads, Mr. Shartow, but we are not enemies. We are friends."

And the pastor departed, leaving Tim "shook up"—to use his own words. It was doubtful that Tim Shartow would ever regain his former attitude toward "them church folks."

On Gertrude's second Sunday as teacher, the two Willies came to test the truth of rumors that had reached them. Charlie and Harry came next and, after Gertrude announced mid-week class outings as a reward for perfect attendance, there was not one absence for thirteen weeks.

To Harold Thornton it had the look of a miracle. The class was like clay in the hands of a potter. There was nothing Gertrude could not do with them. They listened spellbound while she talked, took part in the responsive readings, answered questions, studied their lessons—they even pocketed their Sunday school papers without looking at them until the lesson was over. They sang with a freedom that was **exhilarating** to hear. Even Harry—who sang throughout the song whatever note his voice first caught—never failed to sing. Though his voice added little to the harmony, it powerfully boosted everyone's spirits.

But if Gertrude was doing much for those boys, they were doing as much for her. She had been ordered to rest, to get moderate exercise and plenty of fresh air. She could not have *hired* better helpers than the boys were to her. From the time the first pale blossoms of the bloodroot showed beside the snow, and all through the seasons of violets, wild strawberries and, at last, the goldenrod, the spoils of the woodlands were brought to her.

Their mid-week meetings became long tramps during which Gertrude told them interesting things about insects, birds, and flowers—and they told as much that was new to her. Every one of them had become a conspirator[3] in the plot to keep her out of doors, away from her books. Hardly a day passed by that she did not go somewhere with some of the boys. And as the healthy color began to show in her face, as her strength came back and every pulse beat brought the returning joy of life, Gertrude often felt that her work for the sixth grade class had been repaid a hundredfold.

It was one mid-August afternoon, when the tasseled corn stood high and the thistles had begun to take wing and fly away, that there came the first thoughts of the carols. Harry had to drive cows that day. But the others were with her, and as they came out through Mr. Giertz's woods and looked over the pasture where the sheep were feeding, little Phil began to sing the version of the shepherd's Psalm that she had taught them:

> The Lord is my Shepherd;
> I shall not want;
> He maketh me down to lie—

The other boys joined in, and they sang through to the end. It was beautiful. She had never realized that they could sing so well, and suddenly, as she listened, the plan came full-grown into her mind. She suggested it to them.

The boys were excited. For half an hour they discussed the details, and then while they sat on the grass, she taught them the beginning of "While Shepherds Watched Their Flocks by Night."

That was the first of many open-air rehearsals. When the weather grew colder, they transferred their practices to Willie Giertz's, where there were no near neighbors to whom the secret might leak out.

3 conspirator: someone who secretly plans

There was not one weak voice in the group except Harry's. At first he was a puzzle: what would they do about Harry's voice? That difficulty vanished when Gertrude discovered that with a little less volume, and by standing next to Phil's strong melody, Harry could follow the tune. After that, all went smoothly, and Harry began to improve.

When the program was complete, they had by heart six songs: "While Shepherds Watched Their Flocks by Night," "Away in a Manger," "We Three Kings of Orient Are," "Hark! The Herald Angels Sing," "There Came Three Kings Ere Break of Day," and last, but best, because it seemed especially made for them, the song that began:

> O little town of Bethlehem,
> How still we see thee lie!
> Above thy deep and dreamless sleep
> The silent stars go by.

So at length came Christmas Eve. Little eyes were closing tight in determined efforts to make the morning come more quickly. But in Bethlehem Center were six boys who were thinking less of tomorrow's gifts than of the morning's plan.

Gertrude had fallen asleep thinking of the letter on her bed table. It gave approval for her to return to school for the next term, after the first of the year. But at the first buzz of the alarm clock she was up. Soon she was ready and went softly downstairs and out into the keen morning air. The stars were still bright overhead, and there was no light in the east; but Gertrude wasn't the first one about. At the gate she found Eddie, the two Willies, and little Phil waiting for her. Harry and Charlie soon came speeding along the road. "Are we all here?" asked Harry in a whisper. The boys huddled together, squirming with excitement.

"Yes, we're here," Gertrude answered. "Which place is first?"

"Pastor McKenzie's," announced Charlie, whose part had been to lay out the route. Crossing the road, they passed through the McKenzies' gate. Beneath the study windows, Harry struck a tuning fork against his boot heel, Gertrude hummed the key and then, like one, there rose to greet the dawn of another Christmas day clear voices singing—

> Hark! The herald angels sing:
> "Glory to the newborn King!
> Peace on Earth and mercy mild,
> God and sinners reconciled."

There were sounds from within before they had finished the first stanza. The pastor started to open his window as the "Amen" sounded, but the boys were too quick for him. There was a volley of "Merry Christmas," and his answer barely reached the last chuckling boy as he slipped through the gate.

Beneath the bare apple boughs in Harold Thornton's yard, Charlie, Eddie, and little Phil sang "We Three Kings of Orient Are," while the others joined in the chorus. At the song's close the superintendent, swifter than the pastor, overtook them with a box of candy.

Tears came into Mrs. Martin's eyes as she listened to them singing "Away in a manger, no crib for his bed," and looked on her sick child in his bed. Old Uncle King forgot for a moment his vexing troubles as he listened to "that glorious song of old." Mrs. Fenny cried, as sick people will, when she heard the boys sing the sweet triumphant notes.

So from house to house the singers went, pausing at one because of sickness, at another because those within were lonely. They sang at some for love, as they had serenaded the pastor and the superintendent, and they brought to each some new joy.

The stars were fading out, and the singers had started to return. On their side of the street was the post office and opposite them was the saloon, with its gaudy, gilt sign—Tim's Place. Little Phil was behind Gertrude. As they passed that building—it was home to Phil—his hand just touched Gertrude's sleeve.

"Do you think," he whispered, and she could see the pitiful quiver of his chin as he spoke, "do you suppose we could sing one for my father?"

"Why, surely," she answered. "Which one do you think he'd like best?"

Phil had shrunk behind her and, beneath the gaze of the other boys, his eyes were those of a little hunted animal. "Bethlehem," he said huskily.

And when Harry had struck the tuning fork, they began to sing together—

> O little town of Bethlehem,
> How still we see thee lie!
> Above thy deep and dreamless sleep
> The silent stars go by.

The twenty-fourth of December had been a good day for business in Tim Shartow's place. He had had venison for free lunch. A mandolin[4] and guitar player had been there all evening, and there were several hundred dollars in the till.[5]

But now, in the quiet of the early morning, Tim Shartow sat alone, thinking, and the reaction to last night's business came. Tim remembered how Rob MacFlynn had had too much to drink and had gone home weeping uncontrollably. He would go home and burden his

---

4 mandolin: a stringed instrument
5 till: the place where storekeepers keep their money for doing business

wife, who had toiled all day to earn the money Rob drank up. Tim thought of the fight between Joe Frier and Tom Stacey. Tim did not drink much himself. He despised a drunkard—and these things disgusted him. There was little Phil too—the "saloon keeper's boy." That cut deep. *Wouldn't it pay better in the long run,* Tim was thinking— and then the music floated in from outside.

He didn't hear the words at first, but he had a good ear. Actually, it was the music that had first brought him as a boy into the beer gardens. Stepping to the window he listened, unseen by those outside. There the words reached him:

> How silently, how silently,
> The wondrous gift is given!
> So God imparts to human hearts
> The blessing of His heaven.
> No ear may hear His coming,
> But in this world of sin
> Where meek souls will receive Him still—

Until they sang the "Amen," Tim never stirred from the window.

A storm had been threatening all day. Finally, it descended. The blizzard was raging outside, but within, by the fire in his study, Pastor McKenzie was comfortable. The children were tucked away in their beds, when a knock surprised him.

Who could it be, at this hour, in this weather? he wondered, going to the door. But when he found the saloon keeper on the doorstep, his face tense and **haggard**, the pastor's wonder turned to uneasy question.

"Come in, Mr. Shartow, come in. Good evening. Come out of that weather!"

"I've come for help," Tim Shartow said. "I guess it's the kind you can give."

For a moment the pastor searched Tim's face and then he exclaimed, "God bless you, Tim! Come into the study!"

So, before the close of that day the winter had departed from the saloon keeper's heart. That's how it happened that once again Christ's miracle worked in a man's heart. God's gift was one more time accepted, and once more the dear Christ entered into another heart made meek and ready to receive Him.

– Frederick Hall

Ola and the Wooden Tub

This story took place in Norway many years ago. Some practices in Norway today are different from those you will read about here.

"Hurry, make haste! There's no time to lose! Inger and Kaaren, take these buckets to Selma. And you, Ola, if you don't bring more wood, the fire will be out in no time!"

It was the head laundress, bustling about in the big kitchen of Grandfather's house. The twice-a-year wash day had arrived.

The Otteraen[1] River in the valley below the house was frozen with the first solid ice of early December. The month of heavy rains had just passed, and a few days of clear, crisp, cold weather had followed. Now there appeared on the horizon the first snow clouds that would usher in the dreary winter months. Old peasants guessed that it would be a long hard winter, for wolves had been seen several times, even close to the farms.

In the villages round about, the peasants had done everything to **fortify** the farmhouses, huts, and storehouses against the coming winter blasts. Old rotted logs had been replaced by new ones, freshly tarred. Every nook and crevice where the wind might creep in had been stopped up with clay and straw. During the last clear days

---

1 Otteraen (ó tə rā′ ən)

women had made daily trips to the nearby peat bogs[2] to fetch the winter supply of fuel; in the woods, the men were busy cutting fire logs with saws and axes.

The barn lofts were heaped high with dry, sweet-smelling hay. From the heavy beams of the ceilings in the storehouses hung cured hams, bacon, smoked mutton, sun-dried salmon, and smoked cod. Along the walls stood barrels of precious potatoes and cabbages; other barrels were full of dried cod or pickled herring. The cows and goats had been brought back from the summer farms and were warmly housed in the clean, fresh-smelling barns.

In some of the homes the double windows had already been adjusted. The high porcelain stoves were again in use, and clear, bright fires burned in every fireplace.

Now, just four weeks before Christmas, the semi-annual washing was the only task that remained before beginning the Christmas baking. In Norway, especially in the country, many families have a large supply of homespun linens that lasts from one half-year to the next. The linen is washed only twice a year—once in the early spring and again in early winter, sometime before they begin to bake Christmas and New Year's cakes.

This year Grandmother had hired several peasant women to help with the washing. Some of them, their hair bound in brightly colored kerchiefs, stood in the yard behind the house, washing clothes in huge wooden tubs filled with suds. Others trudged back and forth in their heavy wooden shoes between the kitchen and the tubs, carrying buckets of hot water or baskets of wet linen.

On the kitchen stove, large earthen pots of spicy rice porridge were slowly simmering; that is the only food given on the days when washing is in progress. Grandmother dashed between the linen room and the kitchen, urging the girls and women to work a little faster,

---

2 peat bogs: a bog composed of peat. Peat is partly decomposed and partly carbonized plant matter that can be used as fertilizer or fuel.

and hurrying Hans and Ola, the errand boys, as they brought in piles of firewood for the red-hot stove.

While this was going on, two of the women suddenly came in and announced that they needed at least one more tub.

Another tub! Where should it come from? The nearest large house, called *Haugen*, was nine miles away by the road, and five miles away if one went by the river on skates. Grandfather had gone to the village of Kristiansand early in the morning with the horses. And so the only way to fetch the tub would be by way of the river. Ola would have to go.

But Ola was only eleven years old and small for his age. An ordinary wooden washtub was so large that it would reach almost to a man's waist. How would Ola be able to bring back the heavy tub? Finally Hans suggested that Ola should take his sled and bring it back on that. One of the farm boys at Haugen could carry the tub down to the sled, and when Ola returned, Hans would help him carry the tub up from the river.

About noon Ola started. He had a long way to go, but he loved to skate. The wind was with him, and he felt like a bird as he skimmed over the smooth ice. Frost hung from all the bare branches that skirted the shores. The merry sun changed this world of frost and ice into a fairyland of sparkling diamonds.

In less than an hour he had covered the distance. At Haugen he drank a cup of steaming tea while the tub was found and emptied. This took a little time. Meanwhile he chatted with the boys and men.

When the tub was ready, Per-Eric, one of the farm boys, carried it down to the river and put it on the broad sled. As Ola fastened his skates to leave, Per-Eric jokingly said, "Don't let the wolves eat you on the way back, Ola!"

Ola laughed and waved his mittened hand as he answered, "Watch me, Per-Eric! I shall go back even faster than I came."

A bitter wind blew in his face, and the snow clouds gradually grew denser and blacker. Ola skated as fast as he could, but now the wind was against him, and the sled, **laden** with the tub, was heavy to pull.

He had gone a little more than three miles when it started to snow. The snowflakes blew in his eyes and made it hard for him to see. As he rounded a bend of the river, he suddenly heard a long unearthly howl. Ola hardly dared to look around. When he did look back, he was terrified to see the thin pale figure of a wolf near a clump of pines on the shore. When Ola looked at him, the wolf gave another long howl. It was a **dismal** sound. Somehow Ola thought that it was not only a cry of hunger, but also the call of one wolf to another.

As if in answer to this thought, a few seconds later, far in the distance, the call was answered by another wolf. Ola increased his speed. He remembered the tales he had heard about wolves that followed lonely travelers; how the hungry wolves had gradually surrounded them and had sprung upon them and killed them.

The wolf was now following Ola, running along the shore and steadily gaining on him. Far ahead, on the hill above the river, Ola could see Grandfather's house. He hoped that he would be able to reach the house before the wolf caught up with him. Once he glanced over his shoulder and saw that two more wolves were running in the same direction.

But the wolves went much faster than he could. Soon the first wolf was only a few hundred yards away. Ola looked around in desperation. There was not a sign of anyone who might help him. He was still too far away from the house for his calls to be heard above the shrill whistling of the wind. Nevertheless, he tried two or three times.

"Ha-ans! Ha-ans! Come help me! Come help me, Ha-ans!"

But there was no response. The wind picked up Ola's words and threw them right back at him.

The first wolf was now so close that Ola could see his eyes gleaming like coals, and the others close behind. There was no chance of escape. Suddenly Ola remembered the tub on his sled. Quickly he turned the tub over on the ice and hid himself underneath.

In the house, it was long past the hour when Ola should have returned. Grandfather had come back from Kristiansand just before dusk. Twilight falls very early in Norway in December, for there the

winter days are as short as the summer days are long. Everyone was very much worried, for they had expected Ola to return long before dark.

Grandmother looked often toward the river, hoping every moment that she would see the familiar form of the errand boy racing over the ice. Finally she thought that she saw a tiny moving speck. Grandfather went to fetch his binoculars; and when he looked, a strange sight met his eyes. Far below on the river he saw a wooden tub and an empty sled. The tub seemed to have been turned over, and around it were two or three moving objects that at first he mistook for dogs. But he quickly realized that they must be wolves. *Perhaps,* he thought, *Ola is trapped under the tub.*

Grandfather rushed to get his gun. Hans ran to the storehouse to find his; and two young peasants, who had come in to warm themselves by the fire before returning home, armed themselves with heavy sticks from the woodpile and ran down the hill. Grandmother and the girls watched until they were out of sight; then they hurried to heat flannels and to put hot bricks in Ola's bed. In the kitchen the big copper kettle bubbled merrily for Ola's tea.

While they waited, an old peasant woman sat by the stove, quietly mending. "Well, well," she said, nodding her wise old head, "that Ola's a clever young one! Saving himself from the wolves by hiding under a tub. H'm! That will make a fine tale to tell these winter evenings!"

And before the first flowers showed their faces through the melting snow, the story had been told many a time in the countryside around Kristiansand.

– Ragnhild Chevelier

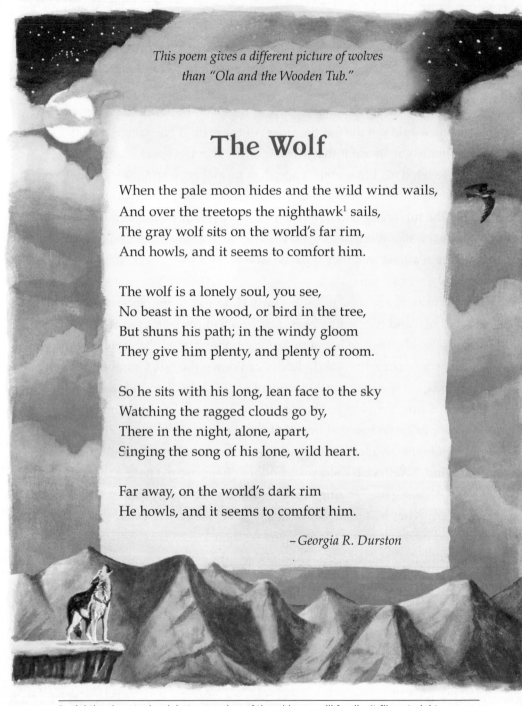

This poem gives a different picture of wolves than "Ola and the Wooden Tub."

The Wolf

When the pale moon hides and the wild wind wails,
And over the treetops the nighthawk[1] sails,
The gray wolf sits on the world's far rim,
And howls, and it seems to comfort him.

The wolf is a lonely soul, you see,
No beast in the wood, or bird in the tree,
But shuns his path; in the windy gloom
They give him plenty, and plenty of room.

So he sits with his long, lean face to the sky
Watching the ragged clouds go by,
There in the night, alone, apart,
Singing the song of his lone, wild heart.

Far away, on the world's dark rim
He howls, and it seems to comfort him.

– Georgia R. Durston

---

1 nighthawk: not a hawk but a member of the whippoorwill family. It flies at night, catching insects in the air.

The poem is told by a child who has been sent to bed. But he has gotten out of bed and gone outside to look at the stars.

Escape at Bedtime

The light from the parlor and kitchen shone out
    Through the blinds and the windows and bars;
And high overhead and all moving about,
    There were thousands of millions of stars.

There ne'er were such thousands of leaves on a tree,
    Nor of people in church or the park,
As the crowds of the stars that looked down on me,
    And that glittered and winked in the dark.

The Dog, and the Plough, and the Hunter,[1] and all,
    And the Star of the Sailor, and Mars,
These shone in the sky, and the pail by the wall
    Would be half full of water and stars.

They saw me at last, and they chased me with cries,
    And they soon had me packed into bed;
But the glory kept shining and bright in my eyes,
    And the stars going round in my head.

– Robert Louis Stevenson

---

1 The *Dog* is the Dog Constellation, called *Canis Major*. The *Plough* and the *Hunter* are British names for constellations. The *Plough* is called the *Big Dipper* in North America and the *Hunter* is called *Orion*.

> *"But the God of all grace, who hath called us unto his eternal glory by Christ Jesus, after that ye have suffered a while, make you perfect, stablish, strengthen, settle you." – 1 Peter 5:10*

A Dangerous Errand

Barbara hurried from her mother's bedroom to answer the knock at the door. Standing shyly outside were two boys, holding a basket between them.

"Oh hello, George, come on inside," she said, greeting the one she knew. She held the door open, and the boys slipped in.

"Mother sent this basket of grapes over for you," George announced, putting the basket on the table.

"How nice of her," said Mother from the bedroom. "She must have heard that I am sick, and grapes are one of the few things I am really hungry for."

George looked puzzled. "Mother didn't say why she was sending the grapes," he said, "but she told us to tell you she wants the basket back. She also said maybe you would give some of the grapes to Cornelis Sternes."

"To Cornelis Sternes?" There was a note of surprise in Mother's voice. Then she said, "Yes, we'll be glad to send some of the grapes over, and we'll see that the basket is returned too. Barbara, why don't you give George a cookie before he leaves?"

"There are two boys, Mother," said Barbara. The second boy hadn't said a word, but stood bashfully just inside the door.

"Oh, I'm sorry, I didn't know. Give him a cookie too, of course."

Barbara hurried to get the cookies from the jar in the corner shelf. She heard Mother ask George, "Who is with you?"

Barbara waited for his answer. She had been wondering too.

"My cousin Willem," George said. "He came with his father and mother to our place yesterday. They live in Amsterdam, but they came for a visit."

Barbara handed a cookie to each of the boys, and they left.

"Did you know Mrs. Claess was sending the grapes?" Barbara asked, picking up the basket and bringing it to show the grapes to her mother.

"No, I didn't."

"Doesn't it seem strange, Mother?"

"She likely just wanted to give us something."

"No, I mean that she told us to give some to Cornelis Sternes. Why would she send them something?"

"That surprised me too," Mother admitted. "They haven't been so friendly since Joos seems to be interested in our faith. But perhaps Mrs. Claess hopes that they will become more open. Though it doesn't seem like her to make mention of the basket."

"But why didn't she have the boys deliver the grapes, instead of telling us to?"

"Well, maybe they were in a hurry."

"I still think it's strange," Barbara said. "Will you send some of the grapes, Mother?"

"Why yes, I suppose we should. Maybe Father could take them tonight when he comes home. Only I don't know if he will want to go. Cornelis especially has been unfriendly lately. Father told me he thinks that Cornelis suspects him of influencing Joos, since they work together sometimes." Joos was Cornelis's oldest son, but he did not share his parents' distrust of the Anabaptists.

Barbara leaned close to her mother. "Do you think Joos will ever become a believer?" she whispered.

"We hope and pray so," Mother answered. "He is very much interested, but it is hard for him, because he knows his parents would be opposed to his becoming one of us."

Barbara felt a glow of pleasure. Her mother must trust her, or she wouldn't be talking like this.

Then she had an idea. "Mother," she said, "couldn't I take the grapes over?"

Barbara waited while her mother smoothed the linen cover with her fingers. "You wouldn't be afraid?"

"No, Mother, why should I be? If anyone asks where I am going, I can tell them. There's nothing wrong with taking grapes to our neighbors." Barbara paused. "It would be different if . . . if I were taking some important secret message like Father often does. Then perhaps I would be afraid."

Mother turned her head so she could see her daughter standing beside the bed. "But remember to be careful with whom you talk when you go through the village. It is not a small matter. One slip of your tongue, and it may cost someone much suffering."

"I'll be very careful, Mother," promised Barbara.

Half wishing she actually were going on a dangerous errand, Barbara put some of the grapes from the basket into a bowl. She covered the grapes that remained in the basket with a light cloth and started off.

Barbara enjoyed the walk through the quiet village. The miller's son passed her, his cart piled high with bags of flour. He smiled at her and waved a friendly greeting. Barbara nearly laughed when she saw his face. Across his forehead was a big streak of flour! *He has no idea how funny he looks.*

Smiling to herself, she walked on. Slowly she passed the market square where merchants and tradesmen spread out their **wares** in open stalls. The ceaseless murmur of voices, the noise of men buying and selling, drifted out to her in jumbled confusion.

When Barbara reached the blacksmith's shop, she quickened her steps. There was something about the place—the harsh, clanging blows and the pounding of iron—that always made her shiver. Too often she had heard stories of believers being tortured with gleaming hot tongs. Barbara trembled.

"I'll walk on the other side of the street on the way home," she told herself. She knew she was being foolish—the blacksmith was a large friendly man who would not hurt anyone. Still, she sighed in relief when she was away from the harsh noises.

Suddenly just ahead of her, she saw a man leaning against the corner of a building. He had a pointed gray beard and twirled a cane in his hand.

Almost without thinking, Barbara slowed her walk. Perhaps he would go on before she got there. But no, he was waiting.

"Where are you going, little girl?" he asked. His face smiled, but Barbara thought his eyes still looked sharp—sharp and cruel.

"I am taking some grapes to the neighbors," answered Barbara. How glad she was that she was not carrying a secret message.

"Are they nice grapes?" the man asked. Before Barbara could answer, he poked the cloth back with his cane and uncovered the grapes.

"You do have some nice grapes," the man said. He smiled again, but the smile did not belong on his face. "Maybe you can help me, little girl," he said, lowering his voice and leaning toward her.

Unconsciously Barbara took a half step backwards.

The man turned the corners of his mouth up again in what was meant to be a smile. "Don't be afraid of me, little girl," he said. "I just want to know something. I would like to become an Anabaptist, but

I am a stranger in town and I don't know where any of them live."

Barbara tried not to gasp, tried not to show her alarm. What would she say if he asked?

But the man went on. "I did hear that one of their best preachers is traveling through here. His name is Leen—Leeneart Bouwens. I'm sure he will be holding a meeting tonight, but unless I can find out where, I cannot go. Perhaps you know where the meeting will be?"

He looked at her, still smiling, but his eyes were sharper than ever.

"No, man . . . no, sir, I do not know," replied Barbara. How thankful she was that she didn't! "I . . . I must go now. My mother will be wondering about me."

Barbara turned away, half expecting the cane to poke out and trip her. She held her breath as she walked, fearful lest the man call her back. She wanted to run and run and never stop running. But she forced herself to walk. Was the man following her? She told herself not to look back. She reached into the basket and pulled the cloth over the grapes again.

A door slammed somewhere behind Barbara. The sharp noise startled her. Was it the man? As she glanced back over her shoulder, her foot tripped on a loose stone. Her hands flew out to break her fall, and the basket of grapes crashed to the street.

Fortunately only a few of the grapes were spilled; the rest were only shaken to one end of the basket. Quickly Barbara gathered the few off the cobblestones and tossed them into the basket. Ashamed for being so jumpy, she reached into the basket to level its contents. Then she saw it—a scrap of paper at the bottom of the basket. She turned the paper over and skimmed the few words.

"Services tonight at the big rock. Same time. Send word to Joos. We can't come because of visitors."

For a long moment Barbara stood staring at the note, too stunned to move. Then with a start she remembered where she was. She took a deep breath. *So that's why they sent the grapes over—to get the note to us. And that's why they mentioned wanting the basket back, so we would be sure to empty it and find the note.*

Barbara stopped, pondering what she should do. What was the use of taking the grapes to the Sterneses now? How would she tell Joos about the meeting without someone hearing? Better to go home again and let Father do it later. She turned to go when another thought struck her.

What if she met the man with the pointed gray beard, and he saw that she still had the grapes? He would guess that something was wrong. Maybe he was watching right now. He would follow her home and—

No, she decided suddenly. *I can't back out now. If I can't talk with Joos alone, I just won't say anything.*

As she started toward the Sterneses again, she remembered the note still clutched between her fingers. What should she do with it? What if the man . . . No, she would not even think about him. Besides, already she had thought of a good place for the note. Crumpling it nervously in her hand, she stooped down to scratch her leg. **Deftly** she slipped the dangerous scrap of paper inside her wooden shoe. She straightened her back and walked on down the street.

Arriving at her destination, she knocked timidly. Joos's mother opened the door. "Come in," she invited.

As Barbara stepped inside, she saw that Joos was just putting on his coat. "I'm going up to the village," he told his mother. "I'll be back in time for the evening meal." He seemed not even to notice Barbara as he brushed past her, opened the door, and went outside.

"Mother sent these grapes over for you," Barbara explained.

"Why, how thoughtful of her!" exclaimed Mrs. Sternes. "Wait until I get something to put them into and you can take the basket right back."

Barbara waited impatiently while Mrs. Sternes transferred the grapes. Perhaps she could still overtake Joos if she went right away.

When she stepped out into the street again, Joos was nowhere in sight. At a brisk pace she set out for home, hoping she wouldn't see the man with the gray beard and the cane that seemed to be especially for poking into other people's business.

Suddenly there was a step at her elbow.

"Barbara."

Still edgy, she jumped at the sound. "Oh, Joos, you startled me."

"I'm sorry. I was waiting in the doorway of the shop back there. I thought maybe you had a message for me."

Barbara lowered her voice. "I have," she whispered. "Services tonight at the big rock. Same time as always. But be very careful," she added, "somehow they found out we are having a meeting. I was questioned on the way down."

"Thanks for telling me. I hope you get home all right, and I think you will. You're a brave girl. Bye." With that Joos was gone.

Remembering the blacksmith's shop, Barbara crossed to the opposite side of the street. *Strange that the street is so deserted this early in the evening,* she mused. But when she remembered the note in her shoe, she was glad the street was empty—at least, empty of men with gray beards, sharp eyes, and poking canes.

She was just passing the blacksmith's shop when she heard the noise. Before she could run, three sweating horses galloped out of the side street ahead and turned toward her. Their riders were armed with long swords, and Barbara knew without asking that they were hunting Anabaptists. She grew weak all over and the scrap of paper in her shoe felt as big as a brick.

Desperately Barbara forced herself to be calm and walk slowly. Maybe the soldiers would not bother to question only a girl carrying a basket.

Her hopes were dashed to the cobblestones as the horses came alongside her and stopped, prancing impatiently.

"The people have melted away as though the **plague** were in the street," one of the men shouted. "All we have to question is one little girl."

"Whoa," said the second soldier, "where have you been, girl, and do you know anything of a meeting tonight?"

Barbara's heart sank down, down, until it seemed it was in her shoe with the note. "I was tak . . . taking some . . . some grapes . . ." she swallowed. "I was taking some grapes to the neighbor's house," She repeated. Then she paused again, wondering how she could answer the last part of the question. "I . . . I took the grapes and . . . and . . . "

"Oh, it's that girl!" shouted a man from the third horse. Barbara looked up and saw that it was the man with the pointed gray beard. He had traded his cane for a horse, and the last trace of the put-on smile was gone. "No use wasting time on her," he said angrily. "I've already questioned her, and she knows nothing. Come on, let's go."

As suddenly as they had come, the horses were galloping down the street. As Barbara hurried home to tell her mother all about what had happened, she could already hear her saying, "You were a brave girl, Barbara. Today God saw fit to spare us suffering. Tomorrow He may not. We do not know. We only have His promise that whatever He allows to come upon us, He will give the strength to bear."

Barbara nodded her head in agreement. *It's true.* Far behind her she could hear the jarring *ring* and the *clang-clang* of the blacksmith's blows.

– Elmo Stoll

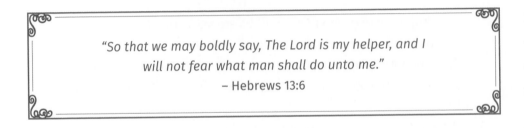

I-ho Ch'üan

When his father left Pao-ting in June 1900, thirteen-year-old Tito stayed home to care for his younger brothers and sisters. His father, Pastor Meng, was going to Peking to meet with other ministers and missionaries to pray for God's work all over northern China.

While Pastor Meng was away, news of the worsening Boxer Rebellion reached Pao-ting. The Boxers called themselves *I-ho ch'üan*, Chinese for "righteous harmonious fists." They believed that Christians were causing the drought that had ruined crops for the last two years. Christians worshiped a foreign God, the Boxers said, and the Chinese gods were angry that they were being neglected.

The Boxers began ripping up the railroad tracks between Peking and Pao-ting. In the villages and on the country roads rang the cry *yang kuei-tzu!* (foreign devil!) as the Boxers began to murder foreign missionaries and anyone suspected of being a Christian.

In Pao-ting, Tito and his brothers and sisters feared their father might never return. But Tito knew that Jesus Christ was with them, even though their father was absent. He cheered his brothers and sisters, and together they prayed for their father's safe return. Soon Pastor Meng arrived home. He gathered his children together and hugged them tightly. Then he called together the small band of Pao-ting Christians. They waited and they prayed, while the Boxers terrorized the villages around.

On June 27, Pastor Meng called Tito into his study. "Tito," he said, "I have asked Mr. Tien to take you away. You must go and hide from the Boxers."

"What?" Tito gasped. "Father, how can I leave you—and my brothers and sisters? I want to stay."

"Yes, Tito, but the Boxers are coming to Pao-ting. They will enter the village soon—maybe tomorrow. We cannot all escape, but you must flee Pao-ting."

"But what will you do?"

"May the Lord's will be done, Tito."

"Father, I am not afraid to die!"

"I know, truly, you are not. I am glad, son. But if we are all killed, who will remain to tell the people about Jesus?"

"But where will I go, Father?"

"Mr. Tien will take care of you, Tito, my son."

Tito clung to his father in the early morning light. He hugged his brothers and sisters, weeping. At last, wise Mr. Tien took Tito's arm.

"Come, Tito," he whispered. "We must leave before the sun rises."

The Boxers attacked Pao-ting that morning. Discovering that Pastor Meng's oldest son had escaped, they scoured the village. Waving swords, picks, and farm tools, they spread out into the countryside, hunting Tito and Mr. Tien.

But they did not find the two, hiding in a cottage on the edge of Pao-ting. There they stayed for several days, but Mr. Tien's relative who owned the cottage finally begged them to leave, fearing that the Boxers might find them in his house.

So they fled into the jagged mountains, to a place seventeen miles north of Pao-ting.

Tito could not stand upright beneath the low ceiling of the dark, wet cave where they crouched in hiding for twenty days. There was no water in the cave and no food. At night they sneaked three miles to the village well to drink. Mr. Tien's uncle, who lived nearby, sometimes brought them a little food to quiet their hunger. Ravenous wolves roved the hillsides around them, howling hungrily during the night; but inside the cave, Tito knew the Lord Jesus was with them.

In his hiding, Tito had hours to wonder—*What has become of my father and my brothers and sisters? Are they well? Are they alive?*

One black night a Christian friend from Pao-ting came to the cave.

"The Boxers have burned everything," he said, crouching beside them. "The church building, the school, the house of every Christian in Pao-ting is ashes."

The messenger hesitated.

"And the believers?" Mr. Tien asked quickly.

"I am the only one to escape."

The messenger continued his story. On the very day Tito and Mr. Tien fled Pao-ting, the Boxers had burst into the chapel where Pastor Meng was praying. They seized him and dragged him to the Buddhist temple. They questioned him. They shouted and screamed at him. They threatened him and tried to force him to deny Christ. When they discovered that his son had escaped, they tortured Pastor Meng to make him tell where Tito was.

But he would not deny his Lord, and he would not tell where Tito had gone. The Boxers became furious. They tortured him more, and finally, they stabbed Pastor Meng to death. Next they turned on Tito's brothers and sisters and on his aunt and her children too. Everyone was killed, the messenger said. Everyone.

And now the Boxers swore that no one from Meng's family would live! They would hunt Tito down and kill him too.

Not many days later, another messenger brought news—the Boxers were nearby. They must run! Mr. Tien and Tito fled southward through rugged mountains and dusty, hostile villages. Tito's legs trudged on weary day after weary day.

They had hoped to reach another Christian mission in the south of Shansi province, but just after they passed through the village of Chang-ma, a group of Boxers attacked them. **Brandishing** swords and rifles, they screamed wildly, *"Kill these devils!"*

The mob surrounded the boy and the old man. Violent hands pulled and shoved at them. Suddenly, a strange man stood at Tito's elbow. "Are you a Christian?" he asked.

"I am," Tito replied bravely, knowing his confession might cost him his life. "From a young age I have believed Jesus."

"Do not be afraid," the stranger said. "I will protect you."

The Boxers grabbed Mr. Tien. They bound his ankles and wrists, **cinching** the ropes tight. They dragged Tito by the hair to the altar in the temple. Fear rushed over Tito, as Boxer knives slashed back and forth before his face and screams rang in his ears. But a quiet voice within him sang—*I'm not ashamed to own my Lord.*

The Boxers strapped Mr. Tien to the altar. He uttered no word for himself, but pled with the Boxers to spare Tito's life: "Everyone in his family is gone. He has no father, no mother, no sisters or brothers. He alone remains."

With his dying words, Mr. Tien begged God to somehow protect Tito.

Just then a man stepped through the crowd. Mr. Chang was a chief man of the village, a leader of the Boxers, one of the dreaded Bachelor Brothers, known for their cruelty. The mob became silent.

"I adopt this boy as my own son."

Everyone gasped!

"Let no one touch him," Mr. Chang ordered. "I take responsibility for his good behavior. He will be my son."

The people stepped back. A murmur rumbled through the crowd, but Tito was released, and Mr. Chang led him home. He told Tito that he had been in Pao-ting when his father was tortured and killed. He boasted that the Boxer Rebellion was spreading over all of China, driving the missionaries out and ridding China of troublesome Christians.

That night Tito was alone in his room. *All of my family is gone,* he thought, *and Mr. Tien is dead too. My uncle who fled to Tung-chow with his family—they must be dead too—and all the other Christians in China.*

He had not had time that night in the cave to feel the full weight of sorrow. But now he lay on his bed in the dark and cried. After a while, he knelt to pray, and the words of a hymn came to his mind. The words seemed true in a way they never had before—*Abide with me, fast falls the eventide; the darkness deepens, Lord with me abide.* He felt very alone.

And yet, the Lord Jesus had been with Tito in the cave. He had been with him as he fled across the mountains of China and when the Boxers threatened him in the Buddhist temple. Tito saw how God had answered his father's prayers and had honored Mr. Tien's pleas for Tito's life. Yes, the Lord Jesus was with Tito that lonely night at Mr. Chang's.

Fierce Mr. Chang began to love Tito as his own son. He might

Chang Sen

Another Chinese pastor who was killed during the Boxer Rebellion was Chang Sen. Chang Sen was an evangelist who had preached to many. He, like Tito and many other Christians, had hidden in a cave in the mountains because the Boxers badly wanted to kill him. When he heard that the Boxers threatened to kill fifty Christians since they could not find him, he came out of hiding to save their lives.

have made a good home for Tito, especially when the Boxer Rebellion suddenly stopped before the end of 1900. However, one day a messenger from Pao-ting came to Chang-ma, bringing news for Tito. His uncle who had fled to Tung-chow was alive, and he wished for Tito to join him in Pao-ting!

When Tito returned home, it seemed like a different village. So much had changed. His father was dead. His brothers and sisters were dead. His aunt and cousins and many of the Christians of Pao-ting were dead too.

But one thing had not changed and would never change. Jesus Christ was with Tito. And He was still with China and the Christians who remained. Tito knew God had spared his life so that he might tell his people about Jesus Christ. And he did.

– Author Unknown

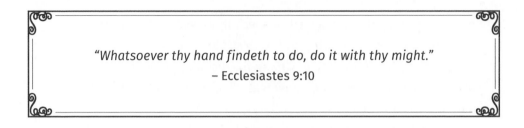

R Is for *Remarkable*

"I want to talk with you about that nephew of yours, William."

Mr. Waddle laid down his newspaper and looked at his wife. "Well?"

"Richard is getting older."

"That isn't his fault, is it, Mandy?"

"He's getting to be a young man, William," Mrs. Waddle declared. "He's had good schooling, he's bright, and he's healthy. Don't you think it's time he quits puttering around with those peach trees?"

"Well . . . " Mr. Waddle said vaguely.

"Maybe he would forget about them, if you wouldn't back him up in it."

"I?"

"No one else approves of Richard's peach experiment. You rented him that five-acre lot and gave him the option of buying it at the end of six years, didn't you? And you loaned him forty dollars to buy trees with. And you told him that he could use your equipment."

Mr. Waddle shuffled his feet uneasily on the porch steps.

"You're Richard's uncle," continued his wife. "He's alone in the world, and you're responsible for his bringing up. You ought to squelch[1] these odd ideas and make him do as other boys of his age do."

---

1 squelch: to stop or put down

"Maybe so. Maybe so."

"Other boys hire out as farmhands or work as clerks in stores or do something else that's fitting to their age. They don't have strange notions about getting land and planting trees and being independent."

"Richard's just *different*, that's all," Mr. Waddle explained. "He pays for his keep, doesn't he?"

"Yes," Mrs. Waddle had to admit.

"He buys his clothes, doesn't he?"

"Yes—lately."

"He's a good boy, isn't he—honest and upright?"

"Yes, yes."

"He's the best strawberry picker and the smartest peach-packer in the neighborhood?"

"Well—yes."

"Then suppose we leave him alone. It may be that he'll surprise us all before he is too many years older."

Richard Russell certainly was different. He was *remarkable*. Mr. and Mrs. Waddle were not the only ones who said it. The schoolteacher said it, and the Peachville neighbors said it too. His oddness showed itself in many ways that "went contrary" to the settled notions of the good Michiganders of Peachville township.

People liked Richard. But they distrusted his oddness. They admired his frank, honest face, his **industry** and cheerfulness. They respected him because he kept his word. But they could not forgive the fact that he was "not like other boys." Fruit farmers were glad to hire him by the day at picking time because of his rapid and skillful work. But they shook their heads doubtfully when he suggested some improvement here, some change there, which, in his opinion, would either hasten the work or make the result more certain.

"Why," said Mr. Pepperton one day to Hank Peters, "what do you think that Russell fellow wanted me to do last week? He wanted me to let him build a machine that would sort peaches into four different sizes! He called the thing a *grader* and said he'd seen a picture of one in some farm paper."

"Did you let him?"

"I? No siree! I wasn't going to have my peaches spoiled by being run through the hopper[2] of a machine. The idea!"

Then Hank Peters shook his head and told Mr. Pepperton how Richard Russell had once urged him to make a basket turntable in the packing shed.

"Sounds just like him!" remarked Mr. Pepperton. "What'd he say the thing would do?"

"That it would save time and work," answered Hank scornfully. "He was working for me that day, fastening on covers, and—as you know—when one end is fastened, you must lift the basket and turn it around to fasten the other side. Well, he worked away for an hour or so. Then all of a sudden, he said, 'Mr. Peters, I could cut out a board the size of a basket bottom, nail an edge around the board to hold the basket in place, and mount the board on a pivot[3] so that it could spin just even with the top of the packing table."

" 'I suppose you could,' said I. 'What of it?'

" 'Why,' he said, 'it would save lifting the basket. All I'd have to do would be set the basket on the pivot board, fasten one end of the cover, spin the basket around, and fasten the other end.'

" 'Young man,' I said, 'I'm paying you a dollar and a quarter a day to work. Don't always be looking for easy jobs.'

" 'I didn't mean it that way,' he answered. 'I was just trying to plan a way that would push the work faster.'

---

2 hopper: a funnel-shaped container for storing or holding things

3 pivot: a device that swings or revolves in a circle. Some common pivots we use are the "lazy susan," the swiveling wheels on grocery carts, and desk chairs that swing back and forth.

" 'Much obliged,' I said, 'but I am not paying wages to inventors this year.' Well—then he was quiet."

Mr. Pepperton laughed heartily at the story and ventured to guess that William Waddle would have a time with Richard Russell before he got through.

The peach trees in Richard's orchard had been planted three years. They had grown into healthy, beautiful trees—the delight of Richard's blue eyes. Each spring he plowed the land and pruned the branches. Every ten days throughout the season, he harrowed the ground. He studied books on fruit raising, **subscribed** to a gardening paper, and kept his eyes and ears open for any information about raising peaches.

At odd times he worked out for the neighbors by the day, earning enough money to pay rent on his land and his living expenses at the Waddles. He turned down several offers to work by the month.

"I can't afford it," he said to one farmer who asked a reason for his refusal. "If I worked by the month, I should have to neglect my trees, and it wouldn't pay me to do that."

The five-acre piece of land that Richard hoped someday to own was valued at 75 dollars an acre, and he paid his uncle four dollars an acre rent. The piece lay back from the road, and there were no buildings on it. The soil was well-drained, high and sandy—**ideal** ground for peaches. It was bordered on three sides by prosperous orchards.

"If you should want more land," William Waddle had said, "you can have the front fifteen acres for the same price. I'm keeping them for you."

"Thank you, Uncle William. I'll pay for the five first," Richard had answered. He believed that if he could hold on until the trees were five years old, the first full crop would pay, or nearly pay, for the five acres.

Two years passed. Richard's trees were entering their fifth season. While the trees were still **dormant**, Richard bought a spray pump, and at the proper time carefully sprayed all his peach trees. When the trees blossomed in the spring, the sight was like a vision of promise to the boy. They looked to Richard as though they would yield an excellent crop.

But the neighbors laughed. They joked about Richard's "squirt gun that would poison all his peaches," for in those days, the art of spraying fruit trees was still widely unknown. Richard, however, had read about spraying and written to the state agricultural experiment station[4] for instructions.

Even William Waddle looked with doubt at the squirt gun. "Better go slowly," he said to Richard.

"But uncle, the people from the experiment station are sure that spraying will prevent the leaf curl disease. And last year, you know, leaf curl disease destroyed one-third of the peach crop in this neighborhood."

"Yes."

"It's an idea that seems worth trying."

"Maybe so. Maybe so," said Uncle William.

Later in the season the dreaded leaf curl attacked almost every peach orchard in the county. The leaves curled up into odd shapes, changed to strange colors, and finally dropped from the trees; many tiny peaches followed the leaves. In Richard's orchard the damage was slight, while in his neighbors' orchards more than half the crop was lost.

"Have you seen Richard Russell's orchard?" asked Hank Peters one morning when he met Mr. Pepperton in town.

"Yes. Have you?"

"Went through it yesterday."

---

4 agricultural experiment station: a station where government employees test new methods of farming

There was an awkward pause. Then Mr. Pepperton coughed. "It begins to look," he said, "as if that Russell wasn't so—" He paused for a word, hesitated again, and coughed again.

"Yes, it does look so," admitted Hank. "Well, I must go. Good-bye, Pepperton."

In early August Richard bought ten dollars worth of lumber, shingles, and nails, and built a small rough packing shed in his orchard. Inside the shed he built a packing table, and on his table he put a spinning pivot board such as he had wished to make for Mr. Peters. He also made a crude peach grader on the principle of an inclined double track[5], with openings between the rails.

The openings were as narrow at the top as the width of a small peach and gradually became wider toward the bottom of the incline. The peaches, when poured into a hopper at the top of the tracks, rolled down and dropped through the openings at different stages of their journey, according to size. The small peaches dropped through first, then the medium size, and the large ones last. Only the very largest peaches reached the basket at the bottom of the incline. The others fell into one of three canvas baskets immediately beneath the tracks.

Uncle William whistled softly as he examined this device. "Bruise them much?" he asked.

"Not unless they are picked overripe, and you know peaches shouldn't be picked that way," replied Richard.

In September the peach harvest began. But no one except Richard had more than half a crop. Richard's trees were, as his uncle expressed it, "loaded." On hearing this statement, Mrs. Waddle sniffed. "He may spoil them in that machine of his, before he gets them sold."

---

5 inclined double track: a track that slopes downward, so the peaches roll

When it came to packing the first peaches, Richard met a difficulty he hadn't expected. The shipping packages commonly used were closed-sided, slat-covered baskets that held one-fifth of a bushel. When packed, the buyer could see only the top layer of peaches. The custom among most growers was to put little peaches in the bottom of the basket, medium-sized peaches in the middle, and big peaches on top.

Richard objected to that custom; he said it was not honest. He wished to pack each size by itself and label the basket accordingly— "Fancy," "No. 1," "No. 2," and "No. 3."

The neighbors laughed at the plan, and they laughed at his grader. "You'll get only trouble for your pains," they said. "The buyers expect to find little peaches in the bottom of the baskets, and they won't believe that your baskets are any different from others."

"I'll label each basket and guarantee it," maintained Richard.

"They won't believe you."

"I'll make them."

His first shipment he graded carefully, labeled correctly, and shipped to a company in Chicago. Richard sent a letter explaining his system of packing with the shipment. Within a few days a check in payment for the peaches came back.

It was a great occasion for Richard. That pink check was the first visible return from his orchard, the first encouragement in five years of planning, working, and hoping.

But when he came to figure the sales of his peaches in comparison with the sales made by various peach growers in the neighborhood, he was greatly disappointed to find that he had made no more for a basket on the average than his neighbors had.

"Never mind, Richard," his uncle said, trying to console him. "It might have been worse."

Richard thanked his uncle, but in his heart he knew his method of packing peaches was the only honest method. It was bound to be accepted, only if—

Oh, that *if!* Richard sat down in his packing shed and thought over the matter. Picking up one of the peach baskets, he looked it over carefully. Turning it over and over, he tried to put himself in the buyer's place and imagine how he would feel if he were purchasing hundreds of baskets of peaches from an unknown shipper.

Would I have time to unpack and examine every basket? he mused. *No, I'm afraid I wouldn't. Would I be willing to trust a label or a guarantee in a letter? Probably not. What would I do then? Pay the shipper the average market price for mixed packing, of course!*

Then he thought, *If I were going to pay a shipper an extra price for an extra product, I'd want to see the fruit packed, or else I'd want to see the bottom and middle layers of every basket after it was packed.*

Seizing a knife, Richard slashed into one side of the basket in his hand and made a long opening about an inch and a half wide in the thin wood. Then, on the other side of the handle, he made a similar opening. Turning the basket around, he cut two openings in the opposite side.

"I've got it!" he cried joyfully and swung the basket around his head as if it were a flag of victory. And sure enough he had "got it." The bottom peaches packed in such a basket could just as easily be inspected as the top peaches; a buyer had only to look to be convinced. Richard did not realize it at the time, but his open-sided basket would become the standard peach-shipping package of Michigan.

That evening Richard explained the idea to his uncle. William Waddle listened attentively, but Mrs. Waddle was doubtful.

"Doesn't it weaken the basket?" asked Mr. Waddle.

"Not that I can see."

"Isn't that a lot of work to cut those slits?" Mrs. Waddle questioned.

"I can do a hundred baskets in forty minutes. I tried it this afternoon."

Mrs. Waddle laid down her knitting and looked at her husband. "William, how much do a hundred baskets cost?"

"About two and a half dollars."

"I hope you haven't spoiled two and a half dollars worth of good baskets," she said.

The following morning Richard shipped one hundred baskets of graded peaches packed in the new way. He sent the shipment to the same Chicago company, with a brief letter of explanation.

In a few days he received a personal letter from the manager of the firm, complimenting him on his "unique, honest packing," and promising extra prices for all peaches so graded and packed. Enclosed in the letter was a generous check, paying Richard more than the regular price.

After supper that night, Richard handed the letter to his uncle. William Waddle read it, winked at Richard, and passed the letter to his wife. She took it gingerly, put on her glasses, and read it through. Then she went back to her knitting.

"Pardon?" said Mr. Waddle, after a long pause.

"I didn't say anything," said Mrs. Waddle.

"Are you going to say anything?" her husband asked.

"Well done, Richard," she said simply. But later in the evening she said good night to him in a gentler tone than usual.

At the end of the peach season, Richard's bankbook showed a balance of four hundred and fifty dollars to his credit. He felt like a wealthy man. It was a joyful moment for the boy when one morning he handed his uncle a check for three hundred and seventy-five dollars, in full payment for the five-acre piece of land.

"I'm proud of you!" Mr. Waddle told his nephew. "I'll have a deed made out at once."

Mrs. Waddle did not say a word. But that morning she made a big spice cake, frosted it carefully, and outlined on top with raisins, a huge *R*. At dinner Richard found the great cake resting on his plate. He gave his aunt a quick look of surprise, but she seemed not to notice.

"Is it for me?" he asked, wonderingly.

She nodded.

Getting up from the table, Richard kissed his aunt affectionately on the cheek.

Uncle William smiled. *I wonder whether that* R *stands for* Richard *or for* Remarkable?

— Walter E. Andrews

It Couldn't Be Done

Somebody said that it couldn't be done,
    But he with a chuckle replied
That "maybe it couldn't," but he would be one
    Who wouldn't say so till he'd tried.
So he buckled right in with the trace of a grin
    On his face. If he worried he hid it.
He started to sing as he tackled the thing
    That couldn't be done, and he did it.

Somebody scoffed: "Oh, you'll never do that;
    At least no one ever has done it";
But he took off his coat and he took off his hat,
    And the first thing we knew he'd begun it.
With a lift of his chin and a bit of a grin,
    Without any doubting or quiddit,
He started to sing as he tackled the thing
    That couldn't be done, and he did it.

There are thousands to tell you it cannot be done,
    There are thousands to prophesy failure;
There are thousands to point out to you one by one
    The dangers that wait to assail you.
But just buckle in with a bit of a grin,
    Just take off your coat and go to it;
Just start in to sing as you tackle the thing
    That "cannot be done," and you'll do it.

– Edgar A. Guest

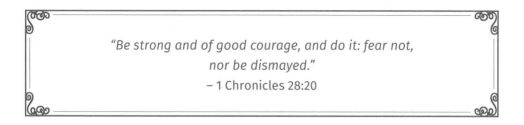

Putting Fear to Flight

The log on the fire popped loudly, but Leif[1] Engstrom didn't look up from the pages of *My Life as an Explorer* by Roald Amundsen.[2] It was three days before Christmas, and all the other boys in the boarding school[3] had gone home for the holidays. Leif was trying to forget that he would spend Christmas away from his family. The school library seemed like a good place to do that, with its plentiful shelves of books, soft armchairs, and the big fireplace.

The log popped again, and a head poked in the library door.

"Hey, Leif, what's going on here?" A tall boy dashed in and began flicking little embers off the carpet onto the hearth. When Leif saw that the popping log had thrown hot embers onto the carpet, he knelt down beside Nils.

"There now, that takes care of it," Nils said, "I don't see any burn holes."

"Thanks, Nils," said Leif. "Guess I was too wrapped up in my reading. Say, I didn't know you were staying here over the holidays."

Nils was two years ahead of Leif in school, so they did not know

---

1 Leif (lāf)
2 Roald Amundsen (rō′ əl ä′ mən sən): a Norwegian explorer. He was the first man to reach the South Pole.
3 boarding school: a school where the students live while they are away from home

each other very well. Nils had never paid much attention to the younger boys, but Leif had always looked up to the only Finnish student in the Swedish school. Nils was outgoing, and a leader among the schoolboys.

"Looks like I'm here for the whole time," Nils said, dropping into the other big easy chair. "Because of the war with Russia,[4] I'm not allowed to travel home to Finland. How about you? I heard your parents have gone to Iceland."

"Yes. My grandmother in Iceland is very ill. They didn't think she would live past Christmas, so my parents sailed last week to be near her. I'm sure I won't get back to Jämtland[5] this Christmas."

"We're the only ones left here during the holidays then." Nils sighed. Leif thought he detected a note of disappointment in his voice.

"What are you reading?" Nils asked.

Leif's eyes brightened. "Amundsen's biography," he answered. "It's really exciting. I'm just to the place where—"

"Never read it," interrupted the older boy. Lounging back in the chair, Nils surveyed the slim pale-faced Leif. "Do you read all the time?"

"Why, no—not all the time," Leif answered slowly. "But there's nothing else to do right now."

"Nothing else? Don't you want to get outside and take a hike or something? I suppose you can't snowshoe or ski or anything, but I wouldn't think you'd want to spend all day in the house."

A nervous smile curved Leif's face. "Oh, I can ski and snowshoe all right. Everybody does where I come from in Jämtland. Sometimes that's the only way to get around."

---

4 In December and January of 1939-1940, Russia invaded Finland. This war and a later war in 1941-1944 are called the Russo-Finnish Wars.

5 Jämtland (yämt' land): a state in west-central Sweden, on the border with Norway. There are many mountains in western Jämtland.

"Oh, I see." Nils's tone was no longer **curt**. A new interest flashed into his eyes. "But what, you don't *like* it? Doesn't this fresh snowfall make you want to get out and try some jumps? Come on out and let's see what you can do."

Leif hesitated; he did not feel at all inclined to leave his comfortable chair and interesting book. On the other hand, he didn't want to disappoint Nils.

"I didn't bring my skis with me to school," Leif said finally.

Nils sprang to his feet. "That's nothing; I'll fix you up. Come on!"

A little glimmer of enthusiasm building, Leif closed his book and followed Nils into the hall and out to the long enclosed porch. They put on their sweaters, wool gloves, and caps. Nils produced two pairs of skis and poles.

Out in the open, Leif shivered as the keen wind struck him. By the time he had adjusted his ski bindings and pulled on his gloves, his fingers were bluish, and he needed no urging to set off at a swift pace. He was at home on skis and glided along with an easy grace.

"You're not *much* good at skiing, are you?" Nils commented after watching Leif for a while. "You can probably jump anything, eh?"

"Oh, I can jump some, but I'm not really much good at anything but just straight away going."

"Huh!" grunted Nils. "You can probably out-ski any of the guys here. Shall we do some cross-country? Let's go up Stenkullen.⁶"

Leif agreed, though he wasn't thrilled about such a climb. Stenkullen rose steeply behind the school. The timber growth on the hillsides was thick, and Leif knew from experience that skiing in the woods wasn't easy. But Nils had no intention of tackling the steep slope directly. He knew of an old logging road that twisted and curved nearly to the summit. They would take this road and then ski back down its winding length.

---

6 Stenkullen (sten kúl' len): The Stone Hill

149

By the time they were halfway up, Leif was out of breath. It was the first time he had been on skis in almost a year, and his muscles were soft from lack of exercise. He did not complain, however, and soon Nils himself stopped for a rest.

"I wish I could handle skis as easily as you do, Leif," he commented. "You just glide along as if you were on skates."

"I may glide, but I'm out of breath!" Leif confessed. "I've used skis ever since I was little, but compared to the boys at home, I'm not a strong skier. Do you think we should go on? I just felt some snow on my face."

"A little snow won't hurt us! We can turn around and ski down in no time at all. Let's not go back just yet."

They skied on. Leif thought it wiser to turn back, but he was afraid to suggest it. Nils might think he was a quitter. A little later, as they climbed the narrow winding road, they came upon a deserted log hut, with a sagging half-open door; but the two boys did not stop to investigate it. Every now and then during the next kilometer, little gusts of stinging snowflakes whirled down from the sky, beat against their faces, and scurried on. Leif's nervousness increased, but Nils merely laughed. "A little snowstorm will make our trip home all the more interesting!"

Scarcely had he said it when from the distance came a curious wailing of the wind, rising swiftly to a dull, threatening roar. Startled, both boys stopped abruptly and stared up the slope. As they did so, something like a white curtain surged over the crest of the hill and swept rapidly toward them. Almost before they could draw a breath, it was upon them, a dense, blinding mass of snow, which whirled about them and blotted out the landscape in a flash.

"Wow!" gasped Nils. "Some speed to that! We had better hurry back while there's still time."

The boys had gone half a kilometer down the road when a sudden heavier gust of stinging flakes blinded them both. Leif instantly slowed to a near stop. When he was able to clear his eyes, Nils was out of sight. An instant later there came a muffled cry ahead of him, and then—silence.

Leif jerked his pole out of the snow and sped forward. At first, he could barely see Nils's ski tracks, but he waited for the storm to lighten a little and then saw what had happened. Nils had misjudged a sharp curve in the trail and plunged off to one side and down a steep slope, thickly grown with trees. At the foot of the slope Leif found him lying, a twisted heap, face down in the snow.

Leif bent over the silent figure. Nils stirred, tried to rise, and fell back with a groan. His left foot was twisted under him. As Leif freed his feet from the skis, Nils made a second effort to rise, but his face turned white, and he sank back with a grunt of pain.

"My ankle," he muttered.

For a moment or two he sat there, face twisted, arms gripping his knees. Then he looked up at Leif, and a **wry** smile twisted his face. "Looks like we're in a mess, doesn't it?"

Leif nodded, unable to trust himself to speak. But Nils's self-control calmed him a little, so that he could think.

"That old cabin back there! If we could get you that far—"

"Good idea," Nils agreed promptly. "I'm afraid I can't walk, but I might be able to crawl."

"Oh, I didn't mean that. If we only had some way of fastening my skis together, you could lie down on them and I could push you."

A gleam of admiration flashed into the older boy's eyes. "You have your nerve!" he said. "Do you know how much I weigh?"

"Doesn't matter. It's all downhill; it won't be so hard. Besides, we can't stay here; we'll freeze."

That was true. Already Leif's teeth were chattering, and even Nils could feel the cold through his thick sweater. He tried to think of some other way, but finally agreed to try Leif's plan. Nils removed the leather laces from his boots, and Leif used them to tie the skis together. Nils sat down on this makeshift sled, and Leif trudged behind and pushed.

It was a toilsome, painful method of progress for both of them. Nils groaned when his swollen ankle was jolted; and Leif, wading knee-deep in the snow, was soon breathless. By the time they reached the cabin, he felt exhausted.

"Couldn't have kept that up much longer," grunted Nils, when they were inside the shelter with the door closed against the storm. His alert gaze traveled swiftly around the hut. There was a rough stone chimney at one end, a shuttered window at the back, and that was all. Snow lay piled on the cold hearth and here and there made little ridges on the logs where it had blown through the many cracks and crevices. It was not much better than the out-of-doors, and Nils's heart sank as he glanced at Leif, leaning exhausted against the wall.

"It's sure to stop pretty soon," Nils said hopefully. "When it lets up a little, we might—"

"I don't believe it's going to let up soon." Leif straightened up suddenly with an air of determination. "We've got to do something—immediately."

Nils stared at him.

"You're not thinking of pushing me all the way down the road, are you?" he protested. "I don't believe you could do it."

"I don't believe I could either," agreed Leif, frankly. "But I could go down and bring back help."

"You—you mean ski down that road? Why, it's six kilometers, and you could miss the trail a dozen times."

"I wouldn't try the road," said Leif quietly. "If I go straight down the hill behind this cabin, it'll land me close to the school. I don't think the whole distance is over a third of a kilometer."

Nils gasped. "You're crazy, Leif! Why, you'll kill yourself trying to ski through those trees."

Leif cut short Nils's protests. He buttoned his collar tightly and yanked on the laces of his boots. "I'm going. The sooner I'm off, the better."

So he stepped out into the storm. Behind the cabin, poised at the top of the slope with the snow whirling around him, he had one horrible moment when he was on the point of turning back. But with a tremendous effort he fought down that feeling. An instant later, a thrust of his ski pole sent him over the edge, gliding downward through the trees with increasing speed.

Strangely enough, he felt that the worst was over. After he had successfully steered through the first fifty meters of woods, his confidence grew, strengthening his courage. After all, even with the blinding snow, this hill was no worse than the smallest of the wooded slopes back home in Jämtland.

At first he managed to keep his speed within a reasonable limit. But just before he left the woods, a sudden turn to avoid a tree flung him off balance. A moment later he flashed out onto the open slope and shot down the steep incline.

Long before he expected it, the snow-covered bulk of a stone wall leaped out of the blinding snow curtain and rushed toward him. He jumped, and soaring through the air, struck the slope again a good four meters beyond the wall.

He tried to figure where he would come out and what hindrances he might yet encounter, but the effort was useless. He knew that the highroad, bordered by another stone wall, ran along the foot of the hill. The school grounds were on the other side of this road. But the speed at which he was traveling made thought almost impossible. Again, with the same terrible swiftness the final barrier loomed ahead. He leaped, and, at the very take-off, a gasp of horror jolted from his lips at the sight of a two horse släde[7] moving along the road directly in his path.

It was all over in a flash. Helpless to avoid the collision, Leif nevertheless twisted his body toward the left. He landed badly, his feet shot out from under him, and he fell backward with a stunning crash.

Two strange faces bent over him, and hands lifted him from where he lay half-buried in the snow. For a moment he was too dazed to speak or even to remember. Then with a rush of relief, he realized what had happened. Regaining speech, Leif blurted out the story of Nils's injury and the need for help.

His rescuers were woodsmen, familiar with the Stenkullen trail and the old log cabin. They took Leif's skis off, helped him into the släde, and drove him to the nearby school. He was stiff and sore, but otherwise unhurt. The woodsmen paused long enough to get some rugs, hot tea, and a heavy coat, and then set off. Two hours later they returned with the injured Nils. They carried him to the school nurse's office. The town doctor had been called and was waiting for Nils's return. He treated Nils for a badly sprained ankle.

The ankle healed slowly, so Leif kept Nils company. Nils had to eat his Christmas Eve dinner in bed, but somehow he did not mind too much, for he and Leif shared it. Leif sat on the other side of a folding table drawn up beside the bed. First they ate cold herring, then ham and cod with potatoes. The cook served a little smoked reindeer as a special treat for the only boys left at school on Christmas Eve, the night Swedish families celebrate Christmas. When they had eaten their meal, Nils and Leif lapsed for a space into a friendly sort of silence.

"Not *much* on skis, are you?" commented Nils after a bit.

"Just lucky, I guess," Leif said.

"*Lucky!*" Nils snorted. "No such thing as *luck*. No, as soon as I can

7 släde (släd): *sled* in Swedish

get around again, you'll have to give me some ski lessons! I thought I was pretty good on skis, but I'm not that good after all."

"I'll show you anything I can, of course," Leif agreed readily. He paused an instant and then went on hesitantly, "I am going to do a lot more of that sort of thing from now on. It was simply disgusting the way I got winded so soon and all tired out."

"That's the way to talk," agreed Nils. "You need to take more exercise, Leif, and stop moping around by yourself so much. We'll fix that up all right. Say, would you read some more of Amundsen's book now? I can't wait to hear what happens next."

– Joseph B. Ames

The Baker's Neighbor

There lived long ago, on a quiet street of a quiet town, a baker. The baker was an industrious man. Every morning, very early, he rose to begin his work. By the time the rest of the town awoke and housewives began to think of breakfast, his breads and rolls and cakes and pies were freshly baked and ready to sell.

The baker was a grim man. The children who came to his shop each morning, sent by their mothers to buy a loaf of bread or several rolls for breakfast, never lingered to talk with him. He never smiled or joked with his customers. He never gave a roll to a hungry-looking boy.

The baker was a greedy man. More than anything else in the world, he loved money. Early each morning, before opening his shop, he went out to his terrace. There, while his breads and rolls and cakes and pies were baking, he counted the money he had made the day before. Lovingly he turned over the coins, touching them, stacking them. Satisfied, he would gather them up and go to open his shop.

On the same quiet street, next to the baker, lived his closest neighbor. This neighbor was a jolly fellow who cared nothing for work or for money. Winning the smiles of the children, laughing with his friends, enjoying the fragrant smells from the baker's shop—these simple pleasures were what the neighbor loved.

Every morning, when he heard the baker's door slam, the neighbor would go out to his own terrace. There he positioned himself precisely where the breeze brought him the fragrance of the baking breads and rolls and cakes and pies. Closing his eyes, he would lean back and relax while he breathed deeply of the fragrant odors.

Every morning when the baker looked up from counting his money, he saw his neighbor. Every morning he became angrier and angrier. The placid satisfaction and sheer pleasure on the face of his neighbor **enraged** the industrious baker. His lazy neighbor was enjoying the results of his own hard work for nothing.

For many weeks the baker endured the tormenting sight. For many weeks he did nothing but clench his fist a little harder, tighten his lips a little closer, each time he saw his neighbor.

One morning the baker could stand it no longer. He marched over to his neighbor's terrace and demanded payment. His neighbor stared in amazement. "Payment? I owe you nothing."

"Every morning my bakery supplies you with pleasant odors from my breads and rolls and cakes and pies," replied the baker haughtily. "It is only right that you pay for them. The ingredients I use are costly."

His jolly neighbor stared again. Then he threw back his head and laughed. He laughed until tears ran down his cheeks. He laughed until other neighbors came running to see what was happening.

When he finally stopped laughing to tell them of the baker's demand, they joined him. Surrounded by a crowd of hooting, laughing neighbors, the **exasperated** baker had no choice. He turned and marched stiffly home.

In the next few days, the quiet town became less quiet. Talk buzzed and hummed from one shop to another, up one street and down the next. Soon everyone knew about the baker and his neighbor.

Now, when children came into his shop, they lingered. Some

would breathe in the odors of the breads and rolls and cakes and pies with delight. Then others would **mimic** the baker. "Pay me for those lovely smells you've just enjoyed!"

Now, when the baker walked down the street, children followed him, sniffing at his clothes and hands. Men and women watched, trying not to smile when the children pled mockingly, "Oh, please, would you give us the smells on credit, sir?"

The baker became angrier every day. He had failed to obtain payment from his neighbor, and now laughter followed him everywhere he went. In desperation, the baker took his case to the judge.

The judge, with a sober face, heard the baker's complaint. "I will hear your case from both you and your neighbor in court next week," he said. The baker went home satisfied.

He was even more satisfied when he heard about the message the judge had sent to his neighbor. The judge had notified the baker's neighbor, telling him which day to appear in court. He had also ordered him to bring one hundred gold coins. In his shop the baker chuckled with satisfaction. He rubbed his hands together in anticipation of counting those hundred gold coins.

Out on his terrace, the baker's neighbor no longer looked jolly. He could not even savor the bakery smells with his usual enjoyment.

On the day of the hearing, the courtroom was crowded. The whole town knew of the case. Everyone wondered what the judge would decide. He told the baker to speak first, explaining his grievance.

The baker told how hard he worked every morning to bake his breads and rolls and cakes and pies. He detailed each step, each costly ingredient that went into the goods he made. Then he told how for many weeks, his neighbor had gleaned pleasure from his own hard work and the expensive ingredients he used. Finally, certain that he had convinced the judge that his neighbor owed him the hundred gold coins, he sat down.

The judge turned to glare at the baker's neighbor. "Is this then true that you have sat on your terrace each morning where the breeze brings the bakery odors to you?"

The neighbor admitted that the baker had spoken the truth.

The judge frowned. "Tell me, how do you find these smells? Are they delightful or annoying?"

The neighbor could not lie. He had to say that he found the smells extremely pleasant and delightful. But immediately he knew it had been a mistake. The judge fixed him with an even fiercer look. "Did you bring with you, as I ordered, one hundred gold coins?"

The neighbor nodded nervously. The baker smiled gleefully.

When the judge ordered the neighbor to give the coins to the baker, the baker could hardly contain himself. He stumbled over his own feet in his hurry to claim the coins. Then he turned to leave.

"Wait," ordered the judge. "You have not counted the money. Come here to the table and do so."

The baker thought it was considerate of the judge to give him the opportunity to count the coins and make certain that his neighbor had not cheated him. He poured the coins out of the bag, a cascade of clinking gold.

The judge, the neighbor, and the spectators watched the baker. It was plain that he loved to touch the coins. Each seemed to cling to his fingers as he reluctantly laid it down and picked up the next. When he had finished, he turned to the judge, a pleased smile on his face. "He has not cheated me," he said, beaming. "The coins number exactly one hundred. I thank you for your justice." Once more he started to leave the courtroom.

Once more the judge stopped him. "Wait," he ordered. "Give the coins back to your neighbor."

In utter surprise the baker obeyed. He handed the bag to his equally astonished neighbor.

With great dignity the judge rose and gathered his robes about him. "I have heard the baker's complaint," he said. "I have heard the neighbor admit that he enjoys the smells from the baker's shop. I have also seen the baker count, with great pleasure, one hundred of his neighbor's gold coins. I therefore declare that justice has been done."

He turned to the open-mouthed baker. "Your neighbor has smelled your smells. You have handled his gold. The case is closed."

For a moment the crowd was utterly silent, amazed by the judge's surprising statement. But when the spectators realized the justice of his decision, their behavior changed. Someone let out a resounding cheer. The courtroom hush completely disappeared beneath the clamor.

Several men carried the baker's neighbor—jolly once more—from the courtroom on their shoulders. The laughing crowd hurried him home to his terrace, where he could enjoy the bakery smells more than ever before.

– retold by Jennifer Crider

> *"But I say unto you, Love your enemies, bless them that curse you, do good to them that hate you, and pray for them which despitefully use you, and persecute you."* – Matthew 5:44

Advertising for a Thief

Betty always loved rainy days when she was visiting at her grandfather's. That was because, for rainy days, she saved the greatest treat of all the wonderful things there were to do in this country paradise. She played in the attic!

This afternoon a steady, beating rain and a northeast wind made the dark September day an ideal one for poking behind the old chests and into the cupboards back by the chimney. Betty had been pretending some of the best parts of the Waverly novels.[1] The gloomy corners, the deep chests, and the closets whose contents could scarcely be seen—even the hanging strings of onions—all helped to create an air of mystery.

Betty was about to settle down on the deep seat of the little window that came almost to the floor and read further in *Redgauntlet*. As she curled up, her hand felt a knob under the windowsill. She pulled out a drawer which she had never found before. Inside were some small old calf-bound[2] books and a yellow newspaper. Betty looked at the newspaper. Such a small sheet and such heavy black type! Then she noticed the curious words of the column headed

---

1 The Waverly novels were written by Sir Walter Scott. Born in Edinburgh, Scotland, in 1771, Scott grew up in the country in his grandfather's home. He wrote many novels. The first was called *Waverly* and the series of novels was named after it. Scott died in 1832.

2 calf-bound: books with calf-skin leather covers

"Advertisements":

> Whoever stole a lot of hides[3] on the fifth of the present month
> is hereby informed that the owner has a sincere desire to be his
> friend. If poverty tempted him to this false step, the owner will
> keep the whole transaction secret and will gladly put him in the
> way of obtaining money by means more likely to bring him peace
> of mind.

What an amazing advertisement! Just then Betty heard her grand-mother coming upstairs to the attic.

"Grandmother!" cried Betty almost before Grandmother had reached the top step. "Listen to this," and Betty read her the strange advertisement.

Grandmother finished pulling out from a trunk the quilts that she wanted before she replied. She sat down on an old chair and said: "I haven't thought of that for years, Betty. It is an interesting story. Grandfather and I put that advertisement in the paper."

"You did? Please tell me about it," begged Betty.

"Well, Grandfather had been working on a **quantity** of valuable hides, tanning them with special care. One night he thought he heard a noise coming from the barn. He went to the kitchen door, but all he saw in the darkness was a man, staggering under a heavy load, entering the yard of the place next door. In the morning the hides were gone.

"At that time, the **tenant** house on that farm was occupied by a wretched family. The father was so discouraged that he was drunk a great deal of the time and seemed perfectly worthless. They were our nearest neighbors, and we used frequently to find their starved cow in our young corn. He would borrow tools and return them broken and do all manner of things that annoyed Grandfather.

"So of course, Grandfather's first **impulse** was to go straight to

3 hide: the skin of an animal

this man and accuse him of the theft. But, as we talked it over, Grandfather said, 'We should think about what the Lord would do.' He cited Jesus' command to love our enemies and do good to those who despitefully use us. Then he suddenly decided on a different course of action.

"We knew that the wife and children were suffering from actual want, which we had tried in vain to relieve. It seemed too bad to add this disgrace to their misfortunes. So Grandfather determined to try putting this notice in the paper.

"We heard nothing of it for three days after the paper was out. Then, just after we had put the cat down in the cellar and were about to light the candle for bed, we heard a knock at the back porch door. It was rainy and cold, just such a night as this will be."

Grandmother unconsciously patted the quilts in her lap.

"I felt certain instantly who it was, and, sure enough, Grandfather opened the door to find our neighbor, Mr. Townsend, with his hat pulled down over his eyes and Grandfather's hides over his shoulder. For an instant he did not speak, then he muttered, 'I've brought these back, Mr. Savery. Where shall I put them?'

" 'Wait until I can light a lantern, and I will go to the barn with you,' Grandfather answered. 'Then perhaps you'll come in and tell me how this happened.'

"While they were out I flew around, down to the pantry for a pumpkin pie, boiled the kettle for coffee, and got down a cured beef to slice. When they came in, I spoke up: 'Neighbor, I thought perhaps a bite of supper would be good for you.'

"He was just inside the door, and I remember he wheeled with his back to me so quickly that I thought he was going right out. Instead, he leaned his arm against the door and buried his face in the crook of his elbow. I declare, I was frightened the way his shoulders shook and heaved. Grandfather motioned to me to keep quiet, and in a few minutes, without turning around, the poor fellow said in a choked voice, catching his breath as a child does after hard sobbing:

" 'It's the first time I ever stole anything. I don't know what's come over me, with the drink and the quarrels! I never thought I'd come to this, but now since I've started downhill everybody gives me a kick—except you. Yet how I hated you for the meals you sent to my wife and children! She's sick—they're starving. I stole the hides, meaning to sell them first chance I got. Then I read your notice in the paper. What's the use—' Mr. Townsend's voice was smothered with those awful sobs.

"Grandfather's voice was just as gentle and friendly, without a bit of that soft pity that would have stirred up the man's bitter pride.

" 'Tonight you may begin a new life, neighbor. Jesus often said to folks—*Your sins are forgiven; go and sin no more.* He offers you the same forgiveness. You're still young, and your life could be completely different from this day on. Promise me that you will not touch liquor for a year, and tomorrow I will **employ** you at good wages. Your boy can help too; at least pick up stones in the south pasture. Forget the hides—that was your first theft and your last. Come now, eat. Keep up a brave heart, man, for the sake of your wife and children.'

"With that our guest sat down at the table, though at first he couldn't eat; and I left them, thinking he might feel easier with no woman about. When I returned he had gone, having finished what I had put before him. Grandfather said he had promised solemnly to lead a different life if Grandfather would only stand by him."

"That was a funny way to treat a thief," said Betty thoughtfully. Her eyes fell on the overgrown little path to the Townsend place, which could still be distinguished in the dark afternoon. "And did he keep good?"

"Indeed he did!" said Grandmother. "He became a faithful follower of Jesus and was our right-hand man for years. It seemed that he loved every animal on this farm because it was Grandfather's."

"It's no wonder everybody loves Grandfather," said Betty. "Let's go downstairs and find him."

– Author Unknown

The Sari With the Silver Border

"Mother, may I have a sari[1] to take back to the States with me?" Bonita asked. "I'd like some kind of a **souvenir** to show Aunt Martha and the girls I'll meet in school."

"Oh, that's a fine idea!" agreed Mother. "It would be something interesting to show your new friends. Do you want a white sari with a red border?"

Two small frown lines appeared between Bonita's eyes. She thought of the village women who owned one white sari and wore it all the time. "I was hoping we could find something special—something unique. The white ones are so—so everydayish."

"Whatever we get, it can't be too expensive," her mother warned. "But I think it is a good idea. It will give you something to remember India and its need of the Gospel." She added teasingly, "Maybe it will help you to remember your parents too, while you are going to school and making all those new friends."

Bonita smiled but did not answer. That hot morning she was not worried about the needs of India. She was too excited about going to the States and meeting lots of new friends in an American school.

---

1 sari (sär′ ē): a cloth worn by some Asian women. One end is wrapped around the waist to form a skirt and the other end draped over the shoulder. The traditional widow's sari today is white.

Her excitement about the trip had nearly made her forget how much she was going to miss her parents.

"Let's go to the market to see what we can find," Mother said. "Father won't be back from buying your plane ticket for a while yet." She and Bonita left the hotel where they were staying in the city while they bought Bonita's ticket and waited for her flight to leave.

The marketplace was noisy; the air, **stifling** and heavy with spices. The merchants—many of them dressed in dirty cloths—crouched on the ground in front of their fruits and hand weavings and ivory carvings. The more well-to-do ones had tiny stalls. All of them yelled to get the people's attention. Bonita mentally compared this market to one in the village where she had lived with her missionary parents for nearly as long as she could remember. The market there was much tinier and not nearly so noisy.

Bonita and her mother approached a corner stall that was piled high with saris. There was a pile of the usual white saris with red borders and a small pile of black ones for widows. The old man crouching behind them eyed Bonita and her mother as they began looking at the saris. He pulled saris from the stack for them to see, pointing out the virtues of various ones.

Finally Mother said, "We're looking for something special for a souvenir to take home to America."

The man's eyes narrowed. He called, "Jehanara!"

A young girl in a black sari appeared from somewhere behind the stall. Bonita knew by her black sari that she was one of the many young widows of India.

"Get your wedding sari," the man ordered.

The girl said nothing but turned around and went through the doorway. She returned carrying a beautiful blue sari with a border of silver threads. The man jerked it out of her hands and passed it to Mrs. Anderson.

Mother looked carefully at the cloth. Bonita held her breath and hoped.

"It was worn only once," the man explained.

"How much do you want for it?" Mother asked.

"Six hundred rupees."[2]

"No." Mother shook her head. "This sari is not worth more than five hundred rupees."

"You Americans have much money," the man whined. "And I am left with my brother's useless widow to support."

As Mrs. Anderson bartered with the man, Bonita began to lose hope. He came down to 560 rupees but would not take less. Finally Bonita and her mother walked on. But they found nothing else that pleased Bonita.

At last they went back to the hotel and found Father, with Bonita's ticket. They told him about their search for a sari. Bonita described the beautiful blue wedding sari with the silver border. But when Mother told him how much the vendor wanted, he agreed, "The man is asking too much."

After dinner, Mother and Father went to their room to lie down. Bonita went to her room and lay down too, but she couldn't rest. All she could do was think about the blue sari. She wanted it so badly!

Bonita jumped up. *I guess I'll go for a walk—I can't rest anyway.* She strolled out into the street and found herself going toward the marketplace. When she came to the stall she and Mother had visited in the morning, the blue sari was there, lying on top of the pile. *If only I could have it to show to my friends in the States! Oh, well, I might as well forget it. Father will never spend that much just for a souvenir.*

She walked on to the far end of the marketplace. There a high wall enclosed the temple gardens. A cow lay across the path to the gate, brushing at the flies with its long tail. Bonita walked around it and

---

2 rupee (rū pē'): a standard unit of money in India. In 2017, it took approximately sixty-seven rupees to equal one American dollar.

through the gate. The cow might lie there all day and no one would disturb it—for cows are **sacred** to the Indians.

At the back of the temple was a high arch. Bonita could see the idol inside in the half-darkness. She stared at its elephant trunk and shuddered. Many of the people of India worshiped this idol as their god. Bonita thought of her own Saviour and wondered how anyone could worship such an ugly idol.

Just then she noticed a girl kneeling before the idol. She wore the black sari of a widow. When she rose to offer the idol a dish holding a glob of fat, Bonita saw that it was Jehanara, the girl from the stall. She set the fat before the idol and then began to write on a scrap of paper. She rolled the paper into a ball, sucked on it to make it into a spitball, and threw the spitball at the idol. Bonita knew this practice: the girl believed that if the wet paper stuck to the statue, her prayer would be answered.

The paper struck the idol and fell to the floor.

Jehanara began to cry. She jumped up and turned to run from the temple, nearly colliding with Bonita.

"Please don't cry," Bonita said. "Maybe I can help you?"

Jehanara looked at her in recognition. "You are the girl from America who looked at my sari." Then she exclaimed, "If you buy my sari—yes!"

"Why, what do you mean? What's wrong?"

"I am a widow. My husband died when I was eight years old. My husband's brother has to take care of me unless he can sell my sari. If he sells my sari, he can send me back to my father. It is not much better at my father's, but at least my brother-in-law is not there to become angry with me and beat me." She covered her face with her hands and began to cry again.

Bonita winced when she saw the red sores on Jehanara's arms. "How old are you?"

"Fourteen."

Bonita was fourteen too. She shook her head sadly. *I'm a Christian. I know the Lord. I have so many things to be thankful for. My life is so full of promise. But Jehanara—she has nothing to hope for—nothing to live for.*

"If only I had not been so wicked in my last life, my husband would not have died!" Jehanara wailed.

"That is not true," Bonita said confidently. "Your husband did not die because of your sins. Only Jesus suffered for someone else. He died to save you and me from our sins."

"Jesus? Who is that?" Jehanara's eyes widened.

As well as she knew how, there in the idol temple garden, Bonita told Jehanara the story of Jesus. She told how God sent Him from Heaven to die on the cross for the sins of all people, so that God could forgive her sins if she trusted in Him.

"Then, if I trust in Him, I won't have to live many lives to suffer for my sins?" Jehanara looked doubtful.

Bonita shook her head. "We have only one life, and if we love and obey Jesus, we can go to live with Him in His home when we die."

"Will your God answer my prayers?"

"Oh, yes. He promised that if we believe on Jesus, He will answer when we pray."

Hope dawned in Jehanara's dark eyes. "I do believe in Him, I do! And I shall pray that your mother will buy my sari!"

The girls knelt together on the walk and prayed, Bonita helping Jehanara to ask God for forgiveness of sins and receive the gift of salvation. Jehanara finished by asking God to make Bonita's mother buy her sari so that she could go home to her father's house.

When they stood, Jehanara was smiling. "It is late. I must go," she said. "But I shall remember Jesus." She ran out of the temple garden.

Bonita walked more slowly as she went toward the hotel. She felt a vague uneasiness. She was glad she had been able to help Jehanara find Jesus. But she was still a fourteen-year-old widow in a black sari. All Jehanara would know of Jesus was the very little Bonita had told her. She would still live with her cruel brother-in-law who would likely not want her to be a Christian. How could she be faithful?

At the hotel Bonita found her parents awake. She told them where she had gone and launched into the story of her meeting with Jehanara. "She wants to follow Jesus, but how can she really when she can't learn more about Him? Can't we do something for her?"

Father looked thoughtful. "I could try. From what you have said, it seems that her brother-in-law is not anxious to keep her."

"I don't need a sari," Bonita said. "You can use the money to help Jehanara."

"We'll see about the sari later," Father said. "But now I think I'll go talk to the man." He left the hotel.

An hour later he returned, and with him was a smiling Jehanara!

"I paid her brother-in-law what she has cost him since his brother's death," Father explained. "He was glad to be rid of her. When we leave the city, Mother and I will take Jehanara back with us."

"And she will have a new sari," Mother promised.

Jehanara beamed shyly, and then she turned to Bonita. "You gave me so much. All I have is my black sari. May I give it to you?"

Bonita nodded. "Yes, I'll take it with me to the States. I would like my friends there to understand how sad life is in India without Jesus."

– Dorothy C. Haskin

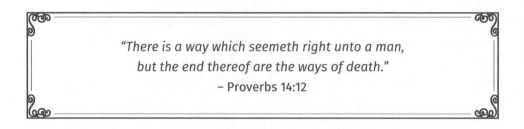
The Flies and the Honey Pot

A jar of honey chanced to spill
Its contents on the windowsill
In many a **viscous** pool and rill.

The flies, attracted by the sweet,
Began so greedily to eat,
They smeared their fragile wings and feet.

With many a twitch and pull in vain
They gasped to get away again,
And died in **aromatic** pain.

O foolish creatures, that destroy
Themselves for **transitory** joy.

– Aesop

172

In All Thy Ways

I Know Christ

I do not know tomorrow's way,
  If dark or gladsome it may be;
But I know Christ, and come what may,
  I know that He abides with me.

I do not know what may befall
  Of grief or gladness, peace or pain;
But I know Christ, and through it all
  I know His presence will sustain.

– *E. Margaret Clarkson*

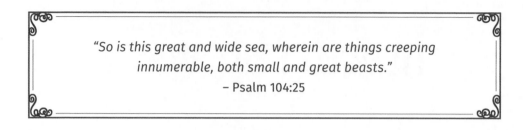

The Ichthyosaur

*Mary Anning was born in 1799 in the English village of Lyme Regis. Her
father, Richard Anning, often took Mary and her brother Joseph for walks
near the cliffs at Lyme Regis. There they would find what Mary's father called
"curiosities": fossils. The limestone and shale cliffs at Lyme Regis contained many
excellent fossils. To supplement his small income as a carpenter, Mr. Anning
sold fossils to collectors and to scientists from London. When her father died,
Mary began to sell fossils too. For many years Mary Anning gently mined the
Lyme Regis cliffs for fossils. This story, taken from the book* Mary Anning's
Treasures, *tells of her first great discovery in 1811.*

One day when Mary was ill with a severe cold, Joseph went hunting alone with Mary's dog Tray. It was nearly dark when he and Tray
returned home. Although he was covered with blue lias[1] dust and his
feet were soaking wet, he wore a triumphant grin.

Mary sat huddled on a stool close to the crackling fire for warmth,
while her mother got supper ready. Seeing the look on Joseph's face,
she cried out, "Joseph! You've found something special. Let me see."

Without a word he pulled from under his jacket a large flat skull
nearly as long as his arm. The eye sockets were enormous, and the
long narrow jaw full of cone-shaped teeth.

---

1 lias (lī' əs): the name given to the layers of limestone and shale in the cliffs at Lyme
Regis, England. The name comes from the way the local people pronounced the word
layers.

"Joseph! The crocodile head!"

Joseph smiled proudly.

"How did—where—oh, tell me everything!"

Joseph laughed aloud at his sister's impatience. Their mother had stopped her work to stare at the skull in utter amazement. Now she sat down with Mary to hear Joseph's story.

"Well, I wasn't having much luck," he began, "so I decided to give up and return home. I was passing Church Cliff when I saw something strange in the face of the cliff. I went over to look at it, and guess who stood guard, without saying a word?"

"Tray, you darling. It was you." Mary reached down and pulled the little dog close to her.

"The strange thing I saw was a jaw," Joseph went on. "As I pushed away loose earth and bits of rock, I could see there was a whole skull. It was farther back and tightly wedged between two layers of rock. I knew I would need help to get it out. I had to hurry, because it was nearly time for the tide to come in.

"I told Tray to stay on guard so I wouldn't lose time finding the spot when I got back. I raced up the side of Church Cliff and up the hill to the quarryman's cottage. I asked him if he and his sons would come with crowbars and help me pry out the skull. Then we all ran back to work. I don't think Tray had moved an inch. The tide was coming in and before we got the skull out, we were standing ankle deep in water. It was a good thing we were close to town.

"And Mary—when we pulled out the skull, it broke off from something else. Probably the backbone. I think the remainder of your crocodile may be there."

"Oh, Joseph, I do hope you are right." Mary's eyes sparkled at the very thought. "I can hardly wait to go look for it."

Mrs. Anning spoke up quickly, "But, Mary, I don't think it will be safe for you to work under the cliff."

"Mother's right, Mary," said Joseph. "Besides, you'll need help to get it out. You'll have to go to the quarrymen and ask them to help you as I did."

It was an impatient Mary who went to bed that night.

By midnight, however, a terrible storm sprang up. Lightning stabbed the darkness with blinding flashes. Ear-splitting thunder rolled again and again across the heavens. Then the rains began. All night they poured down in torrents. And the next day. And the next night. And the day following. Mary grew more impatient every hour.

In the meantime, word of Joseph's discovery had spread. Nearly every villager found time to drop in and marvel at the skull.

"I've heard my grandfather tell about a skull like that, but I've never laid eyes on such a thing before," said one.

Others nodded in agreement. They too had heard of such skulls but had never seen them.

"Is it really a *crocodile's* head?" asked another.

"Well, that's what it was always called," someone else said.

This explanation seemed to satisfy everyone. That is, everyone except Mary. She would wait until their scientist friend from London had passed judgment on it.

At last the weather calmed down, and Mary and Tray hurried off to Church Cliff. What did she see but tons of rock covering the lower part of the sloping cliff and the beach below. The heavy rains had **triggered** an enormous rockslide. If her "crocodile" was there, it was well hidden now. There was nothing to do but wait for another storm to come and carry away the rubble.

Mary was disappointed, but she and Tray moved on until they reached the mudslide. If the storm had been her enemy at Church Cliff, it had been a generous friend here. The collecting was so good that she almost forgot her buried "crocodile" for a time.

The collecting continued to be good for weeks afterward, until the shop was cluttered once more with a wonderful stock of fossils. Joseph had built her more shelves on the walls. On the topmost one perched her most prized possession, the "crocodile" skull. It was still the wonder of the village and of strangers who dropped in. Would she ever find the remainder of it? That question was constantly in her mind.

At long last, another storm—a great gale this time—blew up. Day after day for a week, the wind blew hard from the southwest. It sent the waves crashing much higher than usual on the beach.

Surely all the loose rock at Church Cliff will be carried away now, Mary thought.

As soon as it was possible to go along the beach, she and Tray set off. It was early in the morning before the village came to life. To her great joy, all the clutter of rock at Church Cliff had been swept out to sea, leaving the slopes clean as a pin. The top of the ledge appeared solid and safe.

Without even going close, Mary could see part of a backbone showing. The storm and the tide had certainly **befriended** her this time. She commanded Tray to stand guard. Then she ran as fast as she could up the cliff-side path and through the town to the quarry-man's cottage. He and his sons were just ready to set out for work.

"Oh, sir," Mary was puffing so hard that she could scarcely get her words out, "I have found—the crocodile's backbone—on Church Cliff. But it is too large—for me to get it out by myself. Could I pay you and your sons—to take it out for me?"

The quarryman nodded his assent.

"You will need more men, I think," added Mary.

The quarryman quickly asked one of his sons to go for more help. The other he sent to the top of Church Cliff to check for loose rock before they began working below. Then he gathered up all the hammers, crowbars, and picks he could find and set off with Mary down through the town and back to the base of Church Cliff.

Loyal little Tray was still on guard exactly where Mary had left him. Before long, the quarryman, his sons, and the other helpers were hard at work.

"Please be careful with the bones," Mary called. "They're brittle and break easily."

The men said nothing but nodded in agreement. They worked quickly and carefully, as carefully as Mary herself would have done.

Word soon spread through the town that Mary had found the skeleton. Everyone who could came to watch—shopkeepers, farmers, housewives, chimney sweeps, the candlestick maker, and even the muffin man.

But unfortunately, Mary's friend Mr. Henley was away. Mr. Henley, a fossil collector who knew important scientists in London, would be as excited as Mary over the discovery.

Little by little, the quarrymen removed the rock layer above where the backbone lay. Suddenly one of them shouted, "The whole backbone is here!"

A few minutes later a second quarryman shouted, "I can see the ribs—many ribs!"

It was not long before a third cried out, "I see two feet! The front feet!" Then came an astonished cry: "The two hind feet are here too—but they are much smaller!"

The eager crowd on the beach could barely contain their curiosity, but they had to wait to see for themselves. The rock in which the skeleton was **embedded** was so large that it had to be removed in several pieces. As each piece was taken out, one of the men brought it down to Mary.

Eager hands helped her fit them together. Finally the entire skeleton lay at her feet. It was much longer than she was tall. Everybody was silent for a time as they studied it.

As one of the quarrymen had observed, the front flippers were much larger than the hind ones. Also, at the end of the backbone, the impression of a shark-like tail fin could be seen in the rock. An animal with both flippers and a tail fin?

"What a strange crocodile!" muttered the villagers.

"Its head is like a crocodile's—but certainly the body isn't," said someone.

Mary said nothing. She knew now that it could not possibly be a crocodile. She must send word right away to the scientist in London.

Then everybody tried to help carry the skeleton. It was a joyful procession that Mary and Tray led back to the town. The crocodile that they had heard of for so long was now found. Everybody talked at once. Their town would be famous! Mary would be famous!

Mary blushed deeply.

"But I didn't find the crocodile really," she protested vigorously. "Joseph found the head, and he thought the skeleton might be there too."

The villagers refused to listen to her. They cheered and teased her fondly by turns.

As the merry procession neared the shop, Mary saw her mother appear at the doorway in surprise.

"Why, Mary," she exclaimed, "I knew you had found the skeleton, but I had no idea that so many people would be interested in it."

Mary's helpers carried the slabs of rock containing the skeleton into the shop and placed them on the floor. Then they fitted the pieces together, like a jigsaw puzzle.

Someone reached up to the top shelf for the skull and added it. So large was the whole skeleton that there was barely enough floor space for it. Then someone measured it, from the tip of the snout to the end of the tail. It was over ten feet long! More than twice as tall as Mary.

For the remainder of the day, people streamed in and out to look at the bones of the newfound monster that had lived long ago. The last person to see it that day was Joseph. After he had admired and marveled, Mary told him everything that had happened. Then with great concern, she added, "But Joseph, people keep saying I found it when it was really you."

"Not really, Mary. You started the whole thing. If it hadn't been for you setting up a business in fossils, I wouldn't have been looking for it."

Before she went to bed that night, Mary wrote a letter to her scientist friend in London. She knew that Mr. Henley, who was visiting in the next county, would probably read the exciting news in the newspapers, so she was not surprised two days later to see him jump off the coach almost before it had stopped. As he hurried up the hill to the shop, she stood in the doorway smiling.

"Well, Mary, I knew you'd find it!" Mr. Henley exclaimed. Then he looked at the immense skeleton stretched across the shop floor. "What a size it is!"

Thoughtfully he studied it for some time. Finally he spoke. "No wonder you didn't think it was a crocodile, Mary—with those feet and that fish-like tail fin. But I wonder what it is?"

"I sent word to the scientist," said Mary, "and he will be coming soon to see it."

"And then the monster will be mine?" he smiled at her questioningly.

"Of course, sir."

A few days later, the scientist from the British Museum in London, with his team of assistants, descended upon Lyme Regis and Mary's shop. They congratulated her warmly on her find. They set to work to examine it carefully, bone by bone. Then they made an exact drawing of it so that they could study it when they returned to the museum.

"You are right, Mary. This was not a crocodile," said the scientist when they had finished. "It appears to have been a great fish-like reptile. Because of the tail fin, it would have been able to swim like a fish. We think the feet, or fins perhaps, were covered with skin like flippers. They would have helped to balance the animal. Unlike a fish, however, it had lungs and breathed air.

"You have made a very exciting discovery, Mary; we never knew before that such an animal existed. A brand-new name will have to be given to it. When we decide what the name is, I'll let you know. Then we will send word to other scientists around the world of this amazing discovery."

Later the scientist informed Mary that the name *Ichthyosaurus*[2] had been given to the new fossil reptile. It was a tongue-twisting name, but he explained that it was a Greek word meaning "fish-like reptile."

– Helen Bush

---

2 Ichthyosaurus (ik′ thē ə sȯr′ əs)

The Earth Abideth

The earth abideth for ever.
The sun also ariseth, and the sun goeth down,
And hasteth to his place where he arose.
The wind goeth toward the south,
And turneth about unto the north;
It whirleth about continually,
And the wind returneth again according to his circuits.
All the rivers run into the sea;
Yet the sea is not full;
Unto the place from whence the rivers come,
Thither they return again.

– Ecclesiastes 1:4-7

God Provides Water

¹ Bless the LORD, O my soul.
  O LORD my God, thou art very great; thou art clothed with
    honour and majesty.
² Who coverest thyself with light as with a garment:
  Who stretchest out the heavens like a curtain:
³ Who layeth the beams of his chambers in the waters:
  Who maketh the clouds his chariot:
  Who walketh upon the wings of the wind:
⁴ Who maketh his angels spirits;
  His ministers a flaming fire:
⁵ Who laid the foundations of the earth,
  That it should not be removed for ever.
⁶ Thou coveredst it with the deep as with a garment:
  The waters stood above the mountains.
⁷ At thy rebuke they fled;
  At the voice of thy thunder they hasted away.
⁸ They go up by the mountains;
  They go down by the valleys unto the place which thou
    hast founded for them.
⁹ Thou hast set a bound that they may not pass over;
  That they turn not again to cover the earth.
¹⁰ He sendeth the springs into the valleys,
  Which run among the hills.
¹¹ They give drink to every beast of the field:
  The wild asses quench their thirst.
¹² By them shall the fowls of the heaven have their habitation,
  Which sing among the branches.

¹³ He watereth the hills from his chambers:
  The earth is satisfied with the fruit of thy works.
¹⁴ He causeth the grass to grow for the cattle,
  And herb for the service of man:
  That he may bring forth food out of the earth;
¹⁵ And wine that maketh glad the heart of man,
  And oil to make his face to shine,
  And bread which strengtheneth man's heart.
¹⁶ The trees of the LORD are full of sap;
  The cedars of Lebanon, which he hath planted;
¹⁷ Where the birds make their nests:
  As for the stork, the fir trees are her house.

²⁴ O LORD, how manifold are thy works!
  In wisdom hast thou made them all:
  The earth is full of thy riches.

³¹ The glory of the LORD shall endure for ever:
  The LORD shall rejoice in his works.
³² He looketh on the earth, and it trembleth:
  He toucheth the hills, and they smoke.
³³ I will sing unto the LORD as long as I live:
  I will sing praise to my God while I have my being.
³⁴ My meditation of him shall be sweet:
  I will be glad in the LORD.
³⁵ Let the sinners be consumed out of the earth,
  And let the wicked be no more.
  Bless thou the LORD, O my soul. Praise ye the LORD.

– Psalm 104

Could It Be Done?

Part 1: Secrets of the Soil

This story, like "The Ichthyosaur," is the story of a real person—George Washington Carver. It tells of the early years of Tuskegee Institute, soon after Carver came to help teach young Negroes (as African-Americans were called then) various trades. It is written as if Carver himself were telling the story, but the writer uses his imagination freely to add details, conversations, and thoughts.

This selection by David Collins is from George Washington Carver: Man's Slave Becomes God's Scientist, *a Sowers Series biography from Mott Media.*

In time I knew we'd be doing the impossible with our Tuskegee[1] land. But first our 20-acre plot had to be cleared of weeds and rubbish. Each day my students worked until their backs ached and their muscles begged for mercy. When the land was clear, I had a surprise waiting for the class.

"You see before you a two-horse plow, ready to be put into operation," I said. One of the horses whinnied in the morning sunlight, slapping at a fly on his back with his tail.

"I never did see a two-horse plow," one of the students said, walking around the team of horses. "Everybody here uses just one horse." He shook his head in amazement.

---

1 Tuskegee (təs kē′ gē)

"Who's going to use it?" another asked. "None of us have driven a two-horse plow."

I took my place behind the team of horses and plow. "Step aside, my friends, I have work to do."

Slowly the horses stepped forward as I snapped the reins. The steel blade of the plow slid into the soil, turning it aside as we moved ahead. Like hungry foxes on a rabbit's trail, my students followed me across the plot of land. On our return, we found two farmers watching us.

"Hey, ain't you the professor here—that Carver fellow?" one asked.

"That's who I am," I answered.

"Then what you doin' driving a plow?"

I smiled. "I know of no law, the Lord's or man's, that says I can't. Do you?"

The two men exchanged puzzled looks. "No, I guess not."

"This plowing will be taking us most of the day," I said. "If you care to watch us, feel free. Get your friends too."

That was like throwing corn to crows. Off the men went, returning soon with six more farmers. The idea of a professor plowing seemed quite a fine joke. Laughter rolled across the field like happy music.

"Hope you're not planning to raise anything on this no-good land," came one loud shout.

" 'Cepting weeds," someone else suggested. "Yeah, I guess you can get the best weeds in Alabama on this soil."

There was truth in the farmer's words, and I couldn't help smiling. The hard clay dirt rolled to one side of the plow. How I missed the deep richness of Iowa's soil.

And yet this red dirt offered a challenge. Surely it could be **enriched**. I glanced at the farmers watching. Their faces were curious, reflecting their interest. I had wanted them to see what a two-horse plow could do. If a Tuskegee teacher could turn the soil, surely they could too. At least, I hoped that was what they were thinking. And if we could find a way to grow a useful crop here, couldn't these same farmers learn to make their own land richer and more productive?

When the soil was turned, my students were ready for the next step.

"I'm turning you loose," I told them one morning. "I want you to visit the woods. Gather leaves off the ground. Go into the swamps and creeks. Bring back buckets of mud and muck. Head to the barns and bring back the animal droppings."

"But why?" one student asked, with an astonished look. He obviously thought I had gone mad in the hot sun.

"We must put nutrients back into our land. The things you collect will make the soil rich," I answered. "All of us must help."

In the next week, our 20-acre plot became a dumping ground. I taught the students how to use the two-horse plow, and day after day we turned the clay soil with the buckets of waste brought in. The dirt began to look darker and richer.

I knew my students had only one crop in mind—cotton. Yet it was clear that the constant growing of cotton on our land, and other land throughout the South, had robbed the soil of nutrients. It had lost its power to **nourish**. Like thieves, we had stolen the wealth of the soil that the Lord had provided. Now we had to enrich it again.

On planting day my students came early to our plot.

"Let us bow our heads and ask for the Lord's blessing on our first crop here," I said.

One of the students, Ambrose Lee Harper, stepped forward. "Yes, let's ask the Lord to bring us the best 20 acres of cotton in all the Southland."

I shook my head. "The Lord can do anything," I said, "but I think it is asking too much to grow cotton from the seeds of cowpeas."[2]

My students did not know what to say. Ambrose Lee moved toward me, his eyes angry. "We've cleared this land and mixed the soil to grow

2 cowpeas: sometimes called *black-eyed peas*

cowpeas? Cowpeas is a worthless crop. We thought we was workin' to grow cotton. You fooled us, Mr. Carver."

"I'm sorry, Ambrose Lee. But I know this soil is not right for raising good cotton. It needs refreshing and enriching. A good crop of cowpeas will put nutrients into the soil. Perhaps then we may think about cotton."

Ambrose Lee was not convinced. He turned and walked away. Suddenly he whirled around and shook his fist.

"You're all fools, raisin' cowpeas! Mister Carver, you're the biggest fool of all!"

As I looked to the rest of the students, I wondered how many of them felt the same. Maybe it would be better to plant cotton and to have them all see it would not grow. Would the students learn more? Perhaps. Yet it was wrong to waste the soil. Or was I wrong?

Doubts. And more doubts. Sometimes my mind was filled with them. Was I truly following the path the Lord had chosen for me? Sometimes the urge to paint returned. Other times, when I visited students at the **dormitory**, I sat down at the piano to play. I recalled those happy days at Simpson College. Maybe I was meant to be an artist—or pianist. Had I missed the Lord's directions? Maybe Ambrose Lee was right. Perhaps I was a fool. And if I be a fool, what business did I have leading others as their teacher?

God's Little Workshop

"Here is what I call 'God's little workshop.' No books ever go into my laboratory. What need is there of books? I lean upon the twenty-ninth verse of the first chapter of Genesis . . . 'And God said, Behold, I have given you every herb bearing seed, which is upon the face of all the earth, and every tree, in the which is the fruit of a tree yielding seed; to you it shall be for meat.'"

—*George Washington Carver*

As the cowpeas crept up through the soil into the sunlight, we kept the soil free from weeds. And daily in the lab, we kept adding equipment. Carefully we cut the tops off bottles to make beakers. We made an alcohol lamp from an old ink bottle, then added a wick from twisted plant fibers.

"You don't throw anything away, do you?" my students asked often.

I smiled. "Everything has a use," I answered. "It's finding the use that is exciting."

When it came time to harvest the crop of cowpeas, I found little joy among my students. If they saw any use or excitement in the rows of vegetable stalks, these young farmers kept it well hidden. Slowly they wandered among the cowpeas, picking the peas from each weary stalk.

"Never thought I'd be pickin' cowpeas when I came here to Tuskegee," one boy mumbled. "I guess Ambrose Lee was right."

"Well, the soil may be better now," grunted another student, "but I sure hate the sight of these cowpeas."

"They don't seem ugly when you eat them," I answered. "Come to the cafeteria tomorrow night at seven o'clock. Bring your best appetites."

Once more my students looked bewildered. But they agreed to come.

The pots and pans rattled that Saturday afternoon. I boiled the brown peas, sprinkling in salt and mixing them with several hunks of fresh pork. By 7:00, the table was set, my guests were seated, and I served the food.

"Must we eat these cowpeas?" one boy asked, his face revealing his distaste for the idea. "Cowpeas is livestock food, not people food."

I spooned a serving onto his plate. "Let's give them a chance."

There were few words spoken around the table for a while. I stole glances from face to face. Finally one student spoke.

"Delicious! This is the best meal I ever ate!"

Another head nodded. "Just what I was thinking! But I thought I must be wrong. How could those miserable little cowpeas taste so good?"

"Maybe we should plant cowpeas again," someone suggested.

I shook my head. "No, don't let your stomachs do your thinking. These cowpeas put fresh nutrients back into the soil. Now I'm thinking we could raise a hearty crop of sweet potatoes. They're good eating for men and livestock. We can make starch from them. What we don't use now, we can dry out and have for hungry times later. We should be able to raise about eighty bushels an acre."

The eyes around the table widened. I knew what they were thinking. Fifty bushels in this part of the South was about average. Sixty bushels of sweet potatoes was a healthy harvest. Seventy was unbelievable. But eighty bushels an acre was impossible!

Yet no one challenged my words. Perhaps the cowpeas had helped me win a victory. My students were willing to trust me.

And if they were willing to help me raise the sweet potatoes, we could then plant cotton. The soil would be rich and full of the nutrients needed for the cotton.

"Come on, Professor Carver," one student called out. "Let's find a piano and see if you still play as well as you cook."

"Only if you sing while I play," I agreed.

We gathered around an old piano in the dormitory.

> Praise the harvest, praise the home,
>
> Praise the Lord, where'er we roam . . .

Across the Tuskegee **campus** the music drifted. But unknown to us then, a lone figure was strolling slowly along a pathway. President Booker T. Washington was struggling with a big problem that prevented him from sleeping.

Soon that problem would be troubling me too.

– David Collins

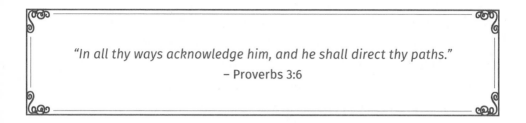

> *"In all thy ways acknowledge him, and he shall direct thy paths."*
> – Proverbs 3:6

Could It Be Done?
Part 2: The School in a Wagon

[Dr. Carver] wanted to write bulletins on farm improvement, but what good were bulletins to farmers who couldn't read? So he made a "bulletin" 20 acres across—the school farm. And if you lived too far away to come and see it, you could expect him in your front yard some morning. "I'm from the institute," he'd say. "My name is Carver." And he'd get to work. —Tom Campbell

Everything at Tuskegee seemed to be going well. Our 20 acres provided 1,600 bushels of sweet potatoes—80 bushels an acre. My students were proud, even overjoyed.

And now, finally, we began planting the "King Crop"—cotton. The tired, sandy clay had become dark rich soil. It turned easily as we plowed and planted. In a few weeks, the hearty stalks grew straight and full of blossoms in the sun.

"We are grateful to You, O Lord," I prayed nightly. "Without You, we are nothing."

Harvest proved the happiest time of all. Each acre produced a 500-pound bale of cotton, compared to the 200 pounds each one had provided before.

But with my joy, I still felt a hurt inside. Each time I saw our leader, Booker T. Washington, I sensed a troubled man. But the cause of his worry remained a mystery to me.

191

My worry was pushed aside by new tasks at Tuskegee. Often I walked by myself into the Alabama countryside. Never had I seen so many kinds of trees! Giant oak, sturdy pine, spreading spruce—22 varieties. I shared my discoveries on paper, writing nature articles for magazines and newspapers. Farmers wrote me questions about the soil, their crops, and all the land around them. Eagerly I answered their letters, hoping they would take good care of the riches the Lord had provided.

Early one morning I slowly walked through a swampy marsh near the Tuskegee campus. I gazed skyward. Spanish moss draped lazily over the branches of sweet gum trees like giant spider webs. Only narrow streaks of sunlight peeked through.

Suddenly I stumbled. My hands flung forward into the sticky mud. Pulling myself up, I jerked a handkerchief from my pocket. I rubbed my muddy hands onto the cloth. A few yards away I saw a large puddle of water. Quickly I walked to it, dipped my handkerchief down to soak, and continued rubbing my hands.

The swamp mud came off easily. But as I dipped the cloth into the water, I noticed the white handkerchief was now bright blue. Yes, as blue as the sky on a cloudless day. I held the cloth up into a sliver of sunlight. The blue looked even brighter.

My heartbeat quickened. Still clenching the handkerchief tightly, I hurried back to the lab on the campus.

From a bucket in the corner, I took a large clump of red clay. Carefully I set it on a tray and poured water over it. The sand and grit washed away. A sticky red paste remained. I pressed my finger into it, then drew a line across a piece of paper nearby. Holding the paper close to the window, I smiled.

"Paint. There is paint in the clay. Blue. Red. Look at that color!" It was hard to control my excitement. Once the clay was washed clean, heated into powder, and mixed with liquid, people could have paint.

They could paint their homes, their barns, their churches, anything they wanted.

Once more I knew the Lord had spoken. There seemed to be no end to His gifts. And I did not mind that He had pushed me to the ground to find this one.

President Washington shared my joy of discovery. "You continue to bring attention to Tuskegee. And at the same time you are bringing respect to our Negro people," he said. "I am glad you are here, Professor Carver."

I was glad I had come to Tuskegee too. And yet, I still longed to share the troubles he carried, to ease his burden.

Carver's Useful Sweet Potato

George Washington Carver was not only a teacher—he was a scientist and inventor. He experimented with many ordinary foods during his years at Tuskegee and found surprising uses for some of them. He discovered over 100 products that could be made from the sweet potato. And, since he was a good cook, he made up many sweet potato recipes too—sweet potato pie, stuffed sweet potatoes, sweet potato balls, sweet potato nuts, and more. With sweet potato flour he made muffins, bread, doughnuts, and biscuits.

Finally, late one night as I walked alone across the campus, my chance came.

Moonlight covered the campus like a silver fog. It painted a shiny surface on the new red brick buildings that dotted the grounds of Tuskegee. As I returned from visiting the students in their dormitory, I heard footsteps behind me. Unlike the quick, steady movement of younger people, these steps were slow, almost plodding. I turned to see the familiar outline of Dr. Washington approaching.

"Making sure the buildings are all locked up?" I called.

Dr. Washington chuckled as he moved closer. "I'm taking a midnight walk. Sometimes sleep does not come so easily to me."

We walked together, not speaking for several minutes. Finally, Dr. Washington stopped. "Are you happy here?"

"At Tuskegee, sir? I am happier here than I have ever been. You have built a fine school here."

There was another long pause.

"But does it ever trouble you that we are here in such a small world?" he asked gently. "Yes, I am proud of Tuskegee. The students who come here take much away. But think of all the young people who cannot come, who still suffer through each day. Somehow I feel we are failing them."

"Failing." How tragic and sad that word sounded. "In what way?" I asked.

"We have worked hard to teach our people to raise good crops, to better their farms and homes." President Washington's voice sounded tired. "But we reach so few. If only we could bring all our people here to Tuskegee—"

"We reach all we can," I interrupted.

"Yes," he agreed. "But for every man we help here, there are ten thousand still untouched. Each time I travel I see them. How I wish we might bring them here and help them."

So that was the mystery, the problem that had troubled him for so long. He carried not only the worries of his own students here at Tuskegee, but also the **plight** of Negroes throughout the South.

Shame swept over me. My life had become so busy that for a time I had forgotten a major reason that I had come to Tuskegee. I, too, should have been carrying more concern for our people.

It was not that I was blind to the world around me. I had seen the beaten, drab cabins sprinkled everywhere in the South. Inside these one- and two-room gray shacks with holes in the walls often lived ten or twelve members of one family. The bed was often a dirt floor, with creek drinking water being shared with pigs and livestock.

"In time, we will reach more people," I told Dr. Washington.

He nodded. "I suppose. But how painful the waiting is. How long they suffer."

I watched him slowly walk away. How much he had done, how hard he had worked. It seemed unfair that he carried such a burden.

Sleep did not come easily for me that night. The hours dragged by. Dr. Washington's words lingered in my mind. "How I wish we might bring them here and help them . . ."

Suddenly I sat up in bed. "That's it!" I exclaimed. "We'll go to them!"

By the time Dr. Washington came to his office the next morning, I had been waiting an hour. I could not control my enthusiasm.

"Our people cannot come to Tuskegee," I exclaimed, "but we can go to them!"

Dr. Washington looked confused. "I have thought of such a thing before, but there is no way. We cannot carry buildings on our backs, Professor Carver. Maybe you had best—"

"No, we need not carry buildings," I interrupted. "But we can carry our knowledge, our tools. We can put a butter churn on a wagon, and a milk tester. Load some garden tools, the newest, the most modern. Carry a new plow—"

President Washington's eyes sparkled and a smile replaced the worried wrinkles I had seen so long.

"—And we can go out in the countryside. We can take Tuskegee right to their doorstep," I added.

"It—it all sounds so fantastic," President Washington exclaimed. "Could it really be done?"

I nodded eagerly. "We can try it. I'll go out on weekends so I can stay in my classroom during the week."

"Let's do try it, Professor Carver. Let's show our people a better way to farm."

Our planning started at once, and it caught fire like dry grass.

A man from the North offered money for the wagon. Invitations poured in from area farmers.

"We hear you are going to be helping farmers," wrote one man. "I have forty acres you may use for anything you wish."

"I have read all your articles in the magazines," wrote another farmer. "Mister Carver, I believe you can do anything with the soil. Please come."

Carefully we planned the wagon and bought the equipment. A cream separator was added to our original list. We bought a new spike-toothed harrow and a diverse cultivator for breaking up hard soil.

Finally, our school on wheels was ready to go.

I picked one of my best students to go with me on the first trip. Early one June morning in 1906, Tom Campbell and I set out. With a snap of the reins, our horse-drawn wagon jerked forward. The other members from my class cheered and shouted.

"Teach them good, fellows!" one student yelled. "Show them what we can do!"

The wagon bounced and bumped along the rutted road. Tom kept a careful watch over our equipment on the back of the wagon.

Within an hour we reached our destination: a rundown cabin at the base of a hill, a mile outside the town of Chechow. A small collection of farmers stood outside. One of them ran forward.

"Doctor Carver, it's you!" A black man with gray-white whiskers helped me off the wagon. The other farmers grouped around us.

"Can we get started at once?" I asked. "Does anyone have a strong horse?"

It seemed the farmers were as eager as we were. One man ran off, returning minutes later with a muscled field horse. We hitched him to our steelbeam plow and began our work.

"When your farmland slopes, you must follow its natural contour,"

I explained. "Never plow in a straight line, uphill and down. By following the curve of the hill, the water will not run off so fast, carrying the precious topsoil away."

The men watched every move Tom and I made as we worked. I only wished Dr. Washington might have been there.

Once the field was plowed, we turned to other matters. We showed the farmers how to fight insects and other diseases of trees and bushes and how to plant useful gardens.

Our program turned also to the wives of the farmers. We showed the womenfolk the best ways to cook and clean, how to make curtains from flour sacks, and weave rugs with corn shucks and grasses.

Everywhere we went, we were welcomed. Our school on wheels was a big success.

"Please come to our town," wrote one mayor. "You may give classes in our town hall, the church building—or anywhere you wish. Just come!"

And so we traveled. Soon Tom took over the wagon himself so I could remain at Tuskegee.

George Washington Carver's Favorite Verses

"Try these and see what a marvelous vision will come to you."
– *George Washington Carver*

"Ye shall know the truth, and the truth shall make you free."
– *John 8:32*

"In all thy ways acknowledge him, and he shall direct thy paths."
– *Proverbs 3:6*

"Study to shew thyself approved unto God, a workman that needeth not to be ashamed, rightly dividing the word of truth."
– *2 Timothy 2:15*

"I can do all things through Christ which strengtheneth me."
– *Philippians 4:13*

"Where there is no vision, the people perish."
– *Proverbs 29:18*

Later, when Tom was married, he and his wife journeyed together. While Tom instructed the men, Mrs. Campbell taught their wives how better to care for their babies. She showed them how to keep their homes **sanitary** and how to prepare nutritious food.

The Lord blessed the movable school. Other institutes in the South started their own schools on wheels. Soon the idea spread into the North and even across the seas.

Best of all, our own people enjoyed real improvements in their way of life. They were conserving their farm soil. They gained an upper hand on the diseases that had once ravaged their families. And once again their farms were growing thick bolls of good white cotton.

– David Collins

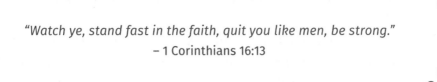

A Chance to Escape

Lijsken Mieuwess[1] lay in the dark, listening. The howling rush of the wind around the cottage walls strove with the whistling at the windows, and the sails of the windmill moaned high above the rooftop. Lijsken pictured the familiar lead-gray clouds creeping inland from the North Sea. It would be a stormy day.

"Dirk," she called to her husband. "Are you going to fasten down the windmill?"

No one answered, but soon she heard the groaning of the sails grow louder, and then stop. Dirk had already gone up and shut off the windmill to keep the sails from being torn apart by the gusting wind.

Lijsken heard Dirk singing in the kitchen, and she got up to begin her day. She and Dirk lived in a small white cottage beside their windmill. From the high mill window they could see a dozen other windmills like theirs stationed across the flat lands of Zeeland. Most of these windmills were built to pump water out of the low-lying fields, into canals, and back into the sea. Dirk and Lijsken's mill, however, was used to grind grain.

"I don't think anyone will come in this weather to grind corn,

---

1 Lijsken Mieuwess (lās' kən myüs)

Lijsken. Perhaps I should go into Vlissingen this morning and see Jelis."[2]

"Yes, Dirk. We should be having a meeting soon—don't you think?"

"Jelis will know when and where. If the rain holds off, I'll go to see him. I have a little flour to deliver to the baker in Scheldt Street anyway."

The clouds rode high on the wind, sprinkling the fields only lightly. Further inland they would soon be pouring down their rain. So, after his morning work was complete, Dirk said good-bye to Lijsken.

"Be careful, Dirk," she warned him. "The authorities are on the alert for Anabaptists now, after all the arrests in Antwerp and Dordrecht. Don't stay long—please?"

"No longer than I must, Lijsken. I love you; I miss you already."

"Hurry then and return to me. I will have herring and good thick soup waiting."

Dirk began his two-mile walk into Vlissingen. He gazed at the fields below the raised roadway and spoke silently to God, praying for Lijsken's safety as she waited alone at the mill.

He was a little anxious for her. Over the last two years so many believers had been arrested and killed in Holland.

2 Jelis (yā′ lis)

Even women had been dragged out of their own homes and thrown into prison.

Some words from Nelleken Jasper's letter echoed in Dirk's mind: "I must yet pass through a great wilderness," she had written from prison in Antwerp, "for it is desolate and perilous here." The letter had been read in the believers' meeting recently. Soon after, they heard that Nelleken had followed the same path her father, mother, and two brothers walked—to be burned at the stake in Antwerp. There was death all over Holland.

Dirk shuddered, and then jumped at the sudden "hello" of a traveler approaching from the side road to Middleburg.

"Going to Vlissingen?" the man asked, shifting the load of leather pouches he bore on his shoulders.

Dirk nodded, trying to compose himself.

"Sorry, I startled you. Mind if I join you?"

"Come along," Dirk said, smiling. "I'm glad for the company."

Noticing that the man was wet, Dirk asked him if he had been caught out in the rain.

The stranger looked down at his coat as if he hadn't known he was wet. "Guess so! Out of Middleburg a few miles it *poured!* I crawled under the closest haystack—but it wasn't close enough. Do you live around here? You are dry."

"I have the mill right back there." Dirk nodded back at his mill, standing tall on the horizon half a mile back. "I see you're a peddler, but I've never met you before. Most of the peddlers stop in at the mill."

"I'm new at peddling." The stranger laughed. "In Zierikzee I had a bakery. But in February I was at an auction in Middleburg, and I bought these purse-maker's tools and some pouches. I paid two guilders and sixpence for all this—and became a purse-peddler! Now I'm out on the road!"

A sudden sickening feeling swept over Dirk. "Middleburg?" he asked timidly.

"Yes. You know Middleburg? That's where the auction was. One good thing that's come out of all this Anabaptist **furor**. A man can get a good bargain at those auctions. Hendrick Alewijns[3] was the Anabaptist's name—a preacher they say he was—and they burned him alive with two others; and the same day I got a new business!" The man smiled broadly, but Dirk was remembering Hendrick Alewijns, the faithful servant of God, who had many times encouraged him and Lijsken and the other brethren around Vlissingen.

"Don't you think?" the peddler was asking. "Don't you think?"

Dirk snapped back from his troubled thoughts. The man was speaking to him. "I'm sorry . . . my mind was wandering. What did you ask?"

"I was saying, don't you think it a shame that Zeeland is overrun with these Anabaptists?"

What should he answer? He mustn't hesitate or the man would become suspicious. Dirk shrugged his shoulders. "I live in the country. So far there have not been any conflicts where we live."

"Ah, the authorities won't overlook the country for long! I heard in Middleburg today that the lords are making a renewed effort to wipe them out. It isn't hard to figure out who they are either, since they refuse to have their babies baptized. They say only adults can believe, so only adults can be baptized!"

"What do you think about it?" Dirk asked, before the man had a chance to ask him.

"Well, I agree with the lords. You can't let every person think for himself. If another church forms, the nation will soon be divided. It's dangerous!"

Dirk had not expected a different answer. This man obviously

3 Hendrick Alewijns (al' wānz)

thought very little of those who wanted only to be faithful to Christ's teachings. The priests and monks had convinced him that every baby must be baptized into the state church so that they could control what people believed.

But Dirk knew better. He had received a copy of the New Testament two years ago. Reading it, he had realized that babies could not become members of the church. *The church is all those who choose to follow Christ in faithful obedience—not babies, who sleep while the water is sprinkled on their heads.*

"Here's where I turn off," the peddler said.

"Good-bye." Dirk nodded to him. "I hope your selling goes well."

Dirk walked south through the streets of Vlissingen, relieved to be alone again. Along the river he came to Scheldt Street and delivered his small bag of fine flour, which the baker would use for special pastries. Then he walked back to Jelis's house. When he knocked, the door swung open, and he stepped in. No one seemed to be home.

"Jelis!" Dirk called. He heard voices in the back of the shop, and a sudden fear filled him. "Ah, talking with that peddler has made me jumpy," he told himself. "Jelis!"

"Who's this?" A man came through the door from the shop. He was leading another man whose hands were tied. The bound man was Jelis! Dirk bolted out the door, slamming it behind him. Down the narrow street he ran, turned and fled down another, then another, until he was gasping for air.

Where could he hide? He couldn't pass through the city gate panting like this! He sped around a corner and ran right into a pair of soldiers.

The room was cold. Frigid and damp. And dark. Dirk strained to see through the tiny opening high in the door. He thought he heard footsteps, but no one came. He thought once he heard Jelis cry out, but he couldn't be sure. His thoughts went back over and over again to Lijsken waiting for him, watching from the cottage door, frightened, worried. Dirk prayed and prayed.

The day ended and night came. Dirk could tell because the darkness grew thicker and the light from the passageway faded. "Lord Jesus," he prayed, "help me to stand firm in faith, like Hendrick and Nelleken and the others have. I am only a man, Lord. Help me not fear torture or death." He could not sleep, though he tried to, sitting up on the wet floor. He prayed more.

In the morning the cell grew lighter. Soon Dirk heard footsteps in the passage. Keys jingled, and the door opened. Three men entered.

"An Anabaptist," sneered the first man, obviously a monk.

"So charged," answered the third man, who was the jailer.

The other man stood silent, staring scornfully. His fur lapels and shining buttons told that he was either a lord or a high church official.

The jailer left the room, closing the heavy door behind him. The monk began questioning Dirk: Who was he? Where did he come from? Was he a citizen of Vlissingen? Why was he in the city? Who else had he seen today? When was he last in church?

When Dirk answered that he had not attended the state church for two years, the monk became angry. "Why don't you attend?"

"I meet with those who follow Christ in true faith," Dirk said.

"And have you been rebaptized?" the richly dressed man asked.

"I was baptized a year ago, on confessing my faith and promising to live for Christ."

"What was wrong with your first baptism?" The monk scowled.

"The Bible tells me to believe, to repent, and be baptized," Dirk answered simply. "When I was eight days old, I could not believe or re—"

"Who baptized you?" the other man interrupted.

Dirk did not answer.

"Who baptized you?" the monk shouted.

"I cannot tell you," Dirk said.

"Can't? You will. You will! I promise you that!" the other yelled.

The men left, but the next day the jailer led Dirk to a room full of weapons and iron tools. The monk was there again, and another man, large and cruel-looking. The monk shouted questions. When Dirk refused to answer, they tortured him, trying to force him to give the names of other believers around Vlissingen.

But finally, when they could not make Dirk betray his brothers or Christ, they seemed to forget about him. Days passed.

Soon he guessed that he had been in prison for nearly a year.

During this year, Dirk had often seen the jailer lead men from their cells toward the prison doors, and later in the day lead them back again. One day the jailer came for Dirk. What a wonderful feeling it was to go outside! The light hurt his eyes at first, but he rejoiced to lift his face toward the sun and feel the salty sea breeze again. If only he could walk on, on, out to the road that led to the mill . . . and Lijsken.

The jailer took Dirk with some other men to his house and gave them work to do, mostly chopping wood and hauling stones. He began to bring Dirk out more often. The jailer's children came to play in the yard while the men worked. Dirk learned their names: Veerle,[4] Thijs,[5] Naomi, and Lorca. Each time he thanked God for the chance to escape his dark cell for a little while.

The jailer always sat near the prisoners, watching every turn of each man's foot, every glance of each man's eyes. Sometimes the prisoners jokingly called him "the watchdog," and sometimes "the hawk." And then one afternoon, something odd happened. The jailer fell asleep.

---

4 Veerle (vir' lə)
5 Thijs (tās)

Dirk understood what the prisoners were planning when he saw them whispering together. They were going to escape! He looked at the jailer, slumped in his chair. He heard the children inside laughing. Then the other prisoners beckoned to Dirk: "Come on! Let's go!" Gingerly they laid down their tools and sneaked off into the trees. Dirk was alone—alone, except for the napping jailer and the sounds of the children's voices in the house. Should he, too, flee? To freedom! To *Lijsken!* They could run until no one would ever find them.

But what about the jailer? Dirk wondered. *What will the city officials do to him when they discover that he has allowed his prisoners to escape?* Dirk felt he would be partly responsible for causing the jailer to suffer and perhaps even to die. No, the jailer had been kind. Dirk would not cause him to suffer.

After the escape, outdoor work ceased. Dirk was again confined day and night to the dark, cold cell. The lords of the city sent more monks to argue with Dirk. They tried to confuse and frighten him. On March 6, 1570, they sentenced him to be tortured on the rack, but he would not deny Christ. At last the city officials knew they would never destroy Dirk's faith.

On May 8, 1571, they burned Dirk Mieuwess at the stake. He did not waver in death, but was **steadfast** as he had been in life. They burned him, not because he was a thief or a murderer, but because he stood for Christ and cared more about the jailer's life than his own.

– David Luthy

Dirk Mieuwess, A.D. 1571

"A Chance to Escape," which you just read, is based on this account of Dirk Mieuwess, taken from the martyr book, the Martyrs Mirror, *which was compiled by T. J. van Braght and published in 1660. As with most books of that time, its title was quite long:* The Bloody Theater or Martyrs Mirror of the Defenseless Christians Who Baptized Only Upon Confession of Faith, and Who Suffered and Died for the Testimony of Jesus, Their Saviour, From the time of Christ to the Year A.D. 1660.

After much persecution, murdering, and burning of the true followers of Christ, a pious brother named Dirk Mieuwess was seized at Vlissingen in Zeeland. After a long imprisonment, the bailiff and jailer permitted him to render them certain services for the benefit of their households, so that he and some of his fellow prisoners were frequently allowed to leave the prison. When the opportunity came, some of the prisoners escaped and advised Dirk Mieuwess to flee with them, which this friend of Christ refused to do. He feared that the jailer, who had permitted him to go out, would get into trouble.

Thus remaining in prison, he was sentenced on the 6th of March in 1570 to be tortured on the rack. The following year, 1571, on the 8th of May, he was burned in Vlissingen. Showing great steadfastness, he offered up his temporal and corruptible body as a sweet-smelling savor unto the Lord of heaven and earth.

He did not suffer as a thief or murderer, nor as one who seeks other people's property, but only for the truth of Christ and a good conscience (1 Peter 2:19). Hence there are sure to him the promises of Christ, who has said, "Blessed are they which are persecuted for righteousness' sake: for theirs is the kingdom of heaven" (Matthew 5:10).

– Thieleman J. van Braght

> "But I say unto you, That ye resist not evil: but whosoever shall smite thee on thy right cheek, turn to him the other also."
> – Matthew 5:39

An Ill Wind

The year is 1778. The American colonies are fighting the Revolutionary War for independence from England. The war will go on until 1783, when England and America sign the Treaty of Paris.

Like so many others in the colonies, the people of Nantucket Island are suffering from the war. Before the war ends, most of Nantucket's whaling ships will be destroyed. English ships will kill or capture 1,200 Nantucket whalemen.

In this story you will read about a privateer—*an armed private ship hired to fight during a war. In the days of the American Revolution, the English king hired many privateers to attack towns along the American seacoast. They stole money and supplies, which King George III used to help pay for the war against the colonies.*

In those days most of the people on Nantucket Island were Quakers who had fled to Nantucket for religious freedom.

Most of Nantucket's soil is sand, so it is not good for farming. However, Quaker settlers made large garden spots and farmed some of the land. Even so, the island could not support its inhabitants. They had to bring food from the mainland. The men of Nantucket decided to fish for cod in the Atlantic Ocean. They became good fishermen and whalers too. In fact, until the 1840s, Nantucket Island was the chief whaling center of the world.

The main character in our story is William Rotch, a real man. In later years, Rotch's son William Jr., moved from Nantucket Island to New Bedford, Massachusetts, and built a house there in the 1830s. That house is still standing. It is now a museum. People who visit the museum can learn about the whaler-Quakers of New England.

"Methinks this west wind **forebodes** us no good," whispered William Rotch to his wife, as he turned from the open window one summer morning in 1778.

"Why, Father, what harm can come from the west wind?" inquired twelve-year-old William Jr., who was always hearing things he was not expected to hear. "I thought the west wind was our friend and brought our whaling ships safely into port."

"Yea, son, so it has been in the past, but we peaceful Nantucket folk can no longer practice our trade. Thou knowest that not one whaling ship has gone out to sea for thirty days. I fear that today's wind may give a British privateer a chance to sail into Sherburne harbor."

"What? A privateer? You mean a full-rigged ship with guns and armed men? Why should they come to Nantucket? They know well that we are Christians and not fighting folk."

"True, son. Yet we are known as a thrifty community and might be worth a visit. These privateers **plunder** where they can."

"Joe Macy told me that vessels flying the British flag have been sighted off the coast a dozen times during the past month."

"That is so, but they could not enter our harbor on the east wind that has been blowing. I shall go down into town to see what the tidings be."

William Jr. started to rise. "Nay," said his father, "stay with thy mother and sisters while I am gone. This may be a serious matter."

Without further words, William Rotch put on his broad-brimmed Quaker hat and strode down the street. Ahead of him groups of anxious and excited townspeople were rapidly moving toward the wharf. Many of the old sea captains had their spyglasses with them to better observe the **formidable** ship coming before the wind into the harbor. All her white sails were set, and a wicked array of guns were visible even to those watchers who had no spyglasses. At the masthead fluttered the British Union Jack, and the decks were crowded with gunners and sailors.

Old Asa Prindle offered his glass to William Rotch without comment. William looked through it at the tall ship as she came about, spilled the wind from her flapping sails, and prepared to anchor where her guns could best command the defenseless town. William saw a fine-looking officer directing the men on deck. The stiff wind carried another officer's voice across the water. He was giving orders to lower away a boat from the ship's side.

The crew scrambled into this boat, followed by the officer. After him came six men with side arms. Rowed by powerful strokes of the oars, the boat rapidly approached the wharf.

"No doubt of it now," said old Asa Prindle. "They've come for plunder."

"Suppose I talk with the commander on behalf of the town?" suggested William. "If I can get him to come to my house, it may be well. Our people have suffered so much loss on account of the war that someone might speak from his heart and anger our visitors into even worse measures than they are now considering."

"Our welfare is safer in thy hands, William, than in our own. Do as Christ leads thee, good neighbor."

"So say we all," agreed many voices from the crowd surrounding William and old Asa.

The ship's boat made for the lee side of the wharf. With a boat hook she was held to the tall piles of the dock while the rope was tied fast. Out jumped the officer and his men. William advanced to meet him with the friendly greeting a loved and long-expected visitor might receive.

"I am William Rotch who bids thee welcome to Nantucket, friend. What may thy name be?"

"Sir Conway-Etherege, in the King's service," replied the officer, stiffly.

"I invite thee to come to my house—and thy friends likewise," said William, regarding calmly the six men with two pistols apiece in their belts.

"My men will await their orders here," replied the officer.

Sir Conway-Etherege thought his way was smoothed before him by this friendly man, who was apparently loyal to the King of Britain. He walked off beside William along the pleasant street up to a row of large houses. William led his guest home and asked him to come in. It was nearly noon.

"I would like thee to take dinner with me," said William.

"Thank you, with pleasure."

William's wife was astonished to see her husband bringing in this unknown and dangerous guest to share their dinner. She gave hasty instructions to the children to ask no questions. Their eyes were shining with suppressed excitement when their father presented his guest, but they obeyed and asked nothing.

Then all sat down together to a homely, ample meal. William treated the commander as a friend and seemed to enjoy his conversation. The islanders had, as the officer knew, been cut off from the outside world by the war. The officer furnished the news of the day from the mainland. From time to time he looked at William **quizzically**, as if he did not quite know how to approach his errand, although it was first in both their minds.

Finally they rose from the table. Sir Conway-Etherege made Elizabeth Rotch a flowery speech of appreciation, and the children followed their mother from the room.

"I take it from your unusual courtesies to me that you are on the King's side, Mr. Rotch," said the officer. "Can you tell me how and where I can best begin my day's work? As you know, I command yon privateer, which has gone up and down the coast bent on plunder. We've been very successful too. Our guns fire on all the important structures and districts of a town before we begin to **negotiate**. As you see, your little hamlet is completely at our mercy. I expect no unpleasant resistance."

"There will be no resistance," said William.

"Then where do you advise me to begin? The afternoon is advancing."

William smiled.

"I don't know of a better place to begin than here in my house. I can better bear the loss than anyone else. We have a store of silver plate, serviceable blankets, also linens. In the cellar, we have supplies of food of various kinds. However, sir, thou art mistaken in supposing me to be on the side of anyone engaged in warfare."

Sir Conway-Etherege was greatly taken aback. He gazed at William with unconcealed curiosity. Never had he run across a man like this.

"Are there any more men like you on Nantucket?"

"There are many better men," answered William.

"Do you say so, indeed! I'd have to see them before I could believe it."

"Then come with me. I shall be glad to introduce some of our islanders to thee."

The officer followed William down the steps and out into the street. This was a new experience for the commander of the privateer; he did not know what to make of it.

William led him into a store. It was quiet, for the townspeople had little money for trade these days. Yet it had once done a large business and was spacious and well stocked.

William led the officer to the owner and introduced them.

"Our visitor wants to know what sort of people we are. I told him that last winter thou distributed four hundred barrels of flour among the poor on the island. And yet I doubt if I, or any man, knows the full extent of what thou hast done to help the needy."

Amazed at this generosity on the part of a man with his living to make, the officer entered into conversation with the storekeeper. The storekeeper told him of gifts of money that had found their way from William Rotch's pockets to households in distress, without anyone suspecting William of being the giver. At this, William hurried the officer out the door. Down toward the wharf they entered a store that sold dry goods.

"Good day, Peter," said William. "This officer from the ship in the harbor wishes to meet the man who gave away blankets, dress goods, and stout shoes last winter when the poor were in dire want."

"He might better turn around and meet thee, William. None of us has done what thou hast done. We only follow thy lead."

William's face was rosier than even the brisk west wind had made it. He led the officer out again into the street.

"My friends are modest," he said. "I can better afford to help others than they can. Dost thou care to meet more of our people?"

"Thank you, no. I find it hard to believe that there are three such men as you in the whole world. A street full of them would be too many. Thank you for your courtesy and forbearance. Farewell, my friend. I will not forget Nantucket."

With that the officer grasped William's hand and shook it heartily. He looked once again up the leafy, beautiful street and out toward the white-capped harbor, where his ship with its deadly guns lay threateningly at anchor.

Groups of men were still watching and talking on the wharf. The sailors and the armed bodyguard wondered what had delayed their commander so long. Ah, here he was coming at last! Well, the excitement of looting and plundering was worth waiting for.

As Sir Conway-Etherege came briskly toward them, they saluted. His orders were quick and short. The sailors took their places at the oars and rowed the officer back to his ship. The ship weighed anchor, trimmed her sails, and sailed quietly out of sight.

– Author Unknown

Thar She Blo-o-ows!

Nantucketers turn up in whaling yarns nearly as often as their whaling ships turned up everywhere in the seven seas. For the Quakers of Nantucket Island were the first Americans to try deep-sea whaling. Actually, Nantucket men began to make their living by **offshore** whaling, hunting whales from the shores of Nantucket Island, soon after they settled there in 1659 and 1660. In those early days, the Nantucket Quakers used long narrow rowboats called whaleboats to chase whales. In these little boats they rowed out from the beaches, just as the Indians had fished for whales from their canoes.

There were plenty of whales around Nantucket Island, and the "half-Quaker, half-sailor" Nantucketers probably would have been content to continue offshore whaling. But on a stormy day in 1712, a Nantucket whaleboat was blown out to sea. Christopher Hussey was the boat's captain. When Hussey finally made it back home to Nantucket, he was towing behind his boat the first sperm whale ever caught by an American. Deep-sea whale hunting had begun.

Quickly the men of Nantucket designed and built tough ships called blubber-hunters; and in less than three years these heavy,

---

deep-sea whalers were hunting whales in deep ocean waters. Each whaler carried several of the long narrow whaleboats on board. It was in these little whaleboats that the Quakers chased whales across the seas.

Whales, of course, are the largest of all animals. The biggest, the gigantic blue whale, grows up to 102 feet long and weighs over 390,000 pounds. At birth, a blue whale calf is 23 feet long and drinks 160 gallons of milk a day.

Whales come in two varieties: toothless and toothed. Almost all of the toothless whales come in the "large economy size." Instead of teeth, these whales have long rows of rough bone-like plates called baleen. The toothed whales, on the other hand, range in size from the monster sperm whale, which can sink a ship, to the porpoises of the dolphin family.

But toothed or toothless, whales are full of oil. Whales have layers and layers of blubber fat—up to a foot thick in some spots. Their flesh, their bones, even the whale's tears and the mother's milk are oily. The larger the whale, the more oil it yields. A single blue whale once yielded 3,050 gallons of oil. Until kerosene was discovered in 1852, most people burned whale oil in their lamps. That's why whalemen called it "black gold." During whaling's Golden Age, from 1825 to 1860, American whalers supplied both American and European lamps with most of their oil.

Barrels of black gold, however, were not the only products of the whaling industry. The gut[1] of sperm whales supplied *ambergris,* a substance which makes perfume last longer. Their huge heads yielded a golden wax, the best of all waxes for candle making. The huge toothless whales also provided baleen, once used to manufacture umbrellas and other items. Baleen is often called whalebone, but it is not really bone; it is flexible like your fingernails. It hangs

---

1 gut: intestines or insides

in hundreds of fringed strips, called plates, from the upper jaw of a toothless whale. Each plate is about a foot wide and may be over 10 feet long. The tiny sea creatures caught on the baleen become the whale's food.

By 1830, Nantucket was the third largest city in New England. It had become the chief whaling port of the entire world. Strangely enough, though Nantucketers had perfected whaling in the ocean deeps, it was deep-sea whaling that finally robbed Nantucket of its first place as a whale-fishing port. The early deep-sea whalers carried only one or two hundred tons of cargo. Before long, whalemen built ships that carried three and four hundred tons. Ships that large could not enter Nantucket's shallow harbor. So, by 1846, another Quaker town passed Nantucket as the world's whaling center. That town was New Bedford, Massachusetts.

The Nantucketers did not stop whaling though. Far from it! Those years were the Golden Age of whaling: 1825-1860. Seven hundred whaling ships were sailing from New England ports. These ships needed skilled captains and able crews. By 1857 New Bedford's fleet employed 12,000 sailors. Many a Nantucket boy "shipped" on his eleventh birthday and became an experienced captain before he was 20 years old.

At one time more than 70,000 Americans made their living from the whaling industry. Thousands of them worked on the ships. Thousands more worked ashore in shipyards and in candle and lamp factories. Many handled and stored oil. Some worked as clerks in shipping houses. Others provided salt pork and sea biscuits, sails, spars, rope, casks, and whaling irons for ships. James Durbee of New Bedford made and sold 58,517 **harpoons** between 1828 and 1868. And he was only one of New Bedford's ten makers of whaling tools. Christopher Hussey's sperm whale had certainly started something!

One toothless whale was always "just right" for whalemen. It traveled slowly, close to the ocean's surface. Its great body was loaded with oil, its enormous mouth filled with 100 pounds of whalebone. Whalemen named it the *right whale.* When oil and whalebone prices were high, a single large right whale was worth $12,000.

But not even a right whale could tumble a crew into their whaleboats as fast as the lookout's cry: "Thar she blo-o-ows, and sparm at that!" The sperm whale's huge head is almost a third of its size and may hold up to a ton of valuable golden oil. Exposed to the air, this oil hardens into a waxy mass. In the nineteenth century, this whale wax made the finest candles. Nantucket's candle factory alone turned out 380 tons of whale-wax candles every year.

Sperm whales provided more than wax. Imagine a captured sperm whale having a tummyache! After all, he eats one ton of clawing octopuses and squid each day. Some sperm whales have a lump of fatty grayish ambergris in their gut. Ambergris sells for as much as $20 an ounce. The *Watchman* of Nantucket once caught a whale that had an 800-pound mass of ambergris in its belly.

Sadly for whales, they are not fish. A whale's heart pumps warm blood, as yours does. Whales have lungs and nostrils. They must come up for air, or they will drown. When a whale comes up to breathe, his warm, wet breath rushes out of his whale-sized lungs through his nostril—"blowhole" to the whaleman. The whale's breath hits the cooler air. It expands and **condenses** into a geyser-like spout, which gives the whale away for miles around. On a calm day you can actually hear a spout from a mile away. To the whaleman, a whale's spout is its nametag. A high slender spout belongs to the rorqual whales, like the blue or minke. A short broad spout belongs to the humpback, a different kind of rorqual whale. These whales are quick divers. They were not worth chasing in the old days. But a slanting spout was another story. That belonged to a sperm whale.

Whatever the kind of whale, once a whaleboat caught up with its gigantic prey, anything could happen. Do you think whalemen enjoyed their old-fashioned "Nantucket sleighride" behind a harpooned whale? The little whaleboat was big enough to carry only six whalemen and their gear. Whales towed the little boats so fast that one sailor was always busy pouring water over the harpoon lines to keep them from burning as they spun out. Woe to the man who was careless enough to catch an arm in those lines!

A Nantucket sleighride might drag a boat several miles over the sea away from the whaleship. If the whale escaped, he carried away yards of stout rope and three or four harpoons. One time a whale drew out 10,440 yards—nearly six miles—of rope before he was caught!

Older whalemen taught young sailors a simple but sobering rule: "Beware the right whale's flukes (tail) and the sperm whale's jaw." A right whale's flukes can shear off the whole front end of a whaleboat. Several times a right whale has splintered three whaleboats to bits with one slap of its massive tail. A sperm whale uses its flukes as a sledgehammer too, but it also uses its massive head as a battering ram. Its jaws snip like scissors on a whaleboat and its crew. And those jaws measure up to fourteen-and-a-half feet deep—over half the length of a whaleboat.

Sperm whales have even sunk a few whaling ships. The *Essex* of Nantucket and the *Ann Alexander* and the *Kathleen* of New Bedford were sunk by sperm whales. After the *Ann Alexander* went down, another New Bedford ship caught the whale that sank her. The sailors found pieces of ship timber stuck in the whale's head and harpoons from the *Ann Alexander* lodged in its body.

Sailors who served aboard graceful, fast-sailing merchant ships thought whalers were clumsy-looking craft. "Built by the mile and chopped off in lengths to suit," they said scornfully. But 35 or 40 men lived on a whaler for two to seven years at a time. To them it was "a sight more comfortin'" to have a ship designed for safety rather than speed. Year after year the whalers safely weathered the worst storms the world's oceans could offer.

Where whales led, whalers followed. They made many discoveries. Nantucket whaleman Timothy Folger charted the Gulf Stream. American whalemen named more than 400 islands in the Pacific Ocean. In fact, it was difficult to make a discovery ahead of Yankee whalers. One foggy day in 1821 two Russian ships claimed an island in the ocean off Antarctica. As the fog cleared, the Russians were startled to see a Connecticut whaler already at anchor between their ships. The little whaler was the famous *Hero,* its captain 21-year-old Nathaniel Palmer. He had just come from finding the Antarctic Peninsula. For years that peninsula was named Palmer Peninsula.

That Golden Age of whaling is long since gone. American whalers no longer sail the seven seas. Yet even today, if you walk the quiet streets of Nantucket or New Bedford, you will see houses built by the whales' black gold. A whaling museum in Nantucket's former candle factory houses old whaling irons, line tubs, sea chests, charts, and whaleboats. There you can see "scrimshaw," the carvings on whalebone that whalemen made on their long voyages.

In Mystic, Connecticut, you can climb aboard the *Charles W. Morgan,* the only remaining wooden whaler. Bring your imagination with you. Can you feel the rolling swells of the Pacific Ocean under her keel? Watch the dancing flames of the ship's furnace light up the ship's **rigging** far above your head. Clouds of oily, foul-smelling smoke rise skyward. Smell the sheets of whale blubber boiling and see the deck beneath your feet grow black with whale grease. To you it is a *squantum,* the old Nantucket word for a picnic! For you are a whaleman, and oil is what you've shipped to find.

– *Edith Dorian and W. N. Wilson*

220

Whales and Stewardship

When God created whales and other large marine animals, He deemed them "very good." He told Adam to rule over these animals and the other things He had made—making humans the caretakers of His good work. How well have humans fulfilled their responsibility?

In 1930 and 1931, whalers in Antarctica killed 30,000 great blue whales, and the survival of the largest animal on earth was threatened. In 1967, countries around the world agreed to protect this whale, but their number is still very low. Scientists estimate that fewer than 10,000 blue whales are left in the world's oceans. In spite of signs that blue whales are successfully having young, they think it will be at least 100 years before blue whales are safe from the danger of extinction.

Another whale in danger is the right whale. Because it is a slow swimmer and feeds on top of the water, it is easy prey for hunters. Right whales also yield huge quantities of oil and baleen, so whalers have killed them in large numbers over the last century. Even though right whales have been protected since 1936, they are very rare today.

In recent years the number of sperm whales has dropped too. Male sperm whales once numbered over 170,000; now there are fewer than 71,000. This whale's protective instinct makes it an easy target. When one is injured, members of its herd gather around. Whalers learned to injure one sperm whale and wait for the others, so they could kill them too.

We know little about the way whales help balance ocean life. Killing whales may affect other animals. For example, blue whales eat millions of tons of plankton. Plankton plays an important role in manufacturing oxygen. If it grows out of control, the earth may have too much oxygen. Or plankton could foul ocean waters, affecting other sea animals.

There is much we do not know about the balances God has created. God has given us many things for our use and enjoyment. We should use them wisely so that we do not destroy them.

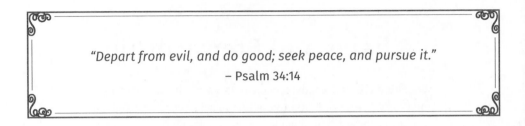

> *"Depart from evil, and do good; seek peace, and pursue it."*
> – Psalm 34:14

The Quakers of Nantucket

Michel Guillaume Jean de Crèvecoeur[1] was born in France in 1735. When he was twenty, he sailed to Canada to serve in the French army. Four years as a soldier convinced Crèvecoeur that war was wrong, so he left the army and moved to New York City. Once there, Crèvecoeur changed his name to J. Hector St. John.

Crèvecoeur found work as a surveyor in America, but he really wanted to be a farmer. In 1769 he married Mehetable Tippet, and they bought a little farm in Orange, New York. Crèvecoeur wrote a book called Letters From an American Farmer. *The imaginary farmer in Crèvecoeur's book tells about life in early America. He writes about farming and the manners of Americans, about life on the frontier and the mistreatment of American Indians.*

Crèvecoeur had long admired the Quakers because they kept peace with all men. He devoted several chapters in his book to describing life and the whaling industry on the Quaker island of Nantucket. Here is a selection adapted from his description of the Nantucket Quakers. It was written during the days when Nantucket was America's most important whaling port.

Nantucket Island was not founded on bloodshed, as so many other settlements have been. It began out of necessity and good will. The Nantucket Friends (Quakers) practice **nonresistance**, justice, good will to all, kindness at home, sobriety, meekness, love of order, and

---

1 Crèvecoeur (krev kər')

fondness for work. They despise the thought of wasting the fruits of their labor on vain luxuries.

At school, the children learn to read and write until they are twelve years old. Then they are made apprentices as coopers.[2] By fourteen they are sent to sea, where they learn navigation. They master the great and useful art of working a ship in all the different situations which the sea and wind require.

The first founders of Nantucket began their whaling career with a single whaleboat, which they used to fish for cod. They fished at a small distance from the shore. Their success at cod fishing led them to think that they might be able to catch whales too, since many whales swam in the waters around Nantucket Island. After many trials and failures, they succeeded.

In the middle of their island, they put up a mast. From this high station, a man was assigned to look carefully toward the sea and watch for spouting whales. As soon as any were discovered, the signal was given and a whaleboat was launched.

It may seem strange to you that so slender a boat, containing only six little men, should dare to chase and to attack the largest strongest animal in the sea! But by long practice these people have become superior to any other whalemen. They know the temper of the whale, and they seldom fail to harpoon their whale and bring the huge leviathan[3] onto the shores.

– J. Hector St. John

---

2 cooper: a person who makes and repairs wooden barrels and tubs
3 leviathan: large sea creature; in this case, the whale

> *"See now that I, even I, am he, and there is no god with me: I kill, and I make alive; I wound, and I heal: neither is there any that can deliver out of my hand." – Deuteronomy 32:39*

I Treated Him;
God Healed Him

Professors in medical schools in the sixteenth century seldom performed surgery. Barbers, not doctors, performed minor operations, pulled teeth, and treated cuts. Barbers who gained skill in closing wounds were called barber-surgeons. The stripes of a barber pole still show the red for blood and the white of bandages.

The greatest of the barber-surgeons was Ambroise Paré.[1] Ambroise Paré was born in a country town in France in 1510. Born into a poor family, he received only a merchant's education, which did not include Latin and Greek, the languages used by scholars and doctors. But his parents did teach Paré about the love of God. Throughout his life he retained the simple humility that is characteristic of all true Christians.

He grew up to be a barber's assistant—the lowest rung on the ladder to becoming a full-fledged doctor. As time passed, Ambroise grew more and more interested in the medical side of his barber profession. In 1529, at the age of nineteen, he took a big step. He decided to become a real doctor.

"The best medical schools are in Paris," Ambroise told his parents. "I'll study there."

1 Ambroise Paré (am broiz pa rä')

But the medical schools in Paris turned him away because he couldn't pass their entrance tests. He had the medical ability, but professors gave the examinations in Latin and Greek, languages Ambroise could neither read nor write. He was intensely disappointed. But he had come to Paris to study medicine, and his spirit refused to be broken by rejection. He found a position as a barber-surgeon at the Hotel of God.

The Hotel of God was a charity[2] hospital, the oldest hospital in the world, and very primitive. The building was dirty, poorly lighted, and damp. Charcoal fires burned in copper pans on the floor to heat it during winter. Sometimes a professor would bring his medical students to the wards and lecture them about the cases there. Students wrinkled their noses at the foul smells and fled from the place as soon as the lectures ended. It was much more pleasant to treat wealthy patients in their homes.

But Ambroise Paré gained a tremendous amount of practical experience in the Hotel of God. He discovered that many of the "facts" the professors taught their students were wrong. Everything Paré learned came to him firsthand.

Three years later France went to war, and Paré was hired as a surgeon. During the war, he gained more experience.

Doctors of Paré's day taught that powder burns from gunshot wounds were poisonous. "Such wounds will prove **fatal** unless treated at once," they declared. But the treatment was a brutal one: they poured boiling oil into the wound to drive out the poison. This terrible **remedy** was horribly painful.

Paré followed this standard remedy until the day a fearful battle broke out. Many men fell from gunshot wounds, and Paré ran out of oil. But he had to treat the wounds somehow. Without much hope, he made a salve of egg yolk, oil of roses, and turpentine. He dressed the

---

wounds in the soothing ointment. Throughout the night he worried about the men. He expected the patients not treated with boiling oil to die of the "powder burn poison," and he hardly slept during the night.

The next morning he made the rounds. To his great relief, the men who had received the soothing ointment were still alive. He discovered, with surprise, that they had rested far more comfortably than those treated with boiling oil. They were doing well and feeling little pain.

"But," he reported, "those treated with boiling oil ran a high fever. Their wounds were hot, swollen, and sharply painful."

It wasn't acceptable medical practice, but—

"Never again," Paré said, "will I so cruelly burn wounded men."

This set him thinking about other ways to relieve pain. Hippocrates,[3] the Greek physician, had taught that doctors should avoid harsh remedies. It was better to do nothing than to take drastic action. But many surgeons failed to remember that they were working on human beings. They cut away without regard for the pain they caused. Paré felt otherwise. "The foundation of medicine must be love," he said.

Paré's most horrible duty as a surgeon involved cutting off arms or legs. After an amputation, doctors seared the stump with a white-hot iron. Otherwise the unfortunate victim would bleed to death. Often soldiers endured the amputation only to die from shock when Paré applied the hot iron.

Wasn't there a less painful way to stop the bleeding?

Finally Paré hit upon a simple, almost painless, solution. He put a spool of silk thread in his medical kit. The test came late one night when a stray bullet shattered a soldier's leg. Paré had no choice but to remove the leg—it was shattered beyond repair. Unless he took

3 Hippocrates (hi pä′ krə tēz′)

immediate action, infection would set in, the limb would fester, and the man would die.

Those were the days before painkillers. An amputation had to be done quickly. A surgeon's skill was judged by his speed. Paré made his cut and sawed through the bone in only three minutes. The soldier endured the amputation fully awake. At the end of the operation, Paré's assistant handed him the hot iron.

"Not this time," Paré said. He passed it back and from his medical bag took the silk thread. Working rapidly, Paré tied off the blood vessels. Bleeding stopped. As simple as that! The patient lived.

When other soldiers heard of the successful surgery, they made Paré their hero. They loved the young surgeon who spared them so much pain. Soldiers were very poorly paid, but they filled a helmet with silver and gold coins to thank him.

But Paré remained humble. He said, "I treated him, but God healed him."

Paré continued to experiment with new ways of healing. His methods saved thousands of soldiers who would have been left for dead on the battlefield.

In Paris, however, doctors resented Ambroise Paré's success. To think, he sewed cuts with needle and thread like a common house-wife mending a tear in cloth. A piece of thread did the work of a white-hot iron! One doctor warned, "To tie the vessels after amputa-tion is a new remedy. Therefore, it should not be used."

Paré decided to write about his medical discoveries. By this time he had learned Latin, but he chose to write in French so common barber-surgeons could read his book. Rather than quoting ancient authorities (as the professors of his day did in their books), Paré packed his book with practical surgical advice. He never tried to use big words to sound more important.

As important as Paré's book was, he couldn't get it published. Doctors in the medical schools resented his fame. They were the experts, they believed, and Paré only a backward barber. An old law was found that said no medical book could be published unless a committee of doctors from the medical schools of Paris approved it. The law was used against Paré.

And so four years passed before Paré got the approval to publish his book. When finally it was published, it sold out immediately. Barbers—and doctors too—clamored for copies. The publisher reprinted it four times within a few years. It was translated into Latin and several other languages, including English.

Some people expressed surprise that he shared his knowledge so freely. After all, his fame and livelihood came from the medical facts he put to work each day. But Paré answered, "The light of a candle will not diminish, no matter how many may come to light their torches by it."

Later Paré met a man named Vesalius[4] in Paris and learned of his study of the human body. Paré translated parts of Vesalius's books from Latin into French. That way other barber-surgeons would have a guide to the human body.

Paré did not have a **formal** education. He never earned a medical degree. Yet he became France's most skillful surgeon. In 1562 he was given the dignified title of First Surgeon of the King.

Today, this humble barber-surgeon is considered to be the founder of modern surgery. He replaced worthless **speculation** in surgery with practical experience. He wrote and translated books about medicine into the language of the common people. His discovery that blood vessels could be tied off to prevent bleeding marked the beginning of modern surgery.

---

4 Vesalius (və sā′ lē əs)

After his death, the people of France raised a statue in Paré's honor. Carved on it are six simple words: *I treated him; God healed him.*

– John Hudson Tiner

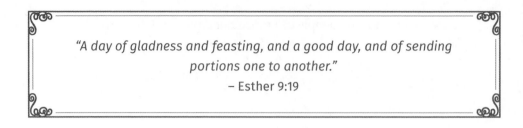

> *"A day of gladness and feasting, and a good day, and of sending portions one to another."*
> – Esther 9:19

Going to Market

The Sabbath[1] begins Friday evening at dusk, and for two days before, Mama was busy with her preparations. On Fridays she cleaned, cooked, and baked. On Thursdays she shopped. Sabbath meals had to be the best of the whole week, so it was most important that she shop carefully. Every Thursday afternoon, Mama went to Riverside Street market, where prices were lower than in her neighborhood stores.

Usually she left Gertie in Papa's care and set off right after lunch. This Thursday Mama was late. The children would soon be home from school, so Mama decided that it would be nice if, for once, shopping for the Sabbath could be a family affair.

"Who wants to come to market with me?" she asked the children as soon as they came trooping in.

"I do! I do!" Everybody wanted to go along.

"Oh! Hasn't anybody any other plans for this afternoon?" asked Mama.

"Nothing as exciting as going to market!" Ella declared, and her sisters all agreed.

But what about Gertie? It was a long walk for little feet.

Gertie spoke up as if she knew what Mama was thinking. "Oh,

---

1 The Sabbath is the Jewish day of rest and worship. It falls on Saturday.

Mama," she pleaded, "me too!"

Mama wasn't going to disappoint her. "All right, but I think it would be a good idea to take the baby carriage along."

"Baby carriage!" Gertie was indignant. "I'm too big for a baby carriage!"

"Of course you are," Mama assured her, "but the carriage will come in handy for all the bundles, and if you should happen to get too tired to keep on walking, why, we can have the bundles move over and make room for a very nice little girl. Now hurry, everybody. Into your hats and coats."

The children danced along, sometimes beside, sometimes just behind Mama. That is, all except Henny. She kept racing ahead and dashing back again, like a small impatient puppy. Already their ears were filled with the shrill cries of street **hawkers**. Already they could smell the good smells, and in another minute, they were themselves part of the crowd.

"Just look at the pushcarts!" exclaimed Sarah.

Heaped high with **merchandise**, they stretched in endless lines up and down the main street and in and out the side streets. They were edged up close to the curb and wedged together so tightly that one could not cross anywhere except at the corners. The pushcart peddlers, usually bearded men in long overcoats or old women in heavy sweaters and shawls, outdid each other in their loud cries to the passersby. All promised bargains—bargains in everything—in fruits and vegetables, crockery, shoelaces, buttons, and other notions, in aprons, in soap and soap powders, and hundreds of other things.

There were stores in which you could buy fish, and stores that carried only dairy products. There were bakeries and meat shops, shoe stores and clothing stores. In delicatessen[2] shops, fat "specials"

---

2 delicatessen (de' li kə te' sən): a store that sells ready-cooked-meats, cheeses, and sandwiches

(frankfurters) hung on hooks driven into the walls. Big chunks of "knubble" wurst (garlic sausage) were laid out in neat rows on white trays bearing the sign "A Nickel a Schtickel" (a nickel for a piece). The counters overflowed with heaps of smoked whitefish and carp and large slabs of smoked red salmon. If one wished, firm plump salt herrings were fished out of barrels for inspection before buying.

But it was not enough that the merchandise sold behind the closed shop doors should be displayed in showcase windows and store-fronts. The shop owners had to come out in the open too. They built stands which they either used themselves or rented out to others. Almost anything could be bought at these stands. There were pickle

stands, where the delicious odor of sour pickles mingled with the smell of sauerkraut and pickled tomatoes and watermelon rind. There were stands where only cereal products were sold—oats, peas, beans, rice, and barley—all from open sacks. At other stands, sugar and salt were scooped out of large barrels and weighed to order. Here coffee was bought in the bean, for every household had its own wooden coffee grinder.

Whenever there was a bit of space too small for a regular stand, one could be sure to find the old pretzel woman. Her wrinkled face was almost hidden inside the woolen kerchief bound around her head. Her old hands trembled as they wrapped up the thick chewy pretzels.

The sidewalks were choked with people. It was not easy for Mama

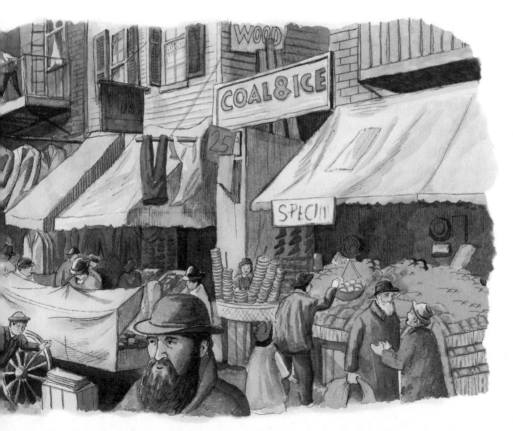

to push the carriage through the narrow aisles left between the pushcarts and stands. The children followed behind in twos, and whenever Mama stopped either to buy or look, they stopped too.

"Say, Gertie," Charlotte cried out, "how would you like a necklace like that?" She pointed to the garlic peddler who was coming toward them. No need for a store, a stand, or a pushcart for this peddler. With a basketful of garlic on one arm and a spicy necklace of the same looped around his neck, he was all set for business.

The dried mushroom peddlers did business in the same way, except that, as Charlotte laughingly said, "They were better dressed." They wore long heavy mushroom bracelets about their arms as well as necklaces.

How sharply the shoppers hunted for bargains! And what bargains, if one could believe the peddlers. How carefully every article was examined to make sure it was perfect! It always was, according to the shopkeepers. How the buyers **haggled** over the price of everything. And how the peddlers proclaimed that the price of anything was the lowest at which they could afford to part with it! But above and through all the noise and confusion, ran a feeling of great good nature and cheery contentment.

Only one tongue was spoken here—Yiddish! It was like a foreign land right in the midst of America. In this foreign land, it was Mama's children who were foreigners, since they alone spoke in an alien tongue—English.

At the next corner, Henny bought a fat juicy sour pickle with her after-lunch penny. She ate it greedily, with noise and gusto, while her sisters watched, their mouths watering. "Selfish! How about giving us a taste, huh?"

Henny pretended that she didn't hear them, but before the pickle was half gone, she stopped teasing and gave them each a bite.

Inside Mama's favorite fish store the smell was not so pleasing. "Gertie," suggested Charlotte, "let's squeeze our noses tight and talk to each other while we're squeezing."

And that's just what they did, talking about anything at all just so they could hear the funny sounds which came through their squeezed noses. "Look at the big fish with goggly eyes," said Gertie.

"I hope Mama is not getting any live fish this week," Charlotte said. "I like to see them swimming around in the bathtub, but I don't like it when Papa cleans them afterward."

But Mama was not getting any live fish this time, only pieces of several

Yiddish

The Yiddish language was first spoken by European Jews hundreds of years ago. Many of their descendants, both in Europe and America, still speak it today.

Yiddish is made up of several other languages—Hebrew-Aramaic and German, with some French, Italian, and Slavic elements.

When millions of European Jews immigrated to the United States in the early 1900s, they brought Yiddish with them. The English language changed Yiddish somewhat, but Yiddish also changed the English language. Many Yiddish words are common in English today.

bagel: a hard, doughnut-shaped roll

chutzpah: great self-confidence, pushiness

schnozzle: nose

schlock: cheap, low quality

schnorrer: a beggar, one who wheedles someone into doing something for him different kinds of fish: whitefish, yellow pike, and winter carp—that meant gefüllte fish (stuffed fish) for the Sabbath. Yum, yum!

"I wish Mama would hurry up," said Gertie. "I can smell the fish right through my squeezed nose. And I do want to buy something for my penny, don't you?"

"Yes, and no fish!"

Out on the street again, the air seemed sharper and colder. Some of the peddlers had been standing in their places since early morning. They stamped their feet and slapped their arms across their chests, trying to warm their chilled bones. But the sweet potato man did not mind the cold. Why should he when he had his nice hot street oven to push before him? When Ella caught sight of him, she said at once, "Just the thing for a cold day."

The sweet potato man stopped before her and pulled open one of the drawers of his oven. There arose on the air such a delicious smell that Ella smacked her lips expectantly. Inside she saw the plump sweet potatoes in their gray jackets. Some were cut open in halves, and their rich color gave promise of great sweetness. For her penny,

Ella got a large half and as she bit into it, she wondered why sweet potatoes baked at home never tasted half so good. When she rejoined the family, four other mouths helped to make short work of that potato.

The chicken market was the next stopping place. It was smelly and noisy with the squawking of fowl. The children gathered about the crates and watched the roosters sticking their long necks through the slats. Mama donned an apron she had brought with her and began to pluck the fowl she selected.

After Mama finished her plucking, the chicken was wrapped up and added to the other bundles in the shopping bag. The family continued on its way.

Gertie turned to Charlotte. "What'll we buy with our pennies?" The answer to that question was just then coming along the street. Candied slices of tangerine and candied grapes mounted on sticks lay in rows on white trays. The peddler stopped when he heard Gertie's delighted cry. "Penny a stick, little darlings," he said. Charlotte chose grape, and Gertie took tangerine. Thus two more pennies were spent.

"I'm almost through," Mama told them, but still Sarah's penny lay warm and snug in her coat pocket. "Aren't you going to spend your penny?" the children asked her. They couldn't be sure because Sarah was saving all her pennies these days—for a book.

But today was something special. She had shared in the goodies her sisters had bought. It would only be fair for her to return their generosity. But what could she get?

"Arbis! Shaynicke, guttinke arbislach! Keuf meine heise arbis!" (Chickpeas! Fine, nice chickpeas! Buy my hot chickpeas!)

The hot-chickpea peddler was singing the words over and over in a funny Yiddish chant as he rolled a small white oven along the streets. Before Mama could stop her, mischievous Henny gave the carriage a big push so that it rolled away from under Mama's hands.

She stooped over it as if she were pushing a great weight and began to chant in imitation:

"Arbis! Shaynicke, guttinke arbislach!"

The children roared with laughter. Even Mama could not hide a smile while she ordered Henny to stop. "Leave her alone, lady," the peddler told Mama. "She's helping me in mine business."

Because he was so good-natured, Sarah decided to give her penny to him. Everyone watched as he fished out the peas. First he took a small square of white paper from a little compartment on one side of the oven. He twirled the paper about his fingers to form the shape of a cone and then skillfully twisted the pointed end so that the container would not fall apart. He lifted the wagon cover on one side, revealing a large white enamel pot. The steam from the pot blew its hot breath in the little girls' faces, so they stepped back a bit while the peas were ladled out with a big soup spoon. The peddler dropped the wagon cover back into place and handed over the paper cup to Sarah. The peas were spicy with pepper and salt, and how good they were! They warmed up the children's tummies and made them very thirsty.

With the purchase of a pound of pumpernickel bread, the shopping tour came to an end. They left behind the life and activity of the market and started the weary walk home. By now the children were tired. Gertie uttered not a single word of protest when Mama lifted her up and put her into the carriage together with the bundles. The others wished they were young enough to join her.

– *Sydney Taylor*

Varifrån Kommer Språken?[1]

allí confundió Jehová el lenguaje de toda la tierra

1 And the whole earth was of one language, and of one speech.

2 And it came to pass, as they journeyed from the east, that they found a plain in the land of Shinar; and they dwelt there.

3 And they said one to another, Go to, let us make brick, and burn them thoroughly. And they had brick for stone, and slime had they for **mortar**.

4 And they said, Go to, let us build us a city and a tower, whose top may reach unto heaven; and let us make us a name, lest we be scattered abroad upon the face of the whole earth.

5 And the LORD came down to see the city and the tower, which the children of men builded.

c'est là que l'Éternel confondit le langage de toute la terre

der HERR daselbst verwirrt hatte aller Länder Sprache

the Lord did there confound the language of all the earth

---

1 Varifrån Kommer Språken? (ver' ē frön köm' ər sprö' kən) Swedish: *Where do languages come from?* The å does not have the ō sound exactly; it is somewhat like the *o* in *ore*. The *r*'s should be rolled slightly.

239

Urah -lk
tpvhwhy
llb

⁶ And the Lᴏʀᴅ said, Behold, the people is
one, and they have all one language; and
this they begin to do: and now nothing
will be restrained from them, which they
have imagined to do.

⁷ Go to, let us go down, and there **confound** their language, that they may not
understand one another's speech.

⁸ So the Lᴏʀᴅ scattered them abroad from
thence upon the face of all the earth: and
they left off to build the city.

⁹ Therefore is the name of it called Babel;
because the Lᴏʀᴅ did there confound
the language of all the earth: and from
thence did the Lᴏʀᴅ scatter them abroad
upon the face of all the earth.

– Genesis 11:1-9

εκει
συνεξεεν
κυριοσ
τα χειλη
πασησ τησ
γησ

A Jingle of Words

Don't you love the common words
    In usage all the time;
Words that paint a masterpiece,
    Words that beat a rhyme,
Words that sing a melody,
    Words that leap and run,
Words that sway a multitude,
    Or stir the heart of one?

Don't you love the lively words—
    Flicker, leap, and flash,
Tumble, stumble, pitch, and toss,
    Dive and dart and dash,
Scramble, pirouette, and prance,
    Hurtle, hurdle, fling,
Waddle, toddle, trot, and dance,
    Soar and snatch and swing?

Don't you love the lengthy words—
    Subterranean,
Artificial, propagate,
    Neapolitan,
Revelation, elevate,
    Ambidextrous,
Undenominational,
    Simultaneous?

Don't you love the noisy words—
    Clatter, pop, and bang,
Scrape and creak and snarl and snort,
    Crash and clash and clang,
Crackle, cackle, yowl, and yap,
    Snicker, snare, and sneeze,
Screech and bellow, slash and howl,
    Whistle, whine, and wheeze?

Don't you love the colorful—
    Amber, rose, and gold,
Orchid, orange, and cerise,
    Crimson, emerald,
Purple, plum, and lavender,
    Peach and Prussian blue,
Turquoise matrix, jade and jet,
    Hazel, honeydew?

Yes, with just the common words
    In usage everywhere
You can capture incidents
    Beautiful and rare.
In words you have a weapon
    More mighty than a gun;
You can sway the multitude
    Or stir the heart of one.

– Betty Scott Stam

Words

Words are things,
    and a small drop of ink,
Falling like dew upon
    a thought, produces
That which makes thousands,
    perhaps millions, think.

– George Gordon,
    Lord Byron

A Word

A word is dead
When it is said,
  Some say.

I say it just
Begins to live
  That day.

– Emily Dickinson

Responsibility

Myself

I have to live with myself, and so
I want to be fit for myself to know;
I want to be able, as days go by,
Always to look myself straight in the eye;
I don't want to stand with the setting sun,
And hate myself for the things I've done.

I never can hide myself from me;
I see what others may never see;
I know what others may never know;
I never can fool myself—and so,
Whatever happens, I want to be
Self-respecting and conscience free.

– Edgar A. Guest

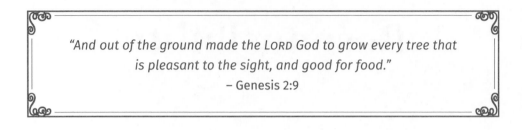

In the Sugar Bush

Part 1

"Yes, of course you can try doing the sugaring," his father said in answer to Peter's question, "but I doubt if I can give you any help."

"I'd like to see how much I can do on my own."

"Don't neglect your other work."

"I won't, I promise. I've done the hens already this morning, so I could leave right after breakfast and go up to the sugar bush on my way to school."

His father looked pleased. So often he had to remind Peter to feed the hens. "That's going a long way around to school."

"But it's quicker than the road for skis," Peter said eagerly. "There's enough snow in the fields to give me a fine run all the way down to the valley."

Father pushed back his chair from the table. Peter started to carry the dishes to the sink.

"I'll take care of everything here," Father said. "You'd best get on your way now."

A smile broke across Peter's face. "Can't I help you?"

"Not now. Not here. Perhaps later."

Peter let out a shout of joy and bent over to lace his boots. He buttoned his coat and pulled his cap down over his ears. At the door he turned back to face his father.

"How soon will we hear from Mother?"

"There may be a letter today."

"Father?"

"Yes?"

"Do you think Uncle Leonard will get better?"

Father nodded. "If he held on to life until your mother got there, she'll nurse him back to health all right."

Peter looked relieved. "Good-bye, Father."

"Good-bye, son."

Every morning that week Peter went to the sugar bush before he went to school. The slim half hour, sliced in between chores and school, counted for valuable preparation toward the work he wanted to do.

The grove of sugar maples stood in the woods a quarter of an hour's walk from the house. Most of the trees were of great age, with huge high crowns and furrowed, shaggy bark, but among them were seedlings and saplings and **robust** young trees. In a clearing stood a small sugar house, its roof swayed by the years that had passed over it and the snows it had borne. Its slab sides had withstood many a tempest roaring through the forest. Heavy snows had piled against them, and summer suns, filtering through the grove, had dried and silvered the wood.

Inside the sugar house was a big evaporator[1] and a storage tank that held the sap and let it into the evaporator by gravity. Against one wall stood an old iron stove that was used for cooking meals or for boiling down the sap when the flow was not heavy. This stove Peter intended to use. Working alone, he would not be able to handle the evaporator and the endless appetite for wood of the fire beneath it.

---

1 evaporator: a long shallow pan for boiling sap. As the sap boils, water evaporates, leaving pure maple syrup behind.

The first day he cleaned the spigots and buckets and set them in readiness on top of the storage tank. The next day he cleaned the stove and repaired the pipe so it would be ready and safe for the hot fire he would have in it. The day after that he sawed and split wood, stacking it in convenient piles. All the time he checked on his equipment and tried to remember every step of the work that his mother had done when he had been with her.

After school Thursday Peter walked up the road with his skis over his shoulder, until he came to the farm lane where the mailbox stood. As he opened it eagerly, its emptiness yawned at him. He tried to tell himself that they could not hope for a letter every day, and yesterday had brought the good news that Uncle Leonard would get better.

At the house, Peter thrust his skis into a snowbank near the door and went out to the barn to give the hens their afternoon feed of grain. He took a basket with him for the eggs. When Peter went to the nests to gather eggs, he turned back reproachfully to the flock. "Only three from the dozen of you!"

The hens cocked their heads and watched him as he placed the eggs in the basket he had brought with him.

"Sap's rising," Peter informed them. "Maybe that will make you feel you ought to get busy and start laying more eggs." He left the hen pen with that encouragement. The hens followed him to the door, then stood in a silent group after he went out. They looked at each other, stretching out their necks and flapping their wings. Then they went solemnly back and scratched among the shavings on the floor, searching for kernels of corn that might have eluded them.

The next morning Peter ate his breakfast quickly and prepared to leave for the sugar house as soon as he had done his chores. Shep looked longingly at him.

"No, Shep, not today," Peter said, stroking her gently.

Reluctantly the dog went back to her place behind the stove.

The sun had not long been risen from behind the mountains. Its light was brilliant across the snow, and its rays were strong and heartening. Widespread in the air was a feeling that everything in nature was reaching out and up to the warmth and brilliance.

"Sap should flow today," Father said as he stood in the doorway and watched Peter adjust the clamps on his skis.

"I plan to tap as many trees as I can," Peter said. He stood up and reached for his ski poles, then thrust them into the snow.

His father watched the boy push off across the flattened snow near the house.

"Bye," Peter shouted, waving one of his ski poles. Then, leaning to the contour of the land, he let the skis give him swift passage across the fields and up the slope toward the woods.

Once at the maple grove, Peter exchanged skis for the snowshoes he kept in the sugar house. Going from tree to tree with his brace and bit,[2] spigots and buckets, he worked fast to make best use of the edge of time that he had.

Bending over on the snow by one

2 brace and bit: A *brace* is a crank-shaped tool that turns a bit, used for drilling holes by hand.

249

of the big trees, he bored a hole in the trunk, careful not to get near a hole made the previous year but keeping the level the same, a good four feet from the ground. It was hard work. Slowly the curled shavings of maple fell onto the snow. When Peter felt that he had gone about two and a half inches into the tree, he cleaned out the hole and drove a spigot into it. Then he attached a bucket to the hook under the spigot, fixed the lid securely in place, and went on to drill another hole. He hung two buckets on every tree, and before the hour he had allowed himself was gone, he had thirty buckets out.

In spigot after spigot the sap gathered slowly, then one drop after another slid down into the buckets. *Drip, drop. Drip, drop.* Before Peter left the grove, a **gratifying** symphony resounded in his ears and echoed through the stillness of the woods.

The sun felt warmer already, and the snow was softening noticeably. The sap had a gentle but steady flow. Given a day, the buckets might have a fair quantity in them before Peter returned to the grove. Peter stooped over the last spigot and, lifting the bucket away, knelt down on the snow and pressed his lips to the spigot, sucking the sap as it came from the tree. It was like clear cool water with a touch of sweetening.

Peter unbuckled his snowshoes and hung them in the sugar house, then clamped on his skis and took up the poles. With one last look around the grove at the buckets hanging expectantly, with one last cocking of his ears to catch the sound of the sap dripping slowly into them, Peter turned and sped on his way through the woods and down across the open fields into the valley. He was fleet and sure, though almost **giddy** with delight at the thing he had started in the maple grove.

At school, the boys and girls were bubbling over with talk of what they were going to do during their week's vacation. At recess it was the main topic of discussion. Some were going away to visit friends or cousins. Many of them would be helping their parents on their farms. As most of the work just then was sugaring, a good deal of time would be spent in the different maple orchards up and down the valley.

Randy's father had a big maple orchard, a team of oxen for the sap gathering, and enough help to keep the boiling going day and night. Randy was proud of the part he played yearly in the sugaring, and he announced confidently that this year his father expected to make all of five hundred gallons of syrup.

"Everything's in our favor so far," he said. Then he turned to Peter. "What are you going to do this week?"

"Sugaring, just like you."

"Is your father going to help?"

"No, he hasn't got time this year."

"How are you going to do it then?"

"By myself."

Randy whistled. Some of the girls looked admiringly at Peter, while one or two of the boys stared at him in open-mouthed astonishment.

"You won't get through very much alone," Randy announced in a superior way.

"Maybe I'll boil down more than you think," Peter replied, feeling jaunty before his friends.

"When are you starting?" Randy asked.

"Starting?" Peter grinned. "I've started. Got things going this morning. Sap's running just as nice as you please into the buckets I set out."

Randy whistled again. "Spry is your middle name," he said; then he clapped Peter on the shoulder. "I'm coming up someday to test your product."

"Come along!"

Mary said, "Maybe we'll all come to taste your syrup, Peter."

"If you do," Peter warned, "I'll find work for every one of you."

They laughed. Some said they wouldn't come, for work wasn't what vacation was for; but there was not one who didn't envy Peter the adventure before him. Master of his own sugar grove! Any boy in the school would have been willing to change places with him, and not a few of the girls.

The bell rang, and they trooped back to the schoolhouse. No one carried his head higher than Peter, and so full of plans was it that he found it hard to keep his mind on his books.

That night, after they had eaten the last of the food Mother had left for them, Peter told his father that he would like to spend the whole next day at the sugar bush.

"All right," his father said. "You've got the weather with you, Peter. That sunset tonight means another day just like this—warm sun as long as it's in the sky and a drop below freezing at nightfall."

"Can't you come up sometime during the day?" Peter asked hopefully.

Father shook his head. "I'm going over to Green Mead Farm to look at a bull. That's a day's journey."

"Will you be back for the milking?"

"Yes, I'll be back in time for that. You won't need to leave your work until you've finished for the day."

Peter started up the stairs. Halfway up he paused. "Father?"

Father looked up from his farm paper.

"Couldn't I take Shep with me?"

"No, she's too near her time," Father said; then he shook his head. "I'm afraid you've set yourself a lonely task."

Peter went on up the stairs, and Father returned to his paper.

Shep got up from her place back of the stove. She looked over at Father, but no word or flicking finger demanded anything of her, so she went quietly up the stairs. Before Peter's closed door she raised a paw and drew it softly down the wood.

Peter heard the faint familiar sound and opened the door.

Shep went into the room. She wagged her plumy tail, then sat down on her haunches and pushed her forepaws along the floor until she could rest her nose on them. Peter sat on the floor beside her and put his arms around her, burying his head in her long coat. She rubbed her nose against him. Shep was lonely too.

– Elizabeth Yates

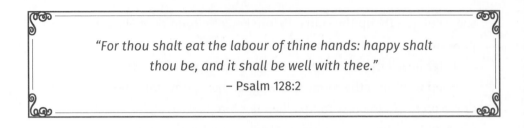

In the Sugar Bush

Part 2

Peter left early the next morning, long before the sun was up, though light was in the sky. He tied his muffler tight around his neck and pulled down the earflaps on his cap. It was as cold as any winter morning, yet the cold was only a reminder of the strength of winter. Spring was in the air. Peter went swiftly on his skis over the crusty surface of the snow, down the pasture slope, across the frozen brook, and up the road into the woods.

A white snowshoe hare darted out from a tree stump, looked with interest at Peter; then wheeled, snapped his hind feet on the hard crust, and disappeared into the woods. Standing still and leaning on his ski poles, Peter looked back at the country he had put behind him. Breathing deep breaths of the frosty air that caught in his throat, he felt like shouting with joy. This was sugar weather: a cold, cold night and a cloudless morning washed with the pale white light of dawn.

The day was crystal clear, and the whole countryside white with its snow covering. The distant mountains stood out like robust walls protecting the valley that stretched away to the east and the south. Peter could see clusters of houses, and here and there a farmstead with smoke coming from a chimney. The light was intensifying behind the mountains. He watched the sun rise in lonely splendor—

tingeing the far hills with rose before the east glowed golden, spreading over the sky, touching the earth.

"Hello, sun!" Peter shouted, feeling that he must speak to someone.

Behind him in the woods, pheasants were calling. Nearby on a branch rang out the **exultant** note of a chickadee. Winging across the valley came a small flock of grosbeaks with their curious undulating flight. They alighted in a tree that had some frozen apples still hanging from its boughs. Soon they would have their fill of seeds if they could get through the wrinkled skins of the fruit. Peter took one look back at his father's farm and saw blue smoke curling from the chimney of the house, hanging for a moment in the cold air, then moving straight up to lose itself in deeper blue. It was like a hand waving, and he waved back to it.

Up at the sugar house Peter got a roaring fire going in the stove. Then he buckled on his snowshoes and went around to the trees to visit his buckets. Some had more in them than others, but all were half full in any case and solid with ice. Two by two, Peter carried them back to the sugar house. He stood them near the warmth of the stove until the ice loosened and was ready to come out; then he tipped the frozen sap into the big boiling pan. The fire soon melted it, and before Peter had brought the last bucket back to the stove, the contents of the pan were already simmering.

Now before him lay the whole stretch of time his father had warned him about. Beyond a few small chores, there was nothing for him to do for hours and hours but **stoke** the fire and wait. It was indeed a lonely task he had set himself.

Peter stood in the warm sunshine in the open doorway of the sugar house. Outside in the grove he could hear the occasional tinkle as a drop of sap gathered in a spigot and fell into a bucket. Behind him was the deep rumbling of the sap as it boiled in the pan. Clouds of steam rose from the pan. The sweet steam developed more and more maple fragrance as time went on. Scum rose to the surface, and Peter skimmed it off. Stirring the sap, he saw with satisfaction that an hour's hard boiling had reduced the level by an inch.

After he had split and stacked some wood for future fires, he cooked his lunch, drawing on a store of supplies he had brought previously to the sugar house. He sat outside on an upturned sap bucket and ate his **leisurely** meal.

Warmed by the sun, he soon took off his coat. The air that had little but silence in it during the colder part of the morning now came alive with the movement of birds. A nuthatch scurried up the trunk of a maple; a downy woodpecker drilled one small hole and then another. Two red squirrels played tag with each other on a maple branch high above the ground. Every now and then they called a halt in their game to cling to the limb and nibble on the sweet icicles formed by chilling winds on flowing sap. Sometimes they sucked a run of sap from a crack in the bark; and often, finding no convenient crack, they slit one for themselves. Peter stretched back in the sun against a tree trunk, waited, and watched.

The clouds of steam were denser when next he went in to stoke the fire. He tasted the boiling sap.

It had more than sweetness to it now; it had flavor—maple flavor.

He made the round of buckets, emptying some of the full ones into the storage container in the sugar house. Now, long past noon, the sun had begun to lose its warmth. The sap stopped flowing into the buckets, for the cold was drawing it down to the roots again. However, the sap in the pan had reached the point where it had to be closely watched. It had boiled down to within a few inches of the bottom. Peter remembered that from then on his mother would never leave it. A moment too long could darken the whole batch.

Peter tasted and tested, pouring some on the snow to see how it hardened. Plunging the thermometer in for certainty, Peter felt sure that it was safe to take the pan off the stove. He poured the syrup through a sieve lined with two thicknesses of flannel and waited while the slow stream came through into the jar he had prepared to hold it.

Peter capped the jar and held it to the light. The syrup was so clear that he could see through it and the color a shade darker than honey. The first sap ever made into syrup with his own hands! A pint boiled down from some twenty gallons of sap!

Wrapping the jar in a newspaper, he stowed it carefully in his rucksack. He melted snow in the big pan on the stove and washed it and his other utensils. He shuttered the windows and closed the door behind him. Outside, he put on his skis, hoisted the rucksack over his shoulders, and smiled as he felt the warmth of the jar of maple syrup against his back.

It was dusky in the woods as he made his way through them, and it seemed good to get into the open fields where daylight still lingered. The snow was hard and crusty, and his skis sang with speed as they cut their way. Never had he gone more exultantly than with the jar containing his first syrup on his back, yet never had he gone more carefully. For all his love of swiftness he would not risk a fall.

At the end of the field he crossed the brook and started up the pasture to his father's farm. If Father had gotten back from Green Mead Farm in good time, he might have supper ready. Peter smiled at the thought. It would be good to talk to someone again. He had not uttered a word all day except in some brief conversation with a woods animal. His ears had in them almost no other sound than the dripping of sap and its rumbling boil.

The snow cracked under his skis. Night closed in about him. It was good to see the lights of the house streaming over the snow to meet him, and he was glad that there was still a little warmth in the jar on his back.

Things were humming in the kitchen. There was a pot of coffee on the stove and a frying pan with bacon sizzling in it. Father, with one of Mother's aprons tied around him and a cookbook open before him, stood by the table mixing something in a bowl.

"You're late," he said.

"It took longer than I thought it would," Peter replied. He bent over to take the jar from the rucksack. "Here's the day's work," he said as he placed it on the table.

His father held it up to the light, turning it round and round, looking at it. "It seems all right," he murmured, "but we can't tell much until we taste it."

"What are you making?" Peter peered into the bowl.

"Pancake batter. Pancakes to go under your syrup. Hungry?"

"I'm as hungry as a horse," Peter answered.

– Elizabeth Yates

258

The Pasture

I'm going out to clean the pasture spring;
I'll only stop to rake the leaves away
(And wait to watch the water clear, I may);
I shan't be gone long.—You come too.

I'm going out to fetch the little calf
That's standing by the mother. It's so young
It totters when she licks it with her tongue.
I shan't be gone long.—You come too.

– Robert Frost

259

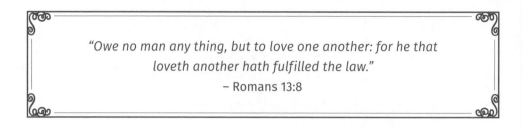

The Meaning of the Word

"R-e-s-p-o-n-s-i-b-i-l-i-t-y," Jakob spelled slowly, his blue eyes
closed tight so he wouldn't see the dictionary page before him. It was
a mouthful of a word all right, and there wasn't much chance the
teacher would get up to anything that size. Still, you never could tell;
when there were only two or three left in a spelling match, she was
apt to jump clean out of the sixth-grade book into words stout enough
to knock you down.

"Jakey!" Mrs. Vanderberg called. "Your supper's getting cold."

Jakob's brows drew together in a frown as black as he could
manage. "Ma, will ya quit callin' me that? You have the fellows doin'
it now. Jaaay-keeee!"

"Ah now, you're still my little boy yet awhile!" His mother laughed,
ruffling his straight fair hair. "Come, so many words you know now
you'll spell down the teacher herself."

"Well, I better," Jakob muttered. Only by some amazing feat
like that could he hope to erase the laughter that followed him now
around the schoolyard. "Oh, Jaaay-keeee, have you mowed down any
haystacks today?"

It had happened way back in early fall, but though now it was
mid-November, nobody had forgotten. Not the fellows, nor his
brother, nor his father.

Ever since Jakob's tenth birthday, he had pestered his father to let him drive the tractor. When a boy wrote his age in two figures, he was practically grown-up, wasn't he? Why, there wasn't another farm-boy his size in the whole county who couldn't run every piece of equipment on his place!

"Too young yet, Jakey," his father kept saying. And even when Jakob's eleventh birthday came and went, "Being grown-up is not something you measure with years."

It just didn't make sense to Jakob. He kept pestering and pouting till at last this fall Pa showed him the workings of the tractor and let him make his first trial run. Boy, that was a day! Jakob felt like a king up there on the high tractor seat. He couldn't keep still about it. All over the house and all over school next day, he bragged about the way he'd handled that little old machine.

Still, he wasn't so crazy about tractor driving that he would add it to his chores. He stayed on at school afternoons, playing ball when he knew Pa and Dirk were starting fall plowing and would have given him a turn at it. But he always got out to the fields by dusk to beg to drive the tractor back to the farmyard. Usually either Pa or Dirk was so saddle-sore by that time that he welcomed the chance to walk and let Jakob take the tractor in.

It was such an evening when half a dozen boys from Jakob's school came bicycling past the Vanderberg farm just as Jakob was driving the tractor down the lane inside the fence. Jakob was drifting along in low gear, keeping well behind the cows that were **moseying** toward the barn, when he heard the whistles and yells from the road.

"Hey-yay, ride 'em, cowboy! Rope that steer!"

Jakob had yelled at them and waved in return. Sitting up a bit straighter, he'd shifted to a higher gear and closed in on the cows. A frisky heifer near the rear got nervous about the buzzing on her tail and pranced out of line. Jakob just couldn't resist the opportunity to show off. In a fine sweeping arc, he swung out of the lane to herd the heifer back into line. The startled cows broke into a clumsy trot and came mooing into the farmyard like a stampede. Nimbly, Jakob circled them, swinging the tractor this way and that.

And then—he made the mistake of taking a peek out at the road to see how it was going over with the boys. Just five seconds of not watching where he was going, and—pow! Something hit him like a bale of mattresses falling off a hundred beds. He'd run smack into the old haystack! Bundles of hay came rolling down on his head and shoulders. Hay got in his mouth and up his nose. Hay packed so solidly around his arms he couldn't reach the tractor controls and shift into reverse. He couldn't yell; he couldn't breathe. He just kept on grinding deeper and deeper into the dusty, scratchy, solid heap until—

Whoof! In a cloud of dust and floating hay, he burst out the other side! Ma was pounding the big triangle[1] in the yard, and Pa and Dirk were coming on the run, and the boys in the road were laughing so

1 triangle: a metal bar bent in the shape of a triangle. Hitting it makes a bell-like sound.

hard they had to lean against each other for support.

That was the last tractor driving Jakob had done. He guessed it was the last he'd ever get to do till he was an old man with a white beard. Pa had made him fork the hay back into its pile all by himself. But that wasn't half as bad as going to school the next day. Jakob's ears burned, just remembering what the boys had said. He'd never live that business down till he did something to make headlines a different way.

Like winning this spelling match, maybe—beating Arie Huibregest who was nearly always the last one up.

Well, he couldn't be any more ready for him, Jakob guessed, closing the dictionary with a big sigh. Words floated in the air around him. When he closed his eyes, words bombarded his eyelids.

In the twilight outside the window, he could see Pa coming slowly up from the cornfield. Corn was the Vanderberg money crop. Pa had planted eighty acres of it this year; then everything had held it back—a wet spring, cold summer, the slow-drying bottomland on which it grew. Not until late August had there been real corn weather with bright sunshiny days, and nights so hot you could fairly hear the leaves rustle as the corn grew higher. Now Pa was worried that it wouldn't dry enough before winter storms struck. The neighbors had all finished harvesting last week, but Pa's corn was slower. It looked plenty dry to Jakob, its long rows golden and rustling, its dry leaves whispering, whispering, like waves washing against a shore. But Pa wasn't quite yet satisfied. Harvest when it was too moist, and it would spoil in the crib; they couldn't have that happen.

Jakob staggered to his numb feet and went out to the big warm kitchen where supper was spread. Dirk was already putting away his second helping of sauerkraut and hot dogs while his eyes ran down the open book beside his plate.

"Books! Books! I never thought to raise such a pair of bookworms!"

Ma scolded, but with pride in her voice. Dirk was in his second year of high school and captain of the debate team. Jakob knew Dirk had a debate coming tomorrow, from the pile of library books on the chair beside him. Dirk tackled school like he tackled farm work, slowly and steadily and thoroughly.

"Hi, Jakey," he said absently.

Jakob opened his mouth to protest and then shut it hastily. Next to Pa, Dirk was the top man around here; even Ma treated him with respect. *How did he get that way?* Jakob wondered with envy. With only a four-year head start on Jakob himself?

"Pa is out looking at the clouds again," Ma said worriedly. "All day it's either the clouds or the weather map."

"There's a blizzard up in Minnesota," said Dirk. "We're sure to get it."

"Ah, not with the corn still in the field!" Ma gave a little anxious sigh and turned back to the stove.

Both boys knew what she was thinking. The big heavy ears of corn were good as gold to meet bills, to make the payment on the mortgage, to buy the new furnace—but not while they hung in the field. If a blizzard came before they could be picked, the stalks would be blanketed with new moisture, and it might well be spring before the field was again ready to pick.

Pa came in the back door, shutting it with firm decision. "Tomorrow we harvest," he said flatly. "The corn is ready, and it is foolish to take any more chance on the weather. We will start with daylight."

"Tomorrow?" yelped Jakob, bouncing upright in his chair. "I can't miss school tomorrow. There's the spelling match!"

Pa looked at him with stern disapproval. "Dirk is all the man I need."

"But Dirk's got a de—" Jakob broke off, silenced by the anger in his brother's glare. Well, all right, he was just trying to help Dirk out! A debate team wasn't much good without its captain, but if Dirk didn't care—

Why was everybody down on him all at once? Pa frowning, Dirk glaring, even Ma looking kind of sad. Jakob gobbled his supper and hiked up to his room. Families sure could be funny sometimes.

When Jakob finally reappeared for breakfast, Pa and Dirk were already in the field. The air was frosty cold and crisp, the sky clear. Huh, thought Jakob, no sign of the blizzard that had caused so much commotion; Dirk could just as well not have missed his debate.

Jakob ate steadily through his usual breakfast of pancakes and sausage and homemade preserves and milk and applesauce, skipped as many chores as he dared, and was ready for the two-mile walk to the country school by eight o'clock. Might as well get started, Jakob figured; there was a bigger dictionary at school, maybe he could brush up on a few more words before the match.

"Responsibility." He tried out his memory on one of yesterday's mouth-fillers. "R-e-s-p-o-n-s-i-b-i-l-i-t-y." Yep, he still remembered it.

Jakob lingered on the doorstep, looking toward the field where the cornpicker had just come to a stop. Dirk was waiting to unhitch the loaded wagon of corn from the picker and hitch it onto the other tractor. Now he started off, rumbledy-bounce, to tow it to the crib. He'd have 25 minutes to back it between the tall legs of the derrick,[2] upend the wagon-box, start the elevator running to carry the corn to the crib, empty the wagon, and have it back at the field before Pa filled another one.

But Pa hadn't started down the next row of corn. He was driving his tractor lickity-bump up to the barnyard. Low on gas, Jakob guessed. Now he'd leaped off and was dragging out the hose from the gas-storage tank.

---

2 derrick: a tower or framework for lifting or lowering heavy things

"Hey, Pa!" called Jakob, remembering the first lesson he himself had been taught about the tractor. "Pa, you didn't turn off your engine!"

Faster than the words, it happened. One second there was Pa holding the nozzle over the funnel, and the next second the flames were rearing up in a red curtain, shutting him off. Gas had sloshed over the hot machine and exploded into fire.

Jakob's legs weighed a ton apiece. It took him seven years to move a step. He had confused glimpses of Dirk running, running from the crib . . . of Pa's hands reaching through the flames, shutting off the ignition . . . of Ma passing him like a tornado wind with a blanket snatched up from the back porch.

Then, as suddenly as it had started, it was over. The last sparks hissed and sizzled down the trail of gasoline drops from the hose that Pa had flung far behind him. Dirk was off to the house for a pail of cold water and some soft cloths, and Ma was examining Pa's burned arms.

Jakob couldn't look. He felt shriveled and small with the pain that was hurting Pa. And he couldn't do anything, not anything. Quiet, soft-spoken Ma had become a commanding general, taking prompt, efficient charge. She backed the old sedan from the garage . . . why, Jakob hadn't even known she could drive! . . . and was helping Pa to the seat beside her.

"Best to run you right in to the hospital," she said firmly. And to the boys, "He'll be all right. Don't fret."

Dirk stepped close to the car. "We'll stick by the corn, Pa," he said, his voice steady and confident. "We'll get it okay. Won't we, Jake?"

Jakob gulped. Warmth crept back into the tight ball of his stomach. He looked at Dirk with gratitude. Jake! And something he could do for Pa after all.

"Sure," Jakob said shakily. "Sure, we'll make out fine, Pa."

He saw Pa's eyes shining back at them, warmly, proudly, as Ma swished down the drive.

"Let's get going, Jake," Dirk said briskly. "I'll take the cornpicker. You handle the tractor. Okay?"

The tractor? Dirk was giving him the tractor without even a crack about keeping the straw out of his hair? Say, Dirk was a good brother! Jakob would show him he was to be trusted.

Driving as carefully as if he were handling a baby carriage, Jakob chugged back to the cornfield. Dirk was still filling the second wagon, the picker stripping off the heavy ears and flinging them onto the moving belt of the elevator that swooshed them upward into the high-sided wagon.

"Ought to run 140 bushels an acre," Dirk said, unhooking the wagon and putting the empty one in its place. He sounded just as though he was talking to Pa.

"Yeah," agreed Jakob, striving to be equally man-to-man. "Sure looks good."

He towed the wagon to the derrick, backed it between the legs without even a bump. Proudly he fastened the derrick hook to the wagonbed, cranked it up, and started the golden flow up the elevator and raining into the crib. Why, this was man's work he was doing, Jakob thought. This was grown-upness. This was what went with the name of Jake.

Far off, the school bell tinkled. It jerked Jakob back to remembrance of the spelling match for which he'd prepared so hard. Disappointment hit him so keenly it hurt. Then he shrugged it off. Helping his family was more important than winning a spelling match.

As the morning hours dragged on, Jakob's glow wore off, and plain aching tiredness took its place. The sun climbed higher and burned the back of his neck. The derrick handle turned harder and harder. Never were hitches so **cantankerous** to handle as those connecting wagon and tractor. Jakob's rumbling stomach reminded him that lunch hour had come and brought nothing but continued work. Why hadn't Ma come back from the hospital? Was Pa worse? On the cornpicker, Dirk was more and more silent, smiling briefly as he unhooked a loaded wagon, saying nothing.

Occasionally Dirk glanced at the sky. Jakob looked too, but there was nothing to see but a dab of cloud on the horizon that he could cover with his hand.

Back and forth. Hitch on, unload, bounce back to the field. One load every 25 minutes. How small a square of corn lay stripped compared to all that waited. Jakob gave a big tired sigh and looked at the cloud again. He put his hand against it, and the cloud mushroomed all around it.

"Hey, Dirk!" Jakob called uneasily. "It's getting bigger!"

Dirk didn't ask him what he meant. He'd been watching too. "Be here by dark," he said briefly.

Jakob looked at the untouched acres of corn. "Dirk, we can't finish it!" he cried.

"Nope," Dirk answered, not stopping. "But we'll get all we can."

Doggedly, Jakob settled down to help, bending his sore shoulders over the derrick handle, cranking faster, hustling between the elevator and the tractor, jouncing, jolting between field and crib. It was a losing battle, and he was ready to cry with weariness, but he couldn't quit. Every extra ear of corn **garnered** in counted a lot.

Suddenly, he straightened and stared unbelievingly at the road. What kind of parade was that coming along? It was a long crawling worm with giraffe heads shooting up every few feet! It wobbled and swayed and curved right up to the Vanderberg gate!

At the edge of the field, Dirk gave a great shout and halted the picker. "Jake, they're coming to help us—all the neighbors! Look at 'em! Seven, eight, nine cornpickers! More than two dozen tractors and wagons!" Dirk's voice choked up. He dropped off the picker and gave Jakob a big hug. "We've got it licked, Jake! We'll beat the blizzard!"

There were tears in his eyes, and tears rolling down Jakob's cheeks, and neither boy cared who saw them.

The parade came churning up around them. Mr. Huibregest rode the lead picker, and Mr. Vellinga the second, and all the other neighbors for miles around followed behind them.

"We heard about your pa's accident," Mr. Huibregest said. "We thought maybe we could help out a little; the sky doesn't look so good, does it?" He gazed out over the harvested acres. "You boys do this much already? You've really been working!"

"Jake here helped fine," Dirk said. "Well as a man."

"I can see that." Mr. Huibregest nodded. He gave Jakob a keen glance. "Guess there's enough of us to handle the unloading now. Why don't you get yourself a breath, Jake? You've done a man's job today."

Gratefully, Jakob staggered toward the back steps while nine cornpickers, and Dirk's the tenth, slashed into the waiting rows of corn with a mighty roar. Jakob felt a big lump welling in his throat at the sight. Let the cloud grow now, let the blizzard come . . . the corn would be harvested before dark!

A man's job. That's what he'd done. For six weary hours, he'd been grown-up, and he'd found out what it meant. Not a thing more or less than that long word he'd mastered yesterday: r-e-s-p-o-n-s-i-b-i-l-i-t-y. He'd missed the spelling match and Dirk his debate, because they felt responsible for their family. All these men had left their own work because they felt responsible for their neighbors. Why, Pa was right! Grown-upness isn't measured by years; it's measured by the number of people you feel obligated to help!

The old sedan rumbled into the driveway, and Ma hopped out, her face tired but shining. "Pa's fine!" she called happily to Jakob. "I stayed till he was over the shock and resting easy. They'll let him come home in no time. And oh, Jakey, the neighbors came, didn't they? Bless them. They'll want coffee and such; I'll go fix it."

She bustled off, and Jakob was left with his mouth open, his protest at the baby name unspoken. Because suddenly he didn't mind it; he even liked it a little. It proved he still had time to work up gradually on this big and sobering business of grown-upness.

Cautiously, he stretched his aching back and flexed his arms. Hey, why didn't he head for the couch, with a couple of apples to crunch on and a good book to read? Nobody could say he hadn't earned a rest.

But his eyes went from Dirk still in the field to his mother hurrying to the kitchen and her neglected tasks, and he sighed a little. It was plain to Jakob that once you get a big word like *responsibility* into your heart, you couldn't ever quite shake it loose again.

"Ma," Jakob called, trailing her into the kitchen. "Is there anything you want me to do?"

– Mildred Geiger Gilbertson

The Runaway

Once when the snow of the year was beginning to fall,
We stopped by a mountain pasture to say, "Whose colt?"
A little Morgan had one forefoot on the wall,
The other curled at his breast. He dipped his head
And snorted at us. And then he had to bolt.
We heard the miniature thunder where he fled,
And we saw him, or thought we saw him, dim and grey
Like a shadow against the curtain of falling flakes.
"I think the little fellow's afraid of the snow.
He isn't winter-broken. It isn't play
With the little fellow at all. He's running away.
I doubt if even his mother could tell him, 'Sakes,
It's only weather.' He'd think she didn't know!
Where is his mother? He can't be out alone."
And now he comes again with a clatter of stone,
And mounts the wall again with whited eyes
And all his tail that isn't hair up straight.
He shudders his coat as if to throw off flies.
"Whoever it is that leaves him out so late,
When other creatures have gone to stall and bin,
Ought to be told to come and take him in."

– Robert Frost

Hunting Graybeard

When I was a boy in Natal, South Africa, the farmers of the district organized a hunt each year, using a hundred native beaters who roused the game with their dogs. A variety of wildlife finds refuge in our valley—monkeys, baboons, deer, and an occasional leopard. But the creature most sought after is the wily gray bushbuck.[1] With his speed and cunning, his savage fierceness when wounded or cornered, he is a quarry worthy of any hunter's gun.

There was one buck we called Graybeard, a magnificent old-timer who year after year survived the hunt. I was ten years old when I had my first glimpse of him, stepping proudly across a small clearing. His horns were long and sharp. His fur was a deep gray speckled with white. Every hunter desired to kill him, and from that day I could think of little else. I somehow felt that my initiation into manhood would consist of claiming Graybeard for my own.

My father had insisted that I wait until I was 14 before I could go hunting. The next three years I spent in a fever of anxiety, fearful that some other hunter would shoot my buck. But Graybeard survived. Once he followed silently behind a younger buck and, as it fell under a blast of shot, he jumped the clearing with one

---

1 bushbuck: a small striped African antelope

272

bound before the hunter could reload. Once he used a pair of does, protected by law from hunters, to shield him as he dashed safely past the line of fire.

The third year the hunters chose their gun stations between the cliffs and the river so cunningly that it seemed as if no game could slip through. After the native beaters scattered into the bush, I heard their excited cries as they sighted Graybeard. I had perched myself on the cliffs, and from my vantage point I watched him run from their dogs straight toward the concealed hunters.

Then he suddenly turned. Scattering the pursuing dogs, he made straight for the line of beaters, who hurled their spears and knobbed throwing sticks at him. Just as I feared he had been struck down, I heard the yelping dogs pursuing him into the bush behind the beaters, and I realized that he had broken through to safety.

That evening the farmers could talk of nothing except how Graybeard had escaped into the bush for another year. Boasts were made regarding the hunter who would claim him in the next year's drive. I smiled, for next year I would be old enough to take my place in the line of guns.

All through that year I **cherished** one bright vision—the picture of myself, a skinny boy of 14, standing astride the magnificent creature which so many hunters had tried unsuccessfully to kill. When my father offered me my first shotgun, I rejected the light 20-gauge which would have suited my frail build and chose instead a heavy 12-gauge, so that I could have a weapon worthy of Graybeard.

On the day of the hunt, I wanted to rush straight to the valley at dawn, but my father forced me to eat breakfast. "Graybeard will still be there," he said, pushing me down into my chair.

In the gray light of early morning, we **congregated** in the valley. The beaters were **dispatched** to the top end, and we hunters drew lots for positions. The best positions were close to the cliffs, because bushbucks tend to climb in their efforts to escape the pursuing dogs. To my disappointment I drew a position down near the river.

Then I heard my father, who had drawn a good stand, say, "I'll change with my boy. I'd like him to have a good place for his first hunt." As he walked past, he patted me on the shoulder. "See that you get the old one," he whispered with a smile.

I scrambled up the steep slope, determined to outdistance the others and find the best possible place to hide. I selected an outcrop of broken boulders, well screened by bush, which gave me a line of fire across a small clearing between me and the cliff.

For a long while there was no sound. Then came the shouts of the beaters, the sound of sticks beaten against the trees, and the yelping of dogs.

First came a doe, blundering past me in panic-stricken flight, then a young buck. I let him pass. Graybeard might be following, and I was determined not to **betray** my position. But there was no further movement, and I wondered if Graybeard had crossed lower down, or perhaps even fallen to one of the shots I'd heard below me.

Then a trembling of the bush caught my eye.

Not ten yards from me, Graybeard stepped to the edge of the trees, silently inspecting the clearing before attempting to cross. I had only to lower the muzzle slightly to cover him. The ambition of my youth was near. Graybeard stood motionless before me. I had only to crook my finger in the trigger to bring him down.

Yet something made me hold my fire. The buck had turned his head and his great ears twitched to catch the baying of the dogs. His moist nose trembled and his eyes, softly luminous,[2] alert without being fearful, seemed to stare right at me.

There was pride and dignity in every line of his body, and I knew suddenly that I could not destroy him. For several breathless

---

2 luminous: shining, glowing

moments he remained where he was, and then the breeze carried my man-smell to him. In two huge leaps he crossed the clearing and was gone. I stayed where I was, filled with delight.

When the drive was over, my father came up the slope. I unloaded my gun and pushed the shells back into the loops on my belt. My father's quick eye took in the details of the stand I had occupied and the full belt of cartridges.

"No luck?" he inquired.

I shook my head.

"That's funny," he said. "The boys sighted Graybeard coming in this direction, and none of the other hunters saw him."

My silence must have aroused his suspicions, for he walked across the clearing and paused beside the deep prints the buck had made in the moist earth as he jumped. I walked away, unable to face the **condemnation** that I imagined on my father's face.

As we drove home, the thought of old Graybeard gathering his does together for another year of safety gave me a thrill of pleasure. But my father's continued silence made the journey strained.

Finally he said, "What happened, son?"

Shyly, stumblingly, I tried to tell him. I described Graybeard as I had seen him—majestic and fearless. I tried to explain why, when the moment had come to fire, I knew I could not buy the hunter's badge at the price of so much splendor.

My father was silent for a moment; then he said slowly: "You've learned something today, son—something that many men live a lifetime without knowing."

– Robin Collins

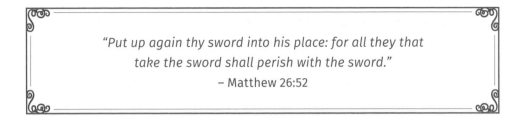

> *"Put up again thy sword into his place: for all they that take the sword shall perish with the sword."*
> – Matthew 26:52

Henry's Own Story

No rain had fallen for about twelve days, and dust dulled the roadside grass to the same gray color as the fence rails. Everything was gray—even the cows lying in the shade of a sugar maple seemed to be shades of gray, rather than red and white.

I had to hustle to keep up with Philipp. He's my next oldest brother, seven years older, and his legs are a lot longer than mine. Plus, I think, he was anxious to get this over with.

We came into a patch of deep shade, and my feet were happy for the coolness of the dirt.

"What do you think they'll do, Philipp?" I asked.

"I don't know, Henry," he said, but he smiled at me anyway.

Philipp's always smiling, and his hazel eyes always sparkle— sometimes with a question and sometimes with a laugh—but they're always alert and honest. That's what people say about Philipp Martin, but I just know he's the best brother you could ever hope to have.

Even though he's older than I am, Philipp often takes me on walks in the woods and tells me stories. He especially loves the stories from the *Martyrs Mirror,* which Father reads to us almost every evening now. But Philipp reads them on his own too. And when we walk in the woods, he tells me the stories he's read.

"The martyrs are the true heroes, Henry," he says. "Just listen to this story about Martin, the painter of Swabia—who knows, Henry, if maybe he wasn't our ancestor!" Then Philipp tells me one of the stories. He knows dozens of them.

But this day he didn't talk. His eyes were fixed straight ahead. I swallowed dryly and hoped we would cross the creek again soon. My legs ached, and my feet were hot. I'm used to walking, all right, but not quite this much.

We had started out before sunup walking from home, going to work with a building crew in the cool of the morning. Many of the men from our church had volunteered to help Morgan Edwards, the Baptist preacher, raise his house. Not that we're Baptists—folks call us Menonists—but we like to be good neighbors. Father says one good *earthly* thing you can do is to help a man build a house for his family. So, even though Father and the older boys had to repair the gristmill today, he sent Philipp and me to help build the house.

The raising went well. Preacher Edwards had already laid the foundation, cut the straight logs, and dragged them down to the building site. We made good time before noon, everyone working smoothly together, each man doing his own job but keeping a rhythm with his neighbor. Everything was going well—until Michael Smyser rode up, that is.

Mr. Smyser is the owner of the Stoneybrook tavern. He's also captain of the local militia, a group of men who train to fight the British soldiers of King George. Well, that's where the trouble came in. Mr. Smyser started talking about fighting the king.

"Edwards," he said to the Baptist preacher, "Jesus never forbade a man to defend himself. I ask you, did the Apostle Peter order Cornelius, the Roman centurion, to quit his soldiering? No! Now, King George is the wickedest brute ever made a king of England—we must defend ourselves against his attacks. In fact, if it comes to war, *we* will be fighting for a *holy* cause!"

Morgan Edwards could see that the men who were helping him raise his new house were feeling a little uneasy. He tried to interrupt Smyser—but Smyser has a reputation for talking fast.

"The first great rule of life," he went on, "is self-preservation! What would come of a nation if every man—" and I thought I saw him look our way—"if every man cowered before **tyrants** the likes of George? Some ignorant fools are saying it's not right to fight! If you and I took that position—why, there would not be a single man left in these thirteen colonies for King George to tax!"

This time Smyser *did* look our way. His cheeks and neck were splotched red. We all wished for a polite way to excuse ourselves, while Mr. Edwards coughed nervously and tried again to interrupt Smyser.

Finally Smyser got around to the reason he'd called at Preacher Edwards' place. He turned full on us: "Every man among you is required to **muster** with the local militia. No more special favors! If you don't turn out . . . well, I wouldn't want to say what is going to happen."

That's when Philipp spoke up. "Mr. Smyser," he said respectfully, but with confidence, "we will never take up arms to harm a man whom God has made in His own image. Jesus said, 'Put up again thy sword into his place: for all they that take the sword shall perish with the sword.' Men will soon repent of all this mustering and war-making."

I never again want to see a man as furious as Michael Smyser looked just then. His face heaved into a terrible scowl, and no one knew what he was going to do. But quickly Jacob Danner stepped forward and said something—I couldn't hear him—quickly but quietly to Mr. Smyser, and Smyser spun around, mounted his horse, and charged off. I sighed in relief, but the men started saying that wasn't the end of the matter.

Mr. Smyser was riding into York to make a complaint about Philipp to the Committee of Observation—the men in charge of the militia. So the noon meal was somber and the conversation sober. Preacher Edwards did most of the talking.

"Life will be different now, friends," he said. "Since last month's battle in Massachusetts, people are beginning to take a harder view of the king. I went down to Philadelphia last week, and people there are nearly in a frenzy. Even some of the Quakers are mustering! They march through the streets, drilling and firing their muskets.[1] They shout threats about King George. And last week one of Philadelphia's leading doctors spoke out against mustering, and a mob seized him. They coated the poor man with tar and feathers, paraded him through the city in a miller's cart, and then drove him out of town!"

As I listened, I remembered the night when we first heard the news about Lexington and Concord. Father had listened to a neighbor tell the story of the battle, and then spoke quietly to us: "War brings a kind of madness, children. People become angry and frightened. Some men can think only about revenge—paying back evil with the greatest evil they can."

Then Father had eased the huge *Martyrs Mirror* down from its shelf. He had read stories of the martyrs to us again and reminded us of their lesson: "The followers of Jesus do not return evil for evil, not even to save their own lives. As for us, life may be harder for a while. Many of our neighbors will find it difficult to understand why we will not take up arms against King George.

"I read a notice in the village today that said that Pennsylvanians must 'furnish themselves with war-like weapons' and 'learn the art of war.' But how can we practice taking up arms? We cannot harm a man whom God has made in His own image! No, 'all they that take the sword shall perish with the sword.' "

---

1 musket: a gun with a long barrel that was smooth inside. It was loaded from the front of the gun and fired by a piece of flint striking against steel, which ignited the powder.

So, you see where Philipp got those words!

Well, back to Michael Smyser. He hadn't wasted any time. Soon after we finished our noon meal, he returned. He said one thing: "Philipp Martin—get walking! You're to appear before the York Committee of Observation immediately!" And then he rode off, leaving us to walk three miles to York in the heat of the day.

Some of the others would have come along, but Morgan Edwards warned against it: "If the lad goes alone, nothing will come of it. If the committee has to face a whole group of you nonfighters, they'll feel forced to act harshly. Philipp, you go on alone. Everything will be all right. Even Smyser will be cooled down before you get there."

Well, *I* was going along, that's for sure. So, first we all prayed together, and then we walked; or rather, Philipp walked and I jogged. When I thought about that doctor in Philadelphia, I got a hollow feeling in my stomach and my mouth felt so **parched** I couldn't get my words out. A redwing blackbird whistled his summer song from the top of a beech tree, but I didn't even look up at him.

Finally we crossed the creek, and I was relieved that Philipp said: "Get your feet in it, Henry. We have time to cool down a bit. There are the roofs of York."

While I stepped into a pool, I looked west toward York, less than a mile off now. Philipp splashed a handful of water at me. We both drank our fill, and I wanted to ask Philipp a question. I couldn't quite figure out how to say what I was thinking though, so I just said, "You seem happy." The dust stuck to my wet feet as we walked on, making a crust of mud along the sides.

Philipp knew what I meant.

"I've been thinking about the martyrs' stories, Henry. I was wondering: why were they so fearless?"

"Hmm." I had to think. "Because they knew what they were doing was right, I guess?"

"Yes. That's it. And because they were doing the right, they knew God was with them, no matter what men did to them. Well, we're doing what's right too."

I still felt glum and a little scared.

"There's nothing more that we can do. Maybe I shouldn't have been the one to speak up, since I wasn't the oldest man there. But I didn't intend to offend Mr. Smyser. And what I said—it didn't hurt anybody, and it was the truth. So, just like the martyrs, we needn't be afraid."

We had passed the stables on the outskirts of York. Ahead of us the courthouse sat beside the green. "Rest here in the green, Henry. I'll go inside and see what they want. I'll be right back."

I didn't want to be left out alone, and I begged Philipp until we were at the courthouse door.

"All right. Just stay in the back then. And let's be praying."

We could hear Mr. Smyser's voice. It led us to a room where a group of men and boys were sitting around in the heat. Mr. Smyser looked up when Philipp came in. He started accusing him right away. If he had cooled down, as Preacher Edwards had said he would, I couldn't tell it. He spoke very fast, saying Philipp was loyal to King George, and that Philipp opposed the new government.

"Some folks would like to cower in safety, hiding in their comfortable houses and big farms, while others fight to protect their liberty," he said. Then he reported in detail what had taken place this morning, and what Philipp had said.

When he had finished, Colonel Hartley, the chairman of the committee, spoke to Philipp: "Is what Mr. Smyser says true? Did you say these things against the cause of freedom?"

"I did not mean to speak against freedom this morning, sir," Philipp answered. "I only said that we could never take up arms to harm our fellow man. I reminded Mr. Smyser that Jesus said, 'Put up

282

again thy sword into his place: for all they that take the sword shall perish—' "

"You needn't preach to us!" Colonel Hartley broke in. "We can read the Bible for ourselves!"

The men sitting at the table—I guessed they were the Committee of Observation—leaned together and whispered a moment. I glanced over the people in the room. The men looked quite rough, and the boys wore scowls or sneers on their faces. One odd fellow, about fourteen I'd say, clutched a pillow against himself in the heat.

Suddenly, most of the committee members stood up and hastily crowded out through the back door. Colonel Hartley and the other man who remained stared down at the table. Oh, how I wished I could see Philipp's eyes! The colonel began to scold him, but somehow, even from the back of his head, I could tell that Philipp's eyes were smiling, alert and honest, as always.

"Philipp Martin," Colonel Hartley was saying, glancing only for a second at Philipp, "people like you are enemies of this country!"

Enemies? I wondered. *How are we enemies? Father's mill grinds grain for all our neighbors; and Father pays his taxes, even the extra taxes we have to pay because we won't fight.*

Colonel Hartley went on, looking around the room as he talked: "This man is loyal to the tyrant King George. This Committee of Observation knows of only one thing to do with a traitor: you shall be covered with tar and feathered like the coward you are!"

The boys in the back of the room snickered, but I felt my heart skip a beat and my stomach drop.

Philipp did not move. I saw his straight back and his hands resting at his sides. Then I noticed the tar box that was sitting on the floor near Colonel Hartley's table. It had all been planned ahead of time!

Mr. Hartley called Philipp to stand before the table, and while Philipp stepped to the front, the Colonel himself slipped out the back door. Only one committee man remained. Drops of sweat covered his forehead.

No one spoke or moved for a long time.

Then the committee man spoke: "Someone in this room must carry out the committee's orders!"

Still, no one moved. At last the man said to Philipp: "If no one here will follow the committee's orders, you will do so yourself, traitor!"

Several of the boys sitting along the side of the room made sounds of disbelief at this command, but Philipp pulled back his shirt and calmly bent over and scooped up a wad of black sticky tar. He dabbed the goo on his shoulder, and then one of the men shouted: "You committee men better do that tarring yerself!"

Other voices jeered at the committee man, "Do it yerself!"

A man near Philipp stood up. "Young man," he said gently, "you go on home. This is enough foolishness for one day."

Philipp didn't wait for any debate. He wiped his fingers on the edge of the tar box and turned for the door. He smiled at me, and I smiled back. Just as we stepped through the door, the boy with the pillow threw a handful of feathers after Philipp, but none of them even came close. We were back out in the sun and heading for home.

We didn't say a word to each other as we hustled out of town. A couple of the youngest boys followed us for a block, but then they dropped off, and we were alone again. As soon as we'd passed the stables, Philipp stooped and wiped his hands on the dusty grass. He wrinkled his nose, but his eyes were alive with joy. Walking briskly toward home, we began to talk about the day's events. We both felt a great urge to get home—now we had our own story to tell.

– *Tim Kennedy*

The Easy Road Crowded

The easy roads are crowded,
And the level roads are jammed;
The pleasant little rivers
With the drifting folks are crammed.

But off yonder where it's rocky,
Where you get a better view,
You will find the ranks are thinning
And the travelers are few.

Where the going's smooth and pleasant
You will always find the throng,
For the many—more's the pity—
Seem to like to drift along.

But the steps that call for courage
And the task that's hard to do,
In the end results in glory
For the never-wavering few.

– Messick

A Smile as Small as Mine

They might not need me;
  But they might.
I'll let my head be just
  in sight;
A smile as small as mine might be
  Precisely their necessity.

– Emily Dickinson

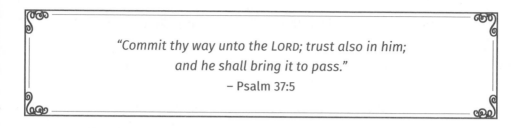

> *"Commit thy way unto the LORD; trust also in him;*
> *and he shall bring it to pass."*
> – Psalm 37:5

Not Meant for Bullets

Part 1

Amos Stoltzfus closed his eyes, again picturing in his mind the smooth, shiny coat, the friendly, inquisitive eyes, and the easy gait of the young colt. He already knew what he was going to name him—Dirk. That was just the name for him, after the man in the big martyr book who turned back to help his enemy and saved him from drowning. That deed had always seemed so noble, and *noble* was the right word for the colt he hoped—

"Hey! Hey! Get out of here," came a sudden shout. "Shoo! What's going on here, anyhow? Where's Amos? Amos! What happened to that boy?"

Amos dashed upstream. He knew what was happening. Matilda—that sneaky cow! A moment ago she had been beside him drinking from the brook. He had taken a few steps downstream, searching for bird nests, and when his thoughts wandered to the colt he hoped would someday be his, sly Matilda had sneaked into the young corn.

His older brother Pete had come along and found her eating corn. He would! *Pete will make the most of this,* Amos thought.

Matilda, hearing Pete's cries and Amos's footsteps, furiously gulped great bites of tender corn. Amos grabbed her leash, and she tore off a few more mouthfuls before yielding to his jerks on the rope.

"Amos!" Pete chided. "Father will not be happy that you let the cow get into the corn."

"Awww, she didn't eat very much," Amos defended himself. "But—I'm sorry," he added.

"No, she didn't get much," Pete agreed. "But it's not to your credit. It's a good thing I came along when I did. No doubt you were dreaming again—about that precious colt!"

Amos opened his mouth, but closed it again. That was exactly what he had been doing. And Pete had even guessed the subject of his dreams!

"You have to be more careful," Pete said, more gently. "You have to be dependable if you expect to get a colt to ride to Grundy's."

Amos sighed. He had heard that so many times! They constantly reminded him: act more grown-up! work harder! be dependable! He wanted the colt so much. Yet growing up to be worthy of him was a difficult assignment.

Amos stretched his neck to see around the bend ahead of him. Summer leaves hung thickly, blocking his view. Amos hoped he might glimpse a deer drinking at the ford. Several times he had spotted one—a rare sight in 1786 in Lancaster County, Pennsylvania.

There was nothing today. A shaft of sunlight filtered through the trees, glinting on the clear water. Amos slowed his pace, enjoying the cool refreshment of the water on his bare feet. He lingered. A frog leaped from the bank, and Amos crouched to stalk him. Suddenly, guiltily, he straightened his shoulders and hurried on. He must not arrive late at Joseph Grundy's. He was thirteen now—old enough to do a man's work. He quickened his step down the narrow trail.

When Amos arrived, he found Joseph and his son John already hewing timbers for their new barn. Joseph looked up with a smile.

"Good morning, Amos. Fine day."

"Yes," said Amos. "Sorry I'm not so early this morning. I had to help Father clean out the spring. Some stones washed in during the storm last night."

"Oh, that's all right," Joseph said pleasantly. "What we don't get done today, we can work on tomorrow."

Soon they were busy. Amos enjoyed working for Joseph. At home, Father usually had Amos help his brothers, who made him feel like he couldn't do things well. But Joseph appreciated whatever Amos did. Maybe it was just that he was hard up for someone and therefore easier to please. John was only ten—not able to take the other end of the crosscut saw, much less to use the adz or the broadax by himself.

My brothers are hard to please, Amos thought sadly. *They forget what it's like to be thirteen and still learning.* Worse yet, they never had been given to dreams. They had no sympathy for that side of Amos at all.

Zinggg-zummm, zinggg-zumm. Back and forth the crosscut saw sang in rhythmic motion. Joseph held his end of the saw a bit higher, so Amos would not need to hold his own end so high. On the return cut, Joseph lifted the saw at just the right moment to keep it from biting in too deeply as Amos pulled. It seemed like Amos was doing as much as Joseph—only the dust falling from each side of the log gave away the secret.

But it didn't really matter—Amos knew he could not keep up with Joseph, who was in the prime of his strength. Each day the muscles in Amos's arms grew stronger. He was on his way to becoming a man. At least physically—sometimes he wasn't so sure otherwise. Pete told him a man was more than someone whose body was grown. A man disciplined himself, and folks could depend on him. A man went beyond dreaming—he had the determination to make his dreams come true.

The saw slowed, then stopped. They wiped the beads of sweat from their faces and caught their breath.

"Well, Amos," Joseph said. "I guess we were reminded yesterday how much we have to be thankful for in this land of freedom."

Amos nodded soberly. He knew Joseph was referring to Sunday's sermon.

Zingg-zummm. As the saw started going again, Amos's thoughts did too. In his mind he was back in church, in the Zooks' new barn. The minister's voice rang in his ears.

"Brothers and sisters, do not forget the sufferings of our Lord. He became poor that we might become rich. He died that we might live. Today, I want to tell you of a man who followed our Lord's example and suffered for the truth. His name was Hans Brael, and you can read about him in the *Martyrs Mirror.* The enemies of truth tortured Hans to force him to betray others in the church, but he refused.

"They locked him in a dungeon for two years. His eyes became so used to the dark that when they brought him out of his dungeon, he was glad to go back because the light hurt his eyes. The dungeon was so damp and filthy that his clothes rotted away, until nothing remained of his shirt but the collar. He took it off and hung it on a nail on the wall.

"Later, the brethren wondered if Hans had remained faithful. 'Send us some token, if only a small piece of straw,' they said. But Hans could find nothing in the dungeon to send. At last he thought of the collar and sent it . . .'"

Zingg-zumm, zingg-zummm. Amos's thoughts paced back and forth with the saw. He had longed for Preacher Dan to go on with the story. What had happened to Hans? Had he been released? Had he escaped? Had he died a martyr? Or—had he given up and denied Jesus?

When the saw stopped, Amos spoke. "Do you know what finally happened to Hans Brael?"

Joseph shook his head. "No. I wish I did. The next time I get a chance to go to Dan's house, I'll ask him. He has a copy of the martyr book—I have seen it. He bought one of the last books before the soldiers came and took them all away.

"I am glad he was able to get it, but I wish I had one too. I was saving for it, but then they were taken. That was ten years ago. I may never get one now. But you are younger, Amos. Perhaps there will be another printing in your lifetime and you may have a *Martyrs Mirror* book someday."

Zingg-zumm, zingg-zumm. Amos's mind ran ahead of the saw. Its rhythm was too slow for the tempo of his thoughts. Could he actually someday own a copy of the *Martyrs Mirror?* Joseph would not tease about something like that.

Amos nearly forgot to pull the saw. Right now it seemed a wild dream. But that was the nature of dreams. One did not dream about things easy to obtain. Dreams were about the difficult, the challenging—even the impossible.

Someday, Amos resolved, *I will own a book of the martyrs myself—then I can read the story of Hans Brael. Someday I will.* If he said it determinedly enough, perhaps he would believe it. That was one secret about dreams—you could not keep them and make them come true, unless you believed them yourself.

The weeks passed. Amos said nothing at home about his dream of someday owning a copy of the great book of martyrs. They would not oppose it—his parents and brothers and sisters—but they would see it as more evidence that Amos was a hopeless dreamer, living in a world of fantasy.

One sultry day in mid-July, Amos again mentioned the book to Joseph. "You said you had hoped to get a copy before the soldiers took them all ten years ago. Why did the soldiers take them?"

"That was during the war," Joseph said. "George Washington's soldiers ran low on musket wadding. Someone told them about the copies of the book at the Ephrata Cloister. So they **confiscated** them."

Amos could hardly believe it. The books seized for bullet wadding?

Joseph went on. "We were dismayed too, but there was nothing we could do about it. The soldiers paid for the books, but that wasn't important. It was the use they were going to—books that were to share Christ's message of peace and nonresistance used in war!

"The brothers at the cloister had worked so hard to translate and print the *Martyrs Mirror.* They had even made the paper themselves— and the ink for printing, out of chimney soot and pokeberry juice. For them it was a service to God.

"Peter Miller did most of the translating. He often slept only four hours a night. But when soldiers arrived with horses and two wagons, the brothers could do nothing—since they really believed the nonresistant message of the book."

"Well, at least Preacher Dan was able to get a copy before the soldiers came," Amos said quietly. "Not everything was lost."

"No, indeed," Joseph said. "Not only he, but many others. They printed around 1,200 to 1,300 copies, and 700 or 800 had been sold before the soldiers came."

Walking home that evening, Amos felt overwhelmed. To harbor in his heart two dreams—two great big oversized dreams—was nearly more than he could contain. The first dream was big enough—to own a colt named after a martyr. The second was bigger—to obtain for himself a copy of the book of martyrs.

"Amos!" Joseph called out as Amos arrived for work. "Preacher Dan just stopped in. He heard yesterday that the brothers at the cloister have bought back some of the martyr books that were seized by Congress. He advised me to find out if it's true."

It took a moment for Amos to grasp what Joseph was saying. Then a wave of joy swept over him. If that was true, if that was true . . . well, if that was true, it was almost too good to be true! "Do you think it *is*?" he asked.

"I don't know. It might be only a rumor. But I intend to find out." Then Joseph's face clouded. "I forgot to tell you—Dan heard that the books are very expensive."

"How expensive?"

"I don't know; but I shouldn't get my hopes too high."

Before Amos left for home that evening, plans were laid. Tomorrow Joseph would travel the 25 miles to the cloister. Before the sun set, he would know if the report was true. If Amos could get permission, he should be at the Grundy house by dawn, and he could go along.

Amos reached home in record time, much too excited to lose any time daydreaming along the way.

After the evening meal was over, Amos shared his news. "Joseph heard something today that he was pretty excited about."

Father looked up. "What was that?"

"Preacher Dan heard that the brothers at the cloister in Ephrata bought back some of the martyr books taken during the war."

Everyone was interested in Amos's announcement. Even Pete wanted to know more—How many copies were bought back? In what condition? What did they cost? Why were they returned?

Amos shrugged. He didn't know.

"But I know how I can find out," he said, restraining his smile. "Joseph invited me to go along to Ephrata with him tomorrow. Then I can answer your questions."

It seemed like a long time before his father spoke. When he did, he simply said, "Yes. You have done well helping Joseph. If he wants you to go along, you may."

Whip-poor-will. Whip-poor-will. Every night during the past few weeks, Amos had fallen asleep to the whippoorwill's call. Tonight, he wished the bird would be quiet. He had been pleased to get permission to go along with Joseph. But now a thought had come to him—what if Joseph did not have enough money? What if they drove all that distance tomorrow, and the book cost too much? Then he had remembered his colt money in the little leather pouch in the upper pigeonhole[1] of Father's high-top desk. Each month Father placed some of Amos's earnings in the pouch.

Amos closed his eyes and rolled over. The leather pouch popped back into his mind. By fall, the colt he had picked out at the Zook farm would be big enough to leave his mother. By then, Amos would have the money to buy him. The Zooks had promised Amos first chance at the colt.

Whip-poor-will. Whip-poor-will. The bird sang on. Amos squeezed his eyes tighter. If he offered his colt money to Joseph, Joseph could buy the book he had wanted for ten years. It might be Joseph's only chance. By the time he saved up more money, the books would be gone. There would always be colts . . .

But the last thing Amos wanted to do was give up his colt—Dirk, his dream.

Joseph would never ask me to make such a sacrifice, Amos thought. Of course, Joseph wouldn't ask it or even expect it. But Amos could offer it, at least if his father agreed.

He had always been eager to take his place among the grown-ups. He had never thought that being a little boy might in some ways be easier than growing up.

The whippoorwill ceased calling, but the **turmoil** in Amos's mind didn't. For so long, he had hoped and planned and dreamed of his horse. He had planned to train Dirk himself, to teach him to come

---

1 pigeonhole: a small open compartment in a desk

when he whistled. Even now, he could imagine the wind singing past his ears as he rode Dirk full gallop along the trail. No, he couldn't— not give up Dirk.

Dirk? Amos opened his eyes. Could he name a colt after the martyr Dirk Willems, who gave up his life for his enemy, if he himself had to be selfish in order to get the colt? Martyrs like Dirk Willems gave up not only their dreams, they gave their lives. Amos knew what he had to do, and it no longer seemed so impossible.

– Elmo Stoll

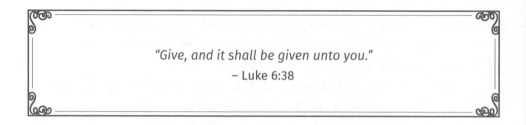
Not Meant for Bullets

Part 2

Amos didn't know whether it was the temperature or excitement that made him shiver on the wagon seat. Four of them were going—Joseph and Amos, and Joseph's two oldest children Rebecca and John.

At last, they were off! The big sorrel mares were full of energy, and Joseph had to hold them back to a walk the first few miles.

Amos didn't listen to the children's chatter. He had too much to think about. Last night he had gladly decided to offer his colt money to Joseph. His mind had been firm when he got out of bed. But now he wasn't so sure. He had worked hard and saved all summer for the colt. Was this really what he wanted to do?

Hours passed. The wagon jostled from side to side in the ruts of the road. Sometimes they had to dodge hanging branches. Rebecca and John sat on the front seat with Joseph, so Amos had the back seat all to himself. He felt like keeping his thoughts to himself too. As long as he didn't tell Joseph about his decision, he could still back out. Father had given him the money. Mother had wrapped it in a cloth and placed it at the bottom of his lunch basket. It would be safe there.

They came to a shallow stream. "Whoa," Joseph called out. "Let's unhitch the horses and let them drink."

As the horses drank great gulps of water, a young man trotted up on horseback. By the number of bags tied to his saddle, Amos decided he must be traveling a great distance. The rider brought his horse to a halt.

"I'm Jacob Bilbrey," he said with a friendly nod. He shook hands with Joseph as his horse drank from the stream. "I've been traveling for two weeks," he explained. "And I've got eight more to go—all the way out to Ohio."

Amos listened to Jacob Bilbrey's story. His parents had moved west ten years ago. Jacob had gone unwillingly and had soon sneaked away from home and returned east. Now he was going back to ask forgiveness from his parents and to do what he could to make up for the lost years.

"Well, Jacob, I'm glad we met you," Joseph said. "We must push on, or we will be late getting home tonight. But I know you will never regret doing the right thing. May the Lord bless you and give you a safe journey."

Jacob's eyes filled with sudden tears. "Thank you," he said huskily. "I need that encouragement. Seems like I have to make the decision again and again. Almost every day the temptation comes to turn back."

"May God give you the strength to stick to it," Joseph said. "Sticking to the right decision is as important as making it in the first place—and sometimes, more difficult."

With a smile and a wave, Jacob leaped back into his saddle and headed west, up the hill. Joseph and Amos hitched the horses to the wagon, and they set off again.

The day grew warmer. They emerged from the forest where open fields lined the road on either side. Amos guessed they must be nearing Ephrata because they passed more houses and met more travelers.

Joseph gently urged the tired horses on, asking them to keep trotting when they wanted to slow down.

Amos remembered what Joseph had told Jacob Bilbrey: sticking to the right decision is just as important as making it—and just as difficult. He thought of Hans Brael sitting in a dungeon until all his clothes rotted away except his collar. When Hans had decided to accept prison rather than give up his faith, was he tempted to change his mind?

I hope he stuck with it, Amos thought. But then he remembered the difficulty of sticking with his own decision, and he felt ashamed.

"Daddy," John was saying. "Aren't we about there? How far is it yet?"

"We're not too far from there, I think," Joseph said. "It's been several years since I've been to Ephrata. I'm not sure myself."

Amos took a deep breath. He could not put it off any longer. "Joseph."

"Yes, Amos."

"I brought some money along in case the book costs more than you have. I would like to help you buy it."

"Oh, did your father send it?"

"Well, er, why yes, he gave it to me. He said it was all right if that is what I really wanted to do."

"But—but, I don't understand, Amos. Whose money . . . ?" Suddenly Joseph looked at Amos. "Amos! Not your colt money! You know I can't let you do that, Amos."

"I've made up my mind," Amos said resolutely. "I want you to have that martyr book more than I want to have the colt. I really do. I made the decision, and I want to stick to it."

Joseph swallowed hard, as if something were lodged in his throat. He looked away. At last he spoke. "I hardly know how I can accept such a sacrifice from you, Amos. But if it is really what you want . . .

well, I don't know how I can refuse it either. I am unworthy. But I'm glad that you value the book so much."

"Well, it's not just the book," Amos said. "It's what it stands for, I guess. It's the stories of people who lived what they believed."

"I know what you mean," Joseph said. "That is why I can't refuse your offer. It is hard to take your money, because you are giving more than money—it is your dream for a colt. But, I can hardly turn it down, for you are giving it for more than just a book."

A cloud darkened the sun, and Amos glanced up in surprise. He had not thought it could rain today, with such a clear sky. But then he saw that the shade had not come from a cloud. A large flock of passenger pigeons was winging its way overhead.

"Pigeons!" Amos called out. "I thought at first we might get rained on."

Rebecca grimaced. "Ugh," she said. "I would rather have rain."

Amos laughed. He understood her annoyance.

Just ahead of them a peddler had parked his wagon by the road under a great chestnut tree. He had an **assortment** of kettles, pots, pans, and knives—knives of every size and description.

"I'm going to ask this fellow where we turn," Joseph said. "This looks different from what I remember."

Amos studied the peddler, who was as fascinating as his wares. Broad-shouldered and tall, he was a giant of a man, with a voice to match.

"Come over here, my friends," he boomed. "Welcome to the shade of the biggest chestnut tree in Cocalico. You have chosen a good spot to rest your horses. Let me sell you a good, sharp knife—here's a big one, well-suited to protect you as you journey."

"Thank you," Joseph said politely, "but I look to God for my protection."

"Come now," the big man said. "Are you implying that God can't use a knife to protect us? It's all the same—the protection of God and the protection of my knife. Anyone who would do me harm will need to deal with both."

"Could you direct us to the cloister?" Joseph asked, not wanting to argue.

The big man's eyebrows shot up. "Ho! So that's why you talk the way you do. If you are friends of those folks, you can find your own way. Cowards!—refusing to help us fight the Redcoats."

"Coward is hardly the right word," Joseph said softly. "Sometimes trusting in God takes more courage than trusting in knives."

The man's face darkened, and his eyes snapped. "Listen, you Tory!" he growled. "I told you I trust in both. If you are so loyal to the enemy, why did we beat them? If God was on your side, why did our side win? Is my knife stronger than your God?"

"You misjudge me," Joseph said, "if you think I am taking sides in warfare. I'm neither a Tory nor a Patriot. I'm a Christian, a peace-loving Christian. Christ's kingdom is spiritual."

Joseph lifted the reins, ready to move on. But the peddler, deter-mined to have the last word, shouted after them: "Know this for sure, that God was with us and gave us the victory. That is sure as, sure as . . . as . . ." The big man rolled his eyes. He saw the great flock of pigeons still flying overhead, just above the sturdy chestnut tree.

With a deep boom, his voice resumed, " . . . as sure as there will always be passenger pigeons flying over this fair land . . . and chest-nuts thriving in our vast forests!"

Rebecca looked straight ahead, her face pale, and pretended not to be afraid. But John kept pleading, "Make the horses go faster, Daddy. Make them run as fast as they can go, so he won't come after us."

"He won't hurt us," Joseph reassured him. "But I must be more careful whom I ask for directions. Apparently feelings run strong in these parts toward those who didn't help fight."

They rounded a bend, came to a fork in the road, and the country-side once again became familiar to Joseph.

Amos drew in his breath with anticipation as he suddenly spied the cluster of tall wooden buildings standing straight and orderly before them. A neat path divided the well-kept garden and led to the nearest building. It was lunchtime, and no one was about.

"We'll unhitch the horses and feed them first," Joseph said.

Amos's fingers flew as he undid the traces. Soon a short man carrying a shovel rounded a corner and spotted them. He came toward them, his face stern behind a long black beard. Joseph explained why they had come, and the man answered, "Wait here. I will fetch someone from the bindery."

After a long time he came back, bringing with him a man with a less severe face. His blue eyes twinkled. He smiled at the children, shaking hands with each of them and asking their names.

"Although 175 unbound copies were returned, many are ruined. Many are missing several pages," the bindery worker told Joseph as they crossed the square. "My two helpers and I have been very busy since the books came back. We have sorted out the better copies and bound them.

"It is good you did not wait any longer to come," he went on. "We only have one complete copy left. A few others are nearly complete—especially one that has only the corners torn off a few pages. Not many words are missing."

He led the way into a building on the opposite side of the square. Inside, unbound books were arranged in great stacks. He led them to a workbench where four bound copies lay side by side.

"We just finished these last week." He pointed to the one on the left. "This is the complete copy. And the one next to it is nearly complete. Both are good copies."

Amos was startled to see the size of the book. He had not expected it to be that big, even though he knew it was the largest book in America.

Joseph stepped over to the bench. He raised the heavy leather cover of the nearest book and slowly turned the pages. The print was sharp, clear, and easy to read. The paper was superior—made of good cloth. How sad to think of the copies that had been torn and wadded by soldiers so that bullets could be shot to maim and wound and kill. The cover and binding were made of strong oak boards beautifully bound in leather.

Joseph opened his mouth, then closed it again. Amos knew what Joseph was thinking: What if the price was greater than their combined savings?

Then Joseph cleared his throat and turned to the man with the blue eyes and pleasant smile. "How much does this complete copy cost?"

"One dollar and sixty pence."

Joseph gasped in surprise, and disbelief crossed his face. "Did you say only a dollar and sixty pence?"

"I did."

"But how can you sell it so cheaply?"

"We did not make them for money—so the price has always been low. But then, after the Continental Army bought them, the value of Continental money fell greatly. We got them back for a good buy and want to pass it along. We are just grateful that we can provide this great book to those who value it."

Amos couldn't take it in. What had he heard? Why, the price of the book was not even half what Joseph had saved for it! He would not need the colt money at all.

Joseph said, "Your policy is generous and wise. I thank you. I have brought enough money for two copies, if you don't mind; this one, and that one there."

Joseph paid for the beautiful books from his own purse, and he and Amos carried them out to the wagon. They wrapped them in a thin woolen blanket to protect the books from the dust and the sun.

Meanwhile the bindery worker brought water for the horses and offered to feed them. He invited the travelers in for lunch.

"Thank you, but we packed an ample lunch," Joseph said, "and we brought feed for the horses. And I can't thank you enough for the good price of the books."

"It gives us as much joy as it gives you," the man said, his eyes shining. Then he sobered. "It was a sad time when the soldiers took them—we never expected to see them again. It seemed so wrong; they were not meant for making bullets."

On the way home, Amos talked on and on about their successful **enterprise**. "I can hardly believe it," he said. "And so cheap!"

"I guess you noticed I could hardly believe my ears when he said the price." Joseph chuckled. "I had to ask him the second time."

"Yes, I noticed! What will you do with the extra copy?"

"Extra copy? What do you mean?"

"You got two copies."

"Yes, one for you and one for me. Nothing extra about that, is there?" Joseph's eyes twinkled.

"But . . . but you never asked me," Amos stammered. "How did you know I wanted to spend my colt money for it?"

"I wasn't figuring on your colt money, Amos," Joseph said. "Didn't you notice? I had enough for both of them."

There had been so many surprises today that Amos didn't think anything more could shock him. But Joseph had. He didn't know what to say. "Oh, but I will be glad to pay you for it. I'm more than glad to. I would much rather have the book than the colt."

"I know," Joseph said. "But I want to give it to you. You were willing to give up your colt money to help me buy my copy. Now that

God has made it possible for me to pay for both, I want to give the second copy to you."

Amos blinked back tears of gratitude. The man at the bindery had said it gave them joy to provide the book to people who valued it. *People who valued it.* He hoped those words would fit him all his life, as he tried to follow the example of those whose stories were in it—those who loved the Lord more than their own lives.

"Thank you, Joseph," he said. "I do thank you more than I can say. And guess what I will read first! The story of Hans Brael. I want to know if he remained true to God."

They rode in silence for a while. Then Amos spoke: "Joseph," he said, "I can't believe I have been so dull."

"About what?"

"About Hans Brael. Of course he remained true! Otherwise he wouldn't be in the book!"

Joseph smiled. "Of course. You're right," he said. "We weren't thinking, were we?"

Amos smiled back. This special book told about people just like him—brave men and women of faith who dreamed great dreams. He hoped he would be like them too—and stick with his dreams to the very end.

– *Elmo Stoll*

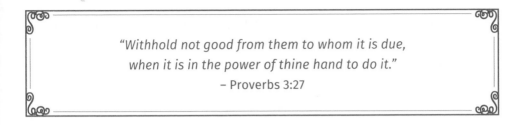

Race Against Death

Dr. Welch's pale face grew very serious as he looked about the hospital room. He knew that he faced a hard fight—and all alone! He was the only doctor in the little town of Nome, Alaska, that bitter, cold winter of 1925.

Already three people had died.

On the hospital beds lay 25 sick people. They had diphtheria, a terrible throat disease. If it should get out of control, it would sweep like wildfire over hundreds of square miles. Eleven thousand people were in danger.

"We've got to have help," Dr. Welch said in a worried voice. "I mean help from the outside!"

"Yes, it's getting away from us," agreed a nurse. "Maybe some town can send us more doctors. If we were only on the railroad or if the sea weren't frozen! This load is too much for you alone."

"It's not the doctors or nurses we need," said Dr. Welch. "It is medicine. I have hardly five shots of antitoxin left, and that is six years old. Maybe it is no good." He clasped his thin fingers. If he could shoot fresh antitoxin into the arms of the people who were well, they would not get sick.

The nurse spoke eagerly, "Can't you radio to the United States[1] for antitoxin?"

---

1 Alaska did not become a state until 1959.

"I could, but it would take six weeks to get here. By that time we may have one of the worst disasters in Alaskan history."

"But couldn't they reach us sooner with airplanes?" broke in the nurse.

"Not through this weather. No pilot could make it, and it is fifty degrees below zero." The doctor looked very grave. "Our only hope is to get antitoxin from some place closer. Take care of that newest patient's throat while I call the radio station."

A few minutes later the cry for help went flashing across the snows. As people heard the bad news, they were much alarmed. Nome, up in the Arctic Circle, was 400 miles from the nearest railroad and frozen in by the sea. Yet help must come at once.

A doctor in southern Alaska heard the message. He happened to have a good supply of antitoxin and immediately wired Dr. Welch: "I am sending antitoxin to Nenana on today's train." Nenana was the town closest to Nome on the railroad.

So the precious 20-pound package was started on its journey. After the 300 miles by train, it must be carried 650 miles over the cruel snowbound trail stretching between Nenana and Nome.

Only dogs could make it.

Again the radio sent out a call—this time for drivers of dog teams. These drivers are known as mushers and their dogs as huskies, the right name for what are sometimes called Eskimo dogs. At once brave mushers picked out their strongest dogs, hitched them to their sleds, and hurried to the trail. The 650-mile trail had never before been covered in less than nine days. But this was a race against death, with 11,000 lives at stake!

At eleven o'clock on Tuesday evening, January 27, the package on which so many lives depended was taken off the train in Nenana. The first musher, waiting with his dog team, took it eagerly and set out on the trail.

The great relay race had begun. Each musher would struggle on until he reached the next man, 25 to 100 miles away.

We do not know much about the first heroes who carried the medicine. We know their names and the routes they took. But the greatest honor has been paid to the two mushers who bore the most dangerous part of the journey. Of course, their skill and daring would not have been enough; the others had to do their part also. But to these two fell the greatest test. Their courage and that of the huskies who led their teams would have been hard to equal.

Shannon was the first musher. Every inch of the trail was familiar to him as he hurried down a frozen streambed toward the Yukon River. Even in the dark he recognized which Indian dwelling he was passing. He knew he was making good time—more than five miles an hour.

Wednesday afternoon Shannon, tired but happy, turned the package over to the second musher. It was time for Shannon to stop; his dogs were worn out. Losing no time, the second stout team plunged down the trail. By seven o'clock in the evening they had reached the Yukon River.

They had covered 150 miles in 20 hours.

If the next teams could only keep up the pace! Just 24 hours later the antitoxin was 350 miles on its way.

Friday afternoon it was placed in the hands of Leonard Seppala, known far and wide as "the king of dog-sled drivers." This daring musher had come out from Nome to meet the medicine, covering 200 miles of difficult trail in four days. Now, with no chance to rest, his picked team of Siberian dogs turned back on the trail.

Seppala hoped to carry the antitoxin all the way back to Nome so that it would get there Saturday afternoon. This would mean covering those 200 miles in one day! Even in the freshly fallen snow! And with temperatures down below zero.

His team came to the edge of the ice-covered Norton Bay. Anxiously he looked out over the frozen surface, for the direct route to Nome lay across this bay. It would be safer to take the land route around it, but that would add almost another 100 miles. If he followed the land, the antitoxin might arrive too late. Seppala decided quickly. It would be the short dangerous way.

"Gee, Togo!" he cried, and the beautiful 48-pound husky dog headed over the ice.

The musher watched the dog with a thrill of pride. Togo was a natural leader. He was a wonder at picking up the trail, and the other dogs knew they must obey him.

Darkness had fallen, and the condition of the ice worried Seppala. Any minute it might break up and drift out to sea. Sometimes before they realized that the ice was free, travelers had been carried for miles on a loose ice cake. Some had been blown out into the Bering Sea and drowned.

Horrible thoughts crowded into Seppala's mind. *Suppose the bay ice should suddenly crack up. We would be carried to open water and drift helplessly all night. Nobody would rescue us. My dogs would freeze to death—and so would I—if we did not drown first. And the antitoxin would be lost, somewhere on the bottom of the sea. They trusted it to me, and I must get through.*

Speed—there lay his safety. Togo picked his way carefully as the team raced along. Each husky seemed to know that Seppala was depending upon him. They loved this master who never struck with a whip.

Midnight came. Seppala wondered whether they were halfway across. How cold it was! Didn't he hear a cracking noise? His heart stood still. Togo raced on as if he knew the danger.

At last the sky turned gray. The musher looked eagerly for signs of land. Ahead lay only an icy stretch.

No! Wasn't that a shadowy coastline a bit to the right? A few minutes later he was sure. Another mile slipped by. They would make it safely—the ice would hold!

"My good dogs!" he cried proudly. "Gee, Togo!"

Togo led the team up on the snowy bank, and the treacherous bay ice was left behind. Seppala hummed a little song. Now if this team he loved could only go the rest of the way.

Suddenly, as he rounded a turn, he saw a dog team and musher waiting on the trail. Much as he would have liked to press on himself, he knew it would be wiser to let this fresh team of dogs take over.

"Hello, Olson," he called, stopping his sled beside the new team. "Here is the antitoxin." he smiled cheerfully as he handed over the package to the new musher.

"Things are worse in Nome—another death!" said Olson. His fingers were busy tying the package to his sled. "You made wonderful time, Seppala."

Olson and his seven dogs were off. Before their 25-mile run was over, these dogs were almost frozen.

With great relief Olson handed the antitoxin to the last musher. Gunnar Kasson, who lived in Nome, had been waiting in an empty cabin for two days and nights. He had not even lain down to rest, because he was afraid he might fall asleep and miss Olson. Thirteen stout-hearted dogs made up his team.

He said to Olson, "I am going to take the antitoxin into the cabin for a few minutes. The terrible wind may have frozen it."

Although the men waited inside the cabin for two hours, the weather kept getting colder—down to 30 degrees below zero. Snow began to fall. Every time they looked outside, the flakes pelted down all the faster. A snowstorm meant dangerous going, Kasson knew. But he said, "There is no use waiting any longer."

Stepping outside, he called his lead dog, "Hey, Balto!"

A handsome husky with a glossy coat ran to his place at the head of the traces.[2] As Kasson fastened the dog into the harness, he said, "Tonight we'll have a hard pull. We have to make it through, boy!"

The dog pricked up his ears and raised intelligent eyes as if he understood.

Thirty-four miles away lay the next town, a little place called Safety. They must reach it before snowbanks could pile up and block the trail.

"Mush!" cried Kasson.

The dogs headed out bravely on the trail that follows the coast. It was terribly hard pulling. Although animals and sled sank into the heavy snow, the team struggled on.

Whew, I never felt a colder wind! thought Kasson, trying to pull his long reindeer coat closer around him. Sealskin boots reached to his hips, and over these he wore sealskin trousers. His head was protected by a reindeer hood. But the fierce 80-mile-per-hour gale whipped right through the skins.

The way led straight into the wind. How could he or the dogs face it? He feared they would all freeze to death. Even though they kept going, how long could they stay on the trail?

Something else made Kasson uneasy. The ice under his feet was in constant motion from ocean ground swells. He turned the dogs in closer to the shore. Now he was crossing the mouth of a frozen river.

Suddenly he realized that Balto was in trouble.

The lead dog had stepped into a pool of water, an overflow that had run up on the ice. Unless Balto's feet could be dried off immediately, the skin would stick to the ice and be torn off. Then he would have to drop out—and he was the only lead dog in the team. It was a bad moment. Just then Kasson saw the one thing which could save Balto's feet—a snowdrift a few yards away.

2 traces: two long straps that attach an animal to the vehicle he is pulling

"Gee, Balto!" he shouted, and the dog turned sharply to the right.

When Balto felt the soft snow, he knew just what to do. He worked his paws in the snow until they were dry. Now the skin was safe. Kasson breathed a sigh of relief.

Starting off again, he headed the team up a 600-foot hill. Here there was nothing to stop the fury of the wind howling off the sea. Kasson's lips set tightly. This hill he had feared more than any other spot. Near the top he discovered that his right cheek had no feeling. It was frozen. He grabbed some snow and rubbed the cheek until it felt alive again.

He was glad to leave the hill behind. Next came a flat stretch six miles long. Would they ever get across it? The wind was picking up masses of snow and hurling them hard and fast. Kasson was choked and blinded. He strained to catch sight of the dogs. The dog nearest the sled was not even a blur. He held his hand before his face—he could not see it!

His heart sank. Lost—he was hopelessly lost. The antitoxin would never reach Nome.

Yet the sled moved steadily on. There was one hope left—that the dogs would keep the trail themselves.

In the lead, Balto never hesitated. Hurrying straight ahead, he scented the trail on the glaring, wind-swept ice. For two hours, Kasson held to the sled and blindly trusted everything to his dogs.

They entered the tiny village of Solomon, but Kasson did not even see the cabins. In this village a message had been waiting for him: "Stop in Solomon until the storm clears. Then go to Safety. Ed Rohn is there with a fresh team. Let him finish the race." Kasson sped on through the storm, not knowing that he had passed Solomon—not dreaming that he had missed an important message.

If anything, the wind grew more bitter in the next 12 miles. Kasson was filled with joy when he finally caught sight of an old log store.

He was in the village of Safety. His dogs had followed the trail!

The houses of Safety were dark.

"Shall I stop for help?" Kasson wondered. "It will mean a long delay. There may not be any dogs in town strong enough to mush through the storm. Balto knows the trail; there is no other dog like him."

Speeding past the dark hotel, the team soon left Safety behind. They had only 21 miles to go on a trail that followed the shore of Bering Sea.

An angry wind whipped in from the sea. "I will tear you off your sled!" it seemed to cry. Kasson clung tighter.

But he was growing very tired. The dogs, too, were slowing up, almost worn out by the long cruel grind. Deep drifts made the pulling terribly hard. Yet they struggled bravely on. They would reach the goal—or die in the traces!

Kasson thought of many things: the rosy flames of a warm fire; how wonderful it would feel when he got to Nome. Would all his dogs make it through? Too bad to lose even one—it must not be Balto! What wouldn't he give for a drink of steaming hot tea! How far away was Nome? Fifteen miles? Twelve miles? How many more sick people had died? He must hurry—hurry—

Just then Kasson felt the sled pitch roughly. He flew headfirst into the snow. As the sled overturned in a great drift, Balto slowed down and stopped the team. The dogs began to bark and fight, tangling up their harness.

Kasson jumped up and put the sled back on both runners. Then, lashing his whip, he quieted the dogs. It took him some time to straighten their harness in the dark. When they were ready to start again, he reached down to see whether the antitoxin was securely fastened.

The antitoxin was gone!

Kasson crawled about on his hands and knees, hunting frantically in the snow. The sled had turned over on the right. Surely he would find the package there—if he had not lost it miles back on the trail. Could that have happened?

No, here it was! His heart began to beat more regularly again. He retied the package, this time very securely.

As they set out, the snowfall seemed lighter. At times Kasson could see a bit of trail ahead. Then in the half-light he saw that two dogs were suffering—the two that had been frozen a few weeks before. The poor creatures were limping stiffly. Stopping the team, he fastened rabbit skin coverings over these two dogs; but it didn't help much, for the cold went right through. If they should die, he would leave them and press on. If all the dogs should die, he would still go on, carrying the antitoxin in his arms. Nome—he must get to Nome!

He wished for morning as the hours dragged by. Now he was running behind the sled, for the team was staggering. "Keep going, Balto!" he cried. "We're almost there!" It seemed that the team could not last another mile.

He strained his eyes, looking for the lumber mill at the edge of Nome.

At last it appeared out of the falling snow. They had made it—they had made it to Nome! It was 5:36 in the morning of Monday, February 2—just five-and-one-half days after the start at Nenana.

The dogs seemed to know that the end of the great race was near. They hurried past the mill, past a row of wooden houses. Kasson heard people shouting, knew they were running after him. He turned to the left—toward the hospital. The next thing he knew, Dr. Welch was wringing his hand. "You got here in time!" said the doctor joyfully. The crowd shouted.

Half-frozen and almost blinded, Kasson dropped down into the snow. With tears in his eyes, he started to pull ice splinters out of Balto's paws.

"Balto!" he cried. "You brought us through!"

– Irma H. Taylor

Glossary

The root word of every word in boldface type in *Calls to Courage* is in this glossary. With each word is the dictionary pronunciation and a definition for the way the word is used in this book. Many of these words have other definitions. The example sentence in italics shows how to use the word correctly. The page number following the sentence indicates where the word is found in the reader.

acquire (ə kwīr′) *v*: to get as one's own. *Howard was pleased to acquire thirty acres of good pastureland for his sheep.* 90

aromatic (a′ rə ma′ tik) *adj*: having a noticeable and pleasing smell. *The scent of the aromatic candle filled the entire house.* 172

array (ə rā′) *n*: an orderly or attractive display. *An array of brightly colored fishing boats docked in the harbor.* 54

assortment (ə sȯrt′ mənt) *n*: a collection of various kinds. *"You should have seen the assortment of pies at the picnic!" Judy exclaimed.* 299

audible (ȯ′ də bəl) *adj*: loud or clear enough to be heard. *The crash in the kitchen was audible even out in the garden.* 49

banish (ba′ nish) *v*: to cause to leave or stay away. *Conrad had to banish Fido from the clubhouse after he chewed up the baseball glove.* 30

befriend (bi frend′) *v*: to make or act as a friend. *Cherilyn befriended the new student in her Sunday school class.* 177

benefit (be′ nə fit′) *v*: to be useful or helpful. *The medicine Dr. Bartow prescribed will benefit Mother in her fight against pneumonia.* 42 *n*: something useful or helpful. *Brother Richard's words of advice were of benefit to us all.* 207

betray (bi trā′) *v*: (1) to give away to the enemy. *A spy might betray his country by telling the enemy important secrets.* 205 (2) to reveal unintentionally. *After the game of hide-and-seek, Keith would not betray his favorite hiding place because he wanted to use it again.* 274

bleak (blēk) *adj*: barren; lacking in life or warmth. *The bleak landscape made Jenna feel lonely.* 78

bluster (bləs′ tər) *v*: to speak noisy, threatening words. *Bullies may bluster angrily but actually be afraid of others.* 89

brandish (bran′ dish) *v*: to wave around in a threatening manner. *Brandishing a stick, Arnold advanced toward the growling dog.* 133

browse (braůz) *v*: to eat leaves, twigs, or other parts of trees and bushes. *Charity kept an eye on the gathering storm clouds while she watched the goats browse among the bushes.* 64

campus (kam′ pəs) *n*: the area of land that contains the grounds and buildings of a school. *When we visited Adam Fielding, he gave us a tour of the college campus.* 190

cantankerous (kan taŋ′ kə rəs) *adj*: irritating or difficult to work with. *Mr. Evans had a reputation of being a cantankerous neighbor, but he became one of our best friends during the years we lived in Franklin.* 268

capable (kā′ pə bəl) *adj*: good at a particular task or job. *Elise proved she was capable of teaching the preschool class.* 26

cherish (cher′ ish) *v*: to love dearly; to hold on to. *Tommy cherished every chance he had to help his father with the work.* 273

cinch (sinch) *v*: to tighten. *Cinching the saddle strap on the donkey's pack, Darren made sure the load wouldn't fall off.* 133

cinder (sin′ dər) *n*: a small piece of partly burned coal or wood. *Trucks from the county spread cinders on the icy roads.* 2

compassion (kəm pa′ shən) *n*: a feeling of sympathy for another. *Compassion moved the people to give food, blankets, and money to the families who had suffered from the flood.* 62

condemnation (kän′ dem′ nā′ shən) *n*: disapproval; the act of pronouncing guilty. *The judge offered only condemnation to the man charged with stealing his uncle's horses.* 275

Pronunciation Key

/a/ **bat**; /ā/ **acorn**; /är/ **star**; /e/ **pet**; /ē/ **eagle**; /er/ **bear**; /ər/ **her**; /i/ **bit**; /ī/ **ivy**; /ir/ **deer**; /ä/ **top**; /ō/ **go**; /ò/ **lost**; /òi/ **coin**; /aů/ **out**; /òr/ **corn**; /ə/ **but**; /ü/ **boot**; /yü/ **use**; /ů/ **foot**; /th/ **thick**; /<u>th</u>/ **this**; /ŋ/ **bang**; /zh/ **measure**

condense (kən dens′) *v*: to change from a vapor to a liquid. *When steam touches a cold surface, it condenses into water.* 218

confiscate (kän′ fə skāt′) *v*: to seize or take away, especially by an order of authority. *Mr. Raymond confiscated Greg's stash of rubber bands.* 292

confound (kən faủnd′) *v*: to mix up or frustrate. *The team hopes that their new strategy will confound their opponents.* 240

congregate (käŋ′ gri gāt′) *v*: to gather in a group. *The boys congregated on the playground after school to see the llamas in Mr. Henry's field.* 273

consist (kən sist′) *v*: to be made of. *Granite is a type of rock consisting mainly of quartz.* 105

cower (kaủ′ ər) *v*: to crouch in fear or shame. *Cameron found Lassie cowering under the table during the thunderstorm.* 46

curt (kərt) *adj*: not using many words; rudely brief. *Lonnie is never curt but always gives you his full attention and answers with a kind word.* 149

deft (deft) *adj*: skillful. *The potter deftly molded a beautiful pitcher out of the clay.* 127

dismal (diz′ məl) *adj*: dreary; causing gloom or sadness. *In the cold drizzle of a February day, the countryside was bleak and dismal.* 117

dispatch (di spach′) *v*: to send quickly to a particular place or for a particular purpose. *Immediately after the storm, rescue workers were dispatched to the area.* 273

dogged (dȯ′ gəd) *adj*: persistent; not giving up. *Each time Seth neared the top of the slippery pole, he lost his grip and slid down; yet he doggedly kept trying.* 268

dormant (dȯr′ mənt) *adj*: asleep or inactive; not growing. *Animals that hibernate are dormant during the winter months.* 140

dormitory (dȯr′ mə tȯr′ ē) *n*: a building used by students as living and sleeping quarters. *At Bible school, young people stay in nearby homes or sleep in a dormitory.* 188

dribble (dri′ bəl) *v*: to flow or fall in little drops. *Honey dribbled from the toast onto the kitchen counter.* 25

embed (im bed′) *v*: to place firmly into something. *Zach winced as his mother probed for the splinter embedded in his finger.* 178

employ (em plòi′) *v*: to hire somebody to work in exchange for payment. *White Oak Mills will employ Curtis as a delivery driver.* 164

enrage (en rāj′) *v*: to make angry to the point of rage. *The tiger grew enraged when its foot got caught in the trap.* 157

enrich (en rich′) *v*: to improve the quality by adding a desirable ingredient. *The drink was enriched with vitamin C.* 186

enterprise (en′ tər prīz′) *n*: an undertaking or project that takes work or effort. *The boys' new enterprise will require several weeks of hard work before they can expect any results.* 303

equip (i kwip′) *v*: to provide what is needed. *Before sailing, the sailors equipped the ship with gear for a three-month journey.* 38

exasperate (ig zas′ pə rāt′) *v*: to annoy or cause great impatience. *The barking dogs exasperated the elderly man, keeping him awake most of the night.* 157

exhilarate (ig zi′ lə rāt′) *v*: to make lively or cheerful; to refresh. *Tom's morning swims in the ocean were always exhilarating, especially in December and January.* 107

extract (ik strakt′) *v*: to take out or withdraw. *Scientists extract medicines from yams, foxglove, and many other common plants.* 7

exultant (ig zəl′ tənt) *adj*: filled with triumph or joy. *Seth gave an exultant shout when he finally reached the top of the slippery pole.* 255

famine (fa′ mən) *n*: a time when food is scarce. *The people of Israel went to Egypt to escape a famine in Canaan.* 62

Pronunciation Key

/a/ bat; /ā/ acorn; /är/ star; /e/ pet; /ē/ eagle; /er/ bear; /ər/ her; /i/ bit; /ī/ ivy; /ir/ deer; /ä/ top; /ō/ go; /ò/ lost; /òi/ coin; /aù/ out; /òr/ corn; /ə/ but; /ü/ boot; /yü/ use; /ù/ foot; /th/ thick; /th/ this; /ŋ/ bang; /zh/ measure

fatal (fā′ təl) *adj* : causing death or ruin. *Doctors have developed vaccines for many of the fatal diseases that took numerous lives in the past.* 225

fluster (fləs′ tər) *v* : to make or become anxious or nervous. *No matter what the mischievous boys did to Emily, she refused to become flustered or angry.* 25

forebode (fȯr bōd′) *v* : to be or give a warning that something undesirable will happen. *The dark cloud in the western sky forebodes a storm.* 210

forlorn (fȯr lȯrn′) *adj* : sad or lonely because of being abandoned. *After the homeless child was adopted into a loving family, his forlorn appearance soon changed.* 99

formal (fȯr′ məl) *adj* : following established rules, forms, or customs. *Andrew's formal education ended at age fifteen when his father died, leaving him to support the family.* 228

formidable (fȯr′ mə də bəl) *adj* : causing fear or awe. *Goliath was a formidable enemy, but David put his trust in God and faced the giant.* 210

forsake (fȯr sāk′) *v* : to turn away from completely. *When people humble themselves, pray, turn to God, and forsake their wicked ways, He will hear them.* 67

fortify (fȯr′ tə fī′) *v* : to make strong. *Kevin and Jorge knew they must fortify their snow fort to keep the other team from knocking down the walls.* 114

frigid (fri′ jəd) *adj* : very cold. *Norwegian sled dogs are able to withstand the frigid temperatures of Antarctica.* 28

furor (fyu̇r′ ȯr′) *n* : an angry public reaction to something; uproar. *Because of the furor in the streets, the police were called in to control the crowds.* 202

garner (gär′ nər) *v* : to gather into storage. *The squirrels busily garnered seeds and nuts for the winter.* 268

giddy (gi′ dē) *adj* : dizzily happy or excited. *Frieda was giddy with delight when she heard the news.* 250

gratifying (gra′ tə fī′ iŋ) *adj*: giving satisfaction or pleasure. *It is always gratifying to accomplish a difficult chore.* 250

grotesque (grō tesk′) *adj*: fantastic, strange, odd-looking. *The bruise on my leg was grotesquely discolored.* 56

gullible (gə′ lə bəl) *adj*: easily fooled. *It is easy to take an unfair advantage of someone who is gullible.* 5

habitat (ha′ bə tat′) *n*: the place or type of place where a plant or animal normally lives. *The African savanna is the habitat of lions, elephants, zebras, and gazelles.* 38

haggard (ha′ gərd) *adj*: having a tired, wasted appearance; weary. *The boy's haggard face peered through the bakery window.* 112

haggle (ha′ gəl) *v*: to bargain or argue about the price of something. *Jenny haggled good-naturedly with Mr. Simmons over the price of his fish.* 234

harpoon (här pün′) *n*: a spear with a barb on the end, used to hunt whales or large fish. *Long ago harpoons were hand-thrown instruments; today many are projected by guns.* 217

hawker (hȯ′ kər) *v*: one who sells his wares on the streets. *Tasha crossed the street to avoid the noisy hawkers.* 231

hospitality (häs′ pə ta′ lə tē) *n*: friendly and generous treatment of guests or visitors. *During their thirteen years of service on the African mission field, Mr. and Mrs. Miller showed hospitality to each person who stopped at their door.* 92

ideal (ī dēl′) *adj*: the best of its kind. *The ideal weather for hiking is a warm, sunny day with a cool breeze.* 139

impulse (im′ pəls′) *n*: a sudden urge to do something. *When Karen saw the woman begging in front of the bookstore, her first impulse was to give her money.* 162

Pronunciation Key

/a/ bat; /ā/ acorn; /är/ star; /e/ pet; /ē/ eagle; /er/ bear; /ər/ her; /i/ bit; /ī/ ivy; /ir/ deer; /ä/ top; /ō/ go; /ȯ/ lost; /ȯi/ coin; /au̇/ out; /ȯr/ corn; /ə/ but; /ü/ boot; /yü/ use; /u̇/ foot; /th/ thick; /t͟h/ this; /ŋ/ bang; /zh/ measure

industry (in′ dəs trē) *n* : diligence in work; steady effort. *Students who study with industry are better prepared for a test.* 137

inflict (in flikt′) *v* : to cause to suffer. *The fire ant is known to inflict a painful sting on its unsuspecting victims.* 45

invade (in vād′) *v* : to enter by force where one is not welcome. *The thistle stubbornly poked its head up through the soil, an invader of Mother's flower bed.* 9

jest (jest) *v* : to joke or tease; to make playful remarks. *"I do not jest," Mr. Sloan declared solemnly. "The matter is very serious."* 94

jovial (jō′ vē əl) *adj* : happy; jolly. *A jovial person can laugh even when he has made a mistake.* 54

laden (lā′ dən) *adj* : heavily loaded. *Mules laden with supplies made the trek to the bottom of the canyon each week.* 117

leisurely (lē′ zhər lē) *adj* : relaxed and unhurried. *After a leisurely lunch at the park, we decided to tour the museum.* 256

merchandise (mər′ chən dīs′) *n* : goods bought and sold in a business. *George stared in wonder at the high shelves jammed with merchandise from all over the world.* 231

migrate (mī′ grāt′) *v* : to move regularly back and forth from one region to another. *Migrating from Mexico to Washington every year, the monarch butterfly travels over a thousand miles.* 28

mimic (mi′ mik) *v* : to imitate precisely. *It was amusing to see the little boy mimic his father.* 158

moderate (mä′ də rət) *adj* : average, mild, or reasonable. *Oregon has a moderate climate: it is not too hot in the summer and not too cold in the winter.* 89

mortar (mȯr′ tər) *n* : material used for bonding bricks. *The mason finished the wall with one last layer of mortar and bricks.* 239

mosey (mō′ zē) *v* : to walk or move unhurriedly. *Ronald spent the forenoon moseying through the village, pausing to chat with neighbors and catch up on the local news.* 261

muster (məs′ tər) *v*: to gather (a group of people), especially for battle or war. *The men were instructed to muster in the town square.* 279

mutual (myü′ chəl) *adj*: having the same qualities in common; shared. *The Morris and Wilson families have a mutual love for singing.* 106

negotiate (ni gō′ shē āt′) *v*: to work together toward an agreement. *Father and Mr. Burns met to negotiate over the price of the tractor.* 212

nonchalant (nän′ shə länt′) *adj*: unconcerned or indifferent. *During the conversation Abe nonchalantly mentioned winning the award.* 56

nonresistance (nän′ ri zis′ təns) *n*: the practice of not using force to resist violence or authority even when it is unjust. *Jesus taught His followers the principle of nonresistance.* 222

nourish (nər′ ish) *v*: to feed and promote growth. *Fertilizer will nourish the plants and increase vegetable production.* 187

offshore (ȯf′ shȯr′) *adj*: located in water at a distance from shore. *I had never been offshore fishing before Monroe invited us to come along on his fishing boat.* 215

pall (pȯl) *n*: something that covers and darkens. *The news of the earthquake in Central America threw a pall of sadness over the reunion.* 96

parched (pärcht) *adj*: completely lacking moisture; dry. *Jim Bridger's throat was parched and his strength was giving out when he stumbled over the hill and discovered the Snake River Gorge.* 281

particle (pär′ ti kəl) *n*: a very small part. *Particles of sand stuck in the hub of my bicycle tire and ruined the bearings.* 56

perspiration (pər′ spə rā′ shən) *n*: sweat. *Perspiration beaded on Anthony's forehead as he tried to recall the next line of his speech.* 25

plague (plāg) *n*: severe, widespread affliction or trouble. *The worst plague ever recorded in Europe was the outbreak of the bubonic plague in Europe during the Middle Ages.* 129

Pronunciation Key
/a/ bat; /ā/ acorn; /är/ star; /e/ pet; /ē/ eagle; /er/ bear; /ər/ her; /i/ bit; /ī/ ivy; /ir/ deer; /ä/ top; /ō/ go; /ȯ/ lost; /ȯi/ coin; /au̇/ out; /ȯr/ corn; /ə/ but; /ü/ boot; /yü/ use; /u̇/ foot; /th/ thick; /t͟h/ this; /ŋ/ bang; /zh/ measure

322

pledge (plej) *n*: a promise to give money. *The students were challenged to make a pledge to help poor children buy supplies for the coming school term.* 2

plight (plīt) *n*: an unfortunate or difficult situation. *Absorbed in his exploration, Neil suddenly noticed the high tide and realized his plight.* 194

plunder (plən′ dər) *v*: to take money or goods by force. *The pirates set off to plunder coastal towns in South America.* 210   *n*: goods or money taken by force. *The plunder taken by Spanish ships in the 1700s amounted to millions of dollars.* 211

prescribe (pri skrīb′) *v*: to order as a treatment for a patient. *My doctor prescribed bed rest and a strong medicine for three weeks.* 104

promote (prə mōt′) *v*: to move to a more important or higher position. *Father was promoted from head mechanic to shop manager after six years of working at Allen Motors.* 67

quantity (kwän′ tə tē) *n*: an amount. *Toby ordered the wrong quantity of wiring for his building project.* 162

quizzical (kwi′ zi kəl) *adj*: puzzled, curious, questioning. *Jack looked at me quizzically when I threw the glass of water over the fence.* 212

ration (ra′ shən) *n*: an allowance of food. *During the war Grandpa's family received a small ration of sugar and butter each week.* 14

ravenous (ra′ və nəs) *adj*: very hungry; greedy. *Gene skipped breakfast and lunch, worked a full nine hours cutting grass, and was ravenous by supper time.* 100

reign (rān) *v*: to rule over. *God promised King David that his family would reign over Israel as long as they followed His commandments.* 66

remedy (re′ mə dē) *n*: a treatment or medicine that relieves pain or cures an illness. *Candace's home remedy of special syrup soothed Janey's sore throat.* 225

restrain (ri strān′) *v*: to hold back. *Two men struggled to restrain the frightened horse.* 87

rhythmic (ri<u>th</u>' mik) *adj*: having a regular pattern of movement or sound. *The saw moved back and forth rhythmically.* 9

rigging (ri' giŋ) *n*: the ropes and chains on a ship used to control the sails and masts. *A sailor is always surrounded by the decks, masts, and rigging of his ship.* 220

robust (rō bəst') *adj*: strong and healthy; vigorous. *Steven is a robust young man who loves outdoor adventures.* 247

sacred (sā' krəd) *adj*: set apart or dedicated for a religious purpose; holy. *Many religions have a place that they consider sacred.* 169

salve (sav) *v*: to ease or quiet. *Mother's kind words salved my aching heart.* 45   *n*: a soothing cream used to relieve pain. *Jerry bought salve at the pharmacy and applied it to his sunburned arms.* 225

sanitary (sa' nə ter' ē) *adj*: clean and free from anything causing infection or disease. *The inspector commended the hospital for its sanitary facility.* 198

scoff (skäf) *v*: to express scorn; to mock or show great disrespect. *People scoffed at Noah when he told them about a flood that would destroy the earth.* 14

scud (skəd) *n*: wind-driven clouds, snow, or mist. *A gray scud drifted in from the northeast.* 71

shanty (shan' tē) *n*: a small crudely built shelter or dwelling. *The rough shanty provided little shelter from the storm.* 79

souvenir (sü' və nir') *n*: something that serves as a reminder. *Charlotte brought home a sand dollar as a souvenir from the ocean.* 166

speculation (spe' kyə lā' shən) *n*: guessing; forming an idea without complete evidence. *Having never met the new teacher, everything we heard seemed to be only speculation.* 228

Pronunciation Key

/a/ bat; /ā/ acorn; /är/ star; /e/ pet; /ē/ eagle; /er/ bear; /ər/ her; /i/ bit; /ī/ ivy; /ir/ deer; /ä/ top; /ō/ go; /ȯ/ lost; /ȯi/ coin; /aü/ out; /ȯr/ corn; /ə/ but; /ü/ boot; /yü/ use; /u̇/ foot; /th/ thick; /<u>th</u>/ this; /ŋ/ bang; /zh/ measure

splint (splint) *n*: a strip of thin pliable wood suitable for weaving. *Johann carefully cut and smoothed each splint for his wife to weave into sturdy baskets.* 68

steadfast (sted′ fast′) *adj*: firmly fixed; faithful. *A steadfast friend will not leave you alone when you need help.* 206

stifle (stī′ fəl) *v*: to press down or smother. *It was difficult to fall asleep in the stifling heat of the tiny bedroom.* 167

stoke (stōk) *v*: to stir up or feed. *Before going to bed, we stoke the woodstove with plenty of logs to last through the night.* 255

subscribe (səb skrīb′) *v*: to arrange to receive something regularly. *The Millers subscribed to a newspaper and several monthly magazines.* 139

tenant (te′ nənt) *n*: a renter; one who occupies a house or land. *The landlord does not allow any tenant to keep pets in the house.* 162

tinge (tinj) *v*: to color lightly. *Mother added a drop of food coloring to the icing, tingeing it a pale yellow.* 255

transitory (tran′ sə tȯr′ ē) *adj*: lasting only for a short time. *The hot weather in the middle of October was transitory; a week later temperatures had dropped, and people wore jackets again.* 172

trigger (tri′ gər) *v*: to set off an action or series of events. *The smoke triggered the fire alarm and caused a few moments of panic.* 176
n: a movable lever that activates a device. *Garret positioned his gun, aimed carefully at the deer, and pulled the trigger.* 46

turmoil (tər′ mȯil′) *n*: a state of great disturbance or confusion. *The turmoil in Jonathan's heart distracted him from his studies.* 294

tyrant (tī′ rənt) *n*: a ruler who exercises power cruelly and unjustly. *The country had been ruled by tyrants for decades.* 279

viscous (vis′ kəs) *adj*: thick; not flowing easily. *Is honey more viscous than molasses?* 172

ware (wer) *n*: goods that have been manufactured for sale. *The traveling salesman stopped his station wagon at each home to show home owners the wares he had for sale.* 125

writhe (rīth) *v*: to twist and turn, especially in pain. *Even after Henry chopped off its head, the copperhead continued writhing in the long grass near the edge of the garden.* 82

wry (rī) *adj*: bent or twisted; humorous in a clever or grim way. *Heather's wry grin told us she saw the humor in the situation.* 151

yield (yēld) *v*: to give way to another; to give up control. *After his experience on the road to Damascus, Saul yielded his life to Christ.* 83

Pronunciation Key
/a/ bat; /ā/ acorn; /är/ star; /e/ pet; /ē/ eagle; /er/ bear; /ər/ her; /i/ bit; /ī/ ivy; /ir/ deer; /ä/ top; /ō/ go; /ò/ lost;
/òi/ coin; /aù/ out; /òr/ corn; /ə/ but; /ü/ boot; /yü/ use; /ù/ foot; /th/ thick; /th/ this; /ŋ/ bang; /zh/ measure

Acknowledgements

Artist: Alex Brover and others

Cover design: David Miller

Editorial committee: Sterling Beachy, Jennifer Crider, Keith E. Crider, James Hershberger, Ava Shank

"A Chance to Escape," adapted from "A Martyr for Faith," from "What the Netherlands Has Given Us," by David Luthy, *Family Life*, March 1970. ©1970 David Luthy, Aylmer, Ontario, Canada. All rights reserved. Used by permission.

"A Dangerous Errand," by Elmo Stoll, from *Step By Step*. ©1968 Pathway Publishers, Aylmer, Ontario, Canada. All rights reserved. Used by permission.

"A Harvest of Gold," adapted from "A Harvest of Gold," by Bonnie Abbs.

"A Jingle of Words," by Betty Stam.

"A Prodigal Son," by Christina Rossetti.

"A Smile as Small as Mine," by Emily Dickinson.

"A Word," by Emily Dickinson.

"Advertising for a Thief," adapted from "Advertising for a Thief," in *The Friendly Story Caravan*. ©1935, 1948, 1949, by Anna Pettit Broomell. Used by permission of Pendle Hill Publications, Wallingford, Pennsylvania. All rights reserved.

"Always 'Ungry," adapted from *A Little Princess* by Frances Hodgson Burnett. Adaptation ©2003 Christian Light Publications, Inc., Harrisonburg, VA. All rights reserved.

"An Ill Wind," adapted from "An Ill Wind," in *The Friendly Story Caravan*. Copyright, 1935, 1948, 1949, by Anna Pettit Broomell.

"Be Like the Bird," by Victor Hugo.

"Beautiful," Author unknown.

"Beavers!" by Tim Kennedy. ©2003 Christian Light Publications, Inc., Harrisonburg, VA. All rights reserved.

"Call of the Wild Geese," adapted from "Call of the Wild" by Todd Lee. ©1990 Todd Lee.

"Check," by James Stephens.

"Could It Be Done? Secrets of the Soil" and "School on Wheels," adapted from *George Washington Carver: Man's Slave Becomes God's Scientist* (a Sowers Series biography), by David Collins. ©1981 Mott Media, Inc. Used by permission.

"Created to Fly," by Robert Doolan. Reproduced by permission from *Creation* magazine, <AnswersInGenesis.com>.

"Crossing the Ice," adapted from "Brooms for Sale," by Thomas H. Raddall. Adaptation ©2003 Christian Light Publications, Inc., Harrisonburg, VA. All rights reserved.

"Dirk Mieuwess, A.D. 1571," by T. J. van Braght.

"Elias," by Leo Tolstoy.

"Escape at Bedtime," by Robert Louis Stevenson.

"God Provides Water," from the KJV Bible.

"Going to Market," adapted from "The Sabbath" from *All-of-a-Kind Family*, by Sydney Taylor. Copyright 1951, by Wilcox & Follett Co.

"Something Told the Wild Geese." Reprinted with the permission of Simon & Schuster Books for Young Readers, an imprint of Simon & Schuster Children's Publishing Division from *Branches Green* by Rachel Field. Copyright 1934 Macmillan Publishing Company; copyright renewed ©1962 Arthur B. Pederson.

"Starfish," by Winifred Welles.

"Thar She Blo-o-ows!" adapted from "Black Gold and Ambergris: Whale" from *Animals That Made U.S. History* by Edith Dorian and W. N. Wilson. ©1964 Edith Dorian and W. N. Wilson. All rights reserved. Used by permission of The McGraw-Hill Companies, NY, NY.

"The Baker's Neighbor," retold by Jennifer Crider. ©2003 Christian Light Publications, Inc., Harrisonburg, VA. All rights reserved.

"The Carolers of Bethlehem Center," adapted from "The Carols of Bethlehem Center" by Frederick Hall. Adaptation ©2003 Christian Light Publications, Inc., Harrisonburg, VA. All rights reserved.

"The Earth Abideth Forever," from the KJV Bible.

"The Easy Road Crowded," by Messick.

"The Flies and the Honey Pot," by Aesop.

"The Honor Box," by Betty Steele Everett. ©1987 Betty Steel Everett, Defiance, OH. All rights reserved. Used by permission.

"The Ichthyosaur," adapted from "The Ichthyosaurus" from *Mary Anning's Treasures* by Helen Bush. ©1965 Helen Bush. First published by Victor Gollancz 1967. Published by Puffin Books 1976.

"The King and the Shirt," from *Fables and Fairy Tales* by Leo Tolstoy, translated by Ann Dunnigan, copyright ©1962 by Ann Dunnigan. Used by permission of Dutton Signet, a division of Penguin Group (USA) Inc.

"The Meaning of the Word," by Mildred Geiger Gilbertson. © 1952, by Mildred Gilbertson. Used by permission of Association For Childhood Education International, Olney, MD. All rights reserved.

"The Meaning of the Word," illustration, William Moyers.

"The Pasture," by Robert Frost.

"The Prodigal Son," from the KJV Bible.

"The Quakers of Nantucket," adapted from "Customary Education and Employment of the Inhabitants of Nantucket" by J. Hector St. John (pseudonym).

"The Road to Canada," adapted from "The Road to Canada," by Anna L. Curtis in *The Friendly Story Caravan*. ©1935, 1948, 1949, by Anna Pettit Broomell. Used by permission of Pendle Hill Publications, Wallingford, Pennsylvania. All rights reserved.

"The Runaway," by Robert Frost.

"The Sari With the Silver Border," adapted from "The Sari With the Silver Border," by Dorothy C. Haskin.

"The Tale of Bramble the King," from the KJV Bible.

"The Wolf," by Georgia R. Durston.

"Varifrån Kommer Språken," from the KJV Bible.

"Whales and Stewardship," by Tim Kennedy. ©2003 Christian Light Publications, Inc., Harrisonburg, VA. All rights reserved.

"What Have We Done Today?" From "What Have We Done Today?" by Nixon Waterman.

"Words," by George Gordon, Lord Byron.

We have attempted to secure permission for all copyrighted material. If further information is received, the publisher will be glad to properly credit the material in future printings.